Ray Stannard Baker
Amherst.

Native American

Native American

THE BOOK OF MY YOUTH

By

Ray Stannard Baker

[DAVID GRAYSON]

☆ ☆
☆

NEW YORK

Charles Scribner's Sons

1941

Foreword

MOST OF my ancestors on both sides had been pioneering for two hundred and fifty years before I was born, exploring, surveying, opening new land, building up small frontier communities. My own generation saw the end of that process. Professor Frederick J. Turner, authority upon the pioneer era, has said that the early 90's marked the end of the frontier in America. I had been brought up on the "last frontier," and I was, presently, to be turned back into crowds, and life in the city. I have had the rare experience of having in my own life passed through all the stages of American development from pioneering to the complicated and dangerous civilization of today; from the intense individualism and the simplicities of the frontier to the advancing, jostling, uneasy, more or less unacceptable socialism of the present hour. When I went to Chicago at the age of twenty-two (1892) I had not the slightest idea that the old free life of the frontier, in which I had grown up, had become a thing of the past, that the American people and I with them were entering into a new world with new problems and a new kind of civilization. My individual reaction to these swift and momentous changes, and my painful, but

v

illuminating readjustments to them, are the real subjects of this book, and my reason for writing it.

I remember a remark made by Robert Louis Stevenson in one of his books or letters—I do not remember where, it was long ago that I read it—to the effect that all the really vital life of a man, when he lived originally, powerfully, beautifully, could be crowded into forty days. Forty days completely worth living!

Well, I have had mine and more; and I am trying to put them into this book. So much I owe to my early American environment, so much to my typically American experience and American training, that I am calling this book *Native American.* "The experience of each new age," says Emerson, "requires a new confession." This is mine.

In this book, then, I am writing of my boyhood and youth on the frontier, of my education, of my earliest ventures as a writer; and in a later volume, if ever I get to the writing of it, I hope to describe my further explorations and discoveries in a new world.

Contents

Contents

Native American

"*My trade and art is to live my life. The man who forbids me to speak of my experience, feeling and practice of it might as well forbid an architect to speak of building as he, and not another, knows it.*"

MONTAIGNE'S ESSAYS

"*The man who writes about himself and his own time is the only man who writes about all people and all time.*"

BERNARD SHAW

"*The next thing to living one's life over again seems to be a recollection of that life, and to make that recollection as durable as possible by putting it down in writing.*"

BENJAMIN FRANKLIN
in his AUTOBIOGRAPHY

☆ 1 ☆

We Migrate

MY MOTHER with her three little boys, one a baby in arms, followed my father from Michigan to the wilderness of northern Wisconsin in the spring of 1875. I was the oldest of the three, then five years old, and it was my first ride on a railroad train; I remember the rumbling trip through Chicago and the masted ships in the river as we crossed it. We spent a night with my uncle's family at Hudson on the lower St. Croix. Beyond this there was no railroad line: and the river steamer, blocked by the winter's ice, had not yet begun to run. We took passage on the ramshackle stage that carried the mail northward. It had a little wood stove in one end of it, kept so hot that the passengers continually changed places, those who were being frozen near the doorway taking their chances of being roasted at the other end by the stove. I was terrified when we were caught in a flooded river which the reckless driver tried to ford, and overjoyed when a number of hulky boys in mackinaw jackets came running from a District School to pull us out. That night, in the cold house my father had made ready for us, I slept in a bureau drawer.

One other incident I must have remembered from hearing it told in later years made an unforgettable and painful impression upon me. On the morning after our arrival at St. Croix Falls, when my beautiful mother, who had gallantly

I

finished the long and exhausting trip with her three restless little boys, looked down into the valley of the St. Croix, across the straggling, unpainted frontier village, she broke down and wept. I seem to remember just how the tears came through her fingers, but this may have been associated with some later incident. When my father tried gently to point out the real beauty of our valley, the rocky cliffs and wooded hills of Minnesota just opposite, and the wild river, choked with the spring flood, roaring through the gorge below, she could only shake her head:

"Oh, Stan," she said, "I cannot live on scenery."

She was of a high-strung, ardent, social nature, sometimes swiftly intolerant in her judgments. She liked comfortable, intimate social affairs. She depended upon her church. She had been in college—Olivet College in Michigan—and beyond many women of her time, had keen intellectual interests. And here she was with her husband and little family in a rough frontier town, far away from her relatives and all her old friends. All about were rough, red-jacketed woodsmen and river drivers, Indians, French-Canadians, and Scandinavian immigrants who spoke little or no English. The village was a mere handful of primitive stores with typical square fronts, a weather-beaten mill, a blacksmith shop or two, a hotel and livery-barn, and a few houses straggling along the hillside. There was no church at all to comfort my mother; there never had been. Occasional services by itinerant preachers, most of them hopelessly ignorant, were held in the bare little schoolhouse.

"Never mind, Alice," said my father, consolingly, "we'll soon have one."

2

And they did: my father was the prime mover in the building of it; and he did it as much, I think, for his Alice as for his God. My mother organized the Omnionian Society among the dozen or more women who came to church, and they sewed and gave oyster suppers and strawberry festivals to help the building fund. And once I saw my mother's tears dropping on the little trousers she was patching; but when my father came in she quickly brushed her eyes and greeted him with a smile.

My father gloried in the hard, new life. It had hope in it, and adventure, and labor and struggle. Even though all the vast wilderness to the north and northwest was still largely uninhabited except by Indians, the lumbermen were cutting the virgin forests of pine and floating the logs down the rivers; and settlers were beginning to come in on the denuded lands. It was a grand moment for bold men: new country was to be opened and conquered, rivers dammed, cities built—but my delicate, sensitive mother was never reconciled. She did not like the rough river-drivers: she feared the Indians.

☆ 2 ☆

The Indians and Rivermen
I Knew

DURING our first years in the St. Croix Valley both the Indians and lumbermen were as familiar to all of us as the
pioneer settlers crawling northward with their ox-teams.
Just beyond our village, a place called Quailtown, there
lived a considerable settlement of Indians: many others were
scattered about the county, especially along the rivers and
on the lakes. They were fragments of the once powerful
tribe of the Chippewa, degraded by liquor and the diseases
of the white man, demoralized by the breakdown of the
stern tribal usages which from time immemorial had constituted the morals and buttressed the religion of a coura-
geous and hardy people. In all the settlements there were
many half-breeds, "half Indian and half river-driver," as the
saying went, and often a dominating white "squaw-man,"
who had all the vices of both races. French was as commonly
spoken as English but most of the Indians were silent in all
languages, including their own. In the after years of my boyhood I had no patience in reading of the "noble red man"
or the heroic Indian of boys' books—I especially detested
Hiawatha—for I remembered vividly the filthy camps of
the Indians I knew and the drunkenness and worse.

The Indians and Rivermen I Knew

In the settlement at Quailtown the dominating figure was an enormous squaw, a pure-blooded Indian called Old Mindy. She was said to be a hundred years old but I suppose was not a day beyond fifty. She had a miscellaneous family of children, one girl having no nose, the dramatic culmination of whose education I shall chronicle in a later chapter. I remember well my first visit to Old Mindy's camp. It was winter and my brother Charlie and I walked up with my father, a mile or so, by the narrow, moccasin-packed trail through the snow. The hovel where the Indians lived was of considerable size, but dark and smoky. It had no floor, but the ground was swept clean: at one end were the rolls of blankets where the Indians slept, at the other a huge, old, iron cookstove.

Our errand was to have moccasins made for my brother and me. In that country the winters were long and cold: there would be weeks when the temperature was never above freezing, with the air so dry and sharp that the snow was like powder and tickled one's nose. For such weather nothing equalled Indian moccasins worn with two pairs of thick woolen socks.

The towering blear-eyed squaw, to whom my father by signs had indicated what we wanted, produced a piece of dark-brown wrapping paper, such as the merchants then used, and this she put on the ground in front of the cookstove. She then directed me to take off my shoes and stand on the paper. I was frankly afraid of her but did what she asked. She took a coal from the hearth and kneeling down beside me—to my great alarm—drew marks around my feet. This she repeated for my brother. She then produced two

5

or three beautiful buckskins from deer the Indians had shot. They had been tanned by the squaws and were as soft and pliable as satin. They also had a fragrant odor of smoke which I have always liked, and which no amount of wear ever obliterated. My father chose the best of the skins and a week later we tramped again to Quailtown to try on our moccasins.

They were beauties, with high legging-tops made of the thinner part of the skin which could be tied in place with buckskin thongs, and ornamented with rows of beads along the instep. They fitted perfectly.

Often we saw groups of Indians trailing into town to trade at Jim Thompson's store—the older men wrapped in blankets and the squaws hatless, but wearing gay calico dresses. In the spring they sometimes brought in maple sugar or syrup to sell. It was black and granular and had a strong flavor of smoke. We boys liked it, but when my father explained to my mother that it must of course be clean because the Indians always strained it through the blankets in which they had slept all winter, we saw no more of it in our house. My mother was even suspicious of the venison they brought in to sell and when my father persisted in purchasing wild rice and bringing it home—for we all liked it better than oatmeal, and to this day I know of no native product of the north country I am more fond of—my mother insisted upon having it washed several times in hot water before it was cooked. In the fall the squaws brought in great pails and baskets of blueberries which they were eager to trade for flour and kukush (salt pork). One of the older Indians whom I saw often was called Lantern-Jaw.

6

The Indians and Rivermen I Knew

I was frightened whenever he looked at me, for he had as evil an eye as ever I saw in my life. Once in Jim Thompson's warehouse I saw him stoop quickly and when he thought no one was looking pick up a handful of potatoes, concealing them under his blanket. When he caught sight of the little boy watching him, he gave him a glance that sent shivers down his spine and effectively sealed his lips. My father called them a "bad lot," and indeed it was rare that a company of them got out of town without a drunken row. Somehow, somewhere, although it was against the law, they could always get liquor.

I remember well the last Indian scare in that country. It was in the spring, probably 1877, not so long after the Custer Massacre on the Little Big Horn in Dakota, which was in 1876. More or less nervousness existed in all the Indian country, and a rumor had come from the wilderness of the upper St. Croix that the Indians were dancing. A day or so later the northern settlers began to arrive in town with their ox teams and their wagons piled high with their poor and scanty but precious possessions—and all the babies. My father pooh-poohed the whole affair, arguing, but to no purpose, with the frightened pioneers, who knew well what had happened to Custer and his soldiers. Finally two or three men of the county, of whom my father was one, started into the north country to find out what the trouble really was. I remember my mother's alarm:

"Why do you go, Stan: do you forget your family of young children?"

I shared in her alarm and remember confiding in our hired man, who was not one to calm a boy's fears.

7

Three or four days later Father returned.

"Just as I thought," said he, "there isn't a particle of danger."

They had seen some of the old men of the tribe: and the story told had its pathos. They were indeed gathering for a great dance, but it was not a war dance. Some of the old men of the scattered tribe, seeing that the Indian was being rapidly dispossessed by the white man, his hunting-grounds despoiled, his camping and fishing places claimed and fenced, and his young men and women, forgetful of the tribal customs, were being corrupted by the new civilization, had decided to call one last ceremonial dance. It was to be religious, not warlike. It was to express the sorrow of the Indian over his lost estate. This news calmed the fears of the settlers and in a few days they were reloading their strange furniture and their crying babies, and the rough, shaggy drivers, gee-ing and haw-ing, were again headed into the mysterious up-country to repossess the little oases of cleared land in the great woods.

It was the last dance of the Chippewa tribe. A few years later most of them were removed to the reservation in the north of the state—a blessing to them and a vast relief to their white neighbors.

Associated in my memory with the Indians are the loggers and river-drivers who swarmed in our town every spring when the "drive" came down—bold, shaggy, rough men in red or blue flannel trousers and mackinaw jackets. They lived in houseboats that were called wannegans and were adept in handling the long, heavy bateaux with which they followed the logs down the river. One of the exciting

8

moments of the year was the shooting of the rapids of the St. Croix, for the wannegans were sometimes wrecked—and the even more blissful experience to boys like us of visiting the "cookee" of the crew who gave us great slabs of dried-apple pie. Much as my old aunts, who presently became a part of our family, objected to our visits to the camps and wannegans of the river-drivers—they considered all river-men beyond the pale of morality—few experiences of my boyhood interested me more. I admired the bold loggers shooting the rapids, often wading up to their waists in the foaming water. I was fascinated by the skill and strength with which they handled their cant hooks, rolling the logs from the rocks where they had stranded. After a day that began with the dawn and lasted till sunset, their vitality still unexpended, they would sometimes engage in rough sports, racing the log-jam in the pool below the rapids where if they missed a step they were cast into the icy water. Or, several of the nimblest of them would mount a huge log of white pine, and "cuffing" it under their spiked shoes, would set it rolling in the water until all were thrown off except the winner, who would be greeted with a roar of enthusiasm from his mates.

I remember their stories, well interlarded with profanity and obscenity, and yet most thrilling to hear. Some of their ribald songs lie in my mind with the memories of Old Mindy the Indian woman, and Gill Jewell, the town idiot. Rough and coarse as they often were I would not have them out of the picture; most of them had a tremendous, coarse, hearty guffaw in them. They were not effeminate, they were primitive. One of these songs concerned the doings of

9

a certain Wild Irishman who must have been the ancestor of Paul Bunyan. The chorus ran thus:

> "Oh Johnny be nimble,
> And Johnny be quick,
> And watch the Wild Irishman
> Turning his trick."

The Wild Irishman performed many miraculous deeds, but I regret I cannot now remember any of the lively verses in which they were chronicled except a part of this one:

> "I'll tell you the facts,
> The Wild Irishman shaved
> With a double-bit axe."

These stories were not told or sung in corners but roared out to a campful or boatload of men—where the tall pines stood and in the evening the smoke of the supper fire rose straight upward through the misty green foliage. I wish sometimes I could hear them again with the lift and glory I felt as a boy—the sagas of strong men, careless of danger, inured to hardship, expecting little of life and getting it.

I have never yet read a narrative regarding these men that seemed true to me. They were not romantic, they were simple and primitive, but, by all that is true, they were *alive*.

I know you pioneers! I have eaten your bacon and beans. I have sloshed at daylight down your wet trails, and returned at dusk through your uncut forests. I have slept well in your grimy camps. I was never one of you, but I knew you and I shall never forget you.

3

Where I Came From

IT WAS in this frontier atmosphere, these pioneer surroundings, that I grew up as a' boy. I was like my father: I loved
it. I loved the forests and the swift rivers and the lumber
camps. I loved fishing and hunting; above all I loved the
long drives with my father into the "up-country."

The fascination I found in these early contacts with the
Indians, the explorers, the lumbermen, the pioneer settlers,
was somehow bred in the bone; they ran in the blood of me.
All the traditions of my family, many vividly retained, told
of the struggle of hardy men with the wilderness, and the
constant danger of Indian attacks. According to the bloody
tally made by our family chronicler, six of my ancestors
were, during their migrations, killed by the Indians, four
were carried off captives into Canada by the French and
Indians, and another after being captured by the Indians
on her way to church (1676) was tomahawked and left for
dead in the woods, but proved so cunning and so indomi-
table that she ultimately escaped and recovered.

I know well how dull the narrative of a man's ancestry
may sometimes appear, especially if he is proud of it, as I
am, but I cannot seem to understand or rightly explain my
own life without reference to my origins.

Native American

I speak with confidence of my ancestry, not because it was remarkable in any way, but because it was not remarkable. Mine is the history of thousands of American families. The only pride I can take in it is that it is typically American. My family, generation after generation, followed the common urge of the pioneers to migrate to the westward, suffered the common hardships of the wilderness, fought the Indians, fought the French, fought the British, hewed out square places in the hard forest, plowed the rough and rooty land with yoked oxen, planted wheat where none had ever grown before, and built forges in the forest and mills on every stream. Wherever those restless pioneers decided to stop and even before they were sure of their own food for the long winters, they built churches for the worship of God, which they soon quarrelled about, and ambitious school-houses where they sent children whose hands were often needed at home. It was a saga of bold, strong and hopeful, if sometimes domineering and dogmatic, men, and brave and devoted, but often lonely, women.

My family, so far as our zealous genealogist can learn, was almost wholly English in its ancestry. One strain of French blood, far back, makes me one sixty-fourth Gallic. One immigrant ancestor was Scotch, another Welsh. All of the earliest settlers came to New England, mostly to Massachusetts, a few to Connecticut.

The tribe I sprang from abhorred crowding. It abhorred crowding in the matter of living space, even more in religious and political patterns and compulsions. Both of these aversions were often active in the same men; while they were looking to the wilderness for new land and new opportunity, they took measures to escape from social or political or intellectual overlordship. My father's family represented predominantly the restless, eager, discontented land-seekers: my mother's family, sprung largely from dissenting ministers and teachers, may be more justly classed among the religious and intellectual pioneers.

My father's earliest ancestor in the name line came to Boston in the 1630's. When it became too crowded there, and in Gloucester, one of the grandsons migrated to new land near New London in Connecticut. Two later generations pioneered at Woodbury and Roxbury, hewing their farms out of the wilderness, building their church on a hilltop, fighting Indians and killing deer.

My great-great-grandfather, Captain Remember Baker, and his cousins, Ethan and Ira Allen, were among the earliest surveyors and settlers in western Vermont. They were leaders of the Green Mountain Boys and had for a time a price set upon their heads by the colony of New York, which claimed ownership to vast tracts of land which they had been granted by the colony of New Hampshire. Instead of surrendering, they responded with a satirical offer of £15 for the capture of the New York authorities. "The gods of the valleys," as Ethan Allen said, "are not the gods of the hills." In one bloody combat with the "Yorkers," Captain Remember had one of his thumbs cut off by the stroke of a sword, and ever afterward, when his rights were questioned, he held up his thumbless hand.

Captain Remember Baker died as fearlessly as he lived. At the outbreak of the Revolutionary War he commanded a scouting party, under the direction of General Schuyler, into British-held Canada. While encamped on the Richelieu (then the Sorel) River, a band of Caughnawaga Indians stole his boat. When he was about to open fire upon them, his flint failed to strike, and an Indian shot him dead. Afterward the band cut off his head and carried it on a pole to the garrison at St. John's, where the British, having found a Masonic emblem among his belongings, bought and buried his head. He was the first American soldier killed on the northern front during the Revolutionary War. "His death," as Allen says in his *History*, "made more noise in the country than the loss of a thousand men toward the end of the American war."[1]

Remember Baker's grandson, who was my grandfather, Luther A. Baker, was also a pioneer. He seemed to have found even the sparsely settled hills of northern Vermont too crowded, and pushed onward with ox-carts into the still vaster wilderness of western New York, where he took up virgin land, opened a farm, fought the British in the War of 1812, and raised a large family of children.

Two of his sons, one my father, Joseph Stannard Baker, were soldiers in the Civil War, my father commanding a cavalry regiment at the age of twenty-four. When the war was over, western New York had been tamed and the two restless brothers migrated to what was then the straggling town of Lansing, Michigan, the state capital. Here I was born on April 17, 1870; and four years later my father, the last pioneer of the family, took another long step westward to the head of navigation on the St. Croix River in northern Wisconsin.

[1] The *New England Quarterly* for October, 1931, contains an account of the life and adventures of Remember Baker, written by me.

Where I Came From

It is to be here noted that all of these hardy men, from the beginning, met their social, economic and even religious problems by escaping from them; they never learned, or had to learn, the difficult modern art of living together in a crowded world.

4

My Adventures on the Frontier

Now THAT I have begun to write, what a flood of early memories crowd upon me, eager for a place in my narrative. How interesting and beautiful those days appear, "a piece of Poetry that may sound to many an unfamiliar ear like a Fable."

I have spoken of the Indians and the rivermen: after them, jogging irresistibly northward with their huge loaded wagons, came the hardy settlers. They also were a part of my life, far more interesting and adventurous than I knew at the time.

My father's business took him for long drives into the "up-country," the wild northern townships of our own county of Polk and the still wilder stretches of Burnett County, which was then largely uninhabited. The roads were mere tracks through the forest, often impassable because of swamp-holes or fallen trees. We always carried an axe with us to chop out a by-pass if necessary. Miles on miles without a sign of human habitation: a country then full of deer and bear, with hundreds of little lakes swarming with fish, which had never yet made acquaintance with a fisherman's hook. Often in the winter during those early years, before there was any such thing as a game law, I have seen hunters coming out of the north with a hay rack piled high with frozen deer they had slaughtered, the legs sticking out stiffly in all directions. Venison in those days was cheaper than any other kind of meat—even the buffalo steaks which were occasionally shipped in, frozen, from the west.

On a great many of his trips my father, who was hard of hearing, took me with him, as he said, to be his ears: but I knew it was for more than this—he liked to have me go. As for me, nothing ever made me happier. I can remember still the thrill I used to have when my father some morning at breakfast would ask:

"Ray, how would you like to make a trip up-country for a few days with me?"

Would I like it! *Would* I!

It was always an intense pleasure to me to be with my father, just to be near him; and it was a pure delight to know that I could help him when he needed it. I think I attained a considerable facility in talking with the Scandinavian settlers who were then coming in on the land, usually on land purchased from my father. Some of them had little or no English, and were too fearful to say a word into Father's blunderbuss of an ear tube. I sat at his elbow when he conferred with the county officers at Grantsburg or helped when we stopped to pay taxes to backwoods township treasurers. He could scarcely have got along without me during the preliminaries of one stormy lawsuit where he refused to take the word of any one but me. The very thought gave me a measure of joy that made me choke and the tears come into my eyes.

On these trips my father was inexhaustibly interesting. He knew the stories connected with many of the little clearings in the forest: he often knew the men and where they came from, and how much they had paid for their land, and where the school was, and how far they had to drive to market. He knew the story of some of the primitive little schoolhouses and the raw new Lutheran churches, and sometimes of spicy quarrels over land lines, and the location of new roads.

"Where is the township cemetery?" I remember asking in one of the new settlements.

"Oh," said my father, "they haven't laid it out as yet. No one has died. Some of them up here have been thinking of shooting old man Perkins as a good beginning."

Sometimes during our long drives my father would suddenly break out, after a long silence, with the kind of prophecies he delighted in, as on one occasion passing through the wilderness that was then the township of Milltown in our own county.

"Ray," he said, pointing with his whip, "I shall not live to see the time, but you will, when all this country will be covered with beautiful farms. There will be fine painted houses and great barns and windmills and good roads and good schools and a rich and contented people."

I believed it of course if Father said it, but it seemed utterly impossible. On all sides were unbroken forests, great trees, jungles of brushwood, marshy brooks, miles and miles of them: even the road was all but impassable, ruts, mudholes and the remainder of huge stumps and roots. And yet, not so long ago, I drove out that very road with my brother Harry in his automobile—a fine pavement all the way. Every word my father said had come true. Great barns and silos, fields overflowing with corn and oats and peas, and herds of cattle as fine as there are to be found in North America. All the things he had dreamed had come to pass and many more that no man, at that time, could have dreamed: an automobile in every garage, radios and telephones and electric lights in every house, and even airplanes whirring overhead. The wilderness we knew as Milltown is now one of the best dairying centers in the state of Wisconsin. And all in fifty or sixty years!

I must speak also of another gift of my father's which helped to make the up-country trips perennially interesting. He had a singularly keen nose: I never knew any man with a better one. It was a great beak of a nose with long narrow nostrils, although I do not know that that had anything to do with his gift. He would break a long silence, after miles of unbroken forest, lift his head with sudden awareness and say to me:

"I smell open fields."

In a few minutes we were sure to come to a settler's cabin, a log barn, or a clearing. Among the free odors of the forest he had caught some vagrant odor of the work of men.

When we were tramping or surveying in that country, I have seen him stop suddenly, draw in a long breath, and remark:

"Marshes," or, "A stream yonder."

Part of this strange keenness of sense, often noted by those who knew that sturdy old cavalryman, may have been based, as our talents sometimes are, upon a defect. It is well known that when one sense is defective the others fly to the rescue, and my father's singular development of the sense of smell may have been due in part to his loss of hearing, though I believe it to have been, to a far larger degree, a native gift. All his life long he enjoyed with more than ordinary keenness the odor of flowers, and would often pick a sprig of balsam or sweet fern and carry it along with him in his hand, sniffing at it from time to time, and he loved the lilac, as I do after him.

I recall once on a wild Northern lake, when we were working along the shore in a boat, how he stopped suddenly and exclaimed:

"Ray, do you hear anything?"

"No, Father. What is it?"

"Indians."

Sure enough, in a short time I heard the barking of their dogs and we came soon upon their camp, where, I remember, they were drying deer meat upon a frame of poplar poles over an open fire. He told me that the smoky smell of the Indians, tanned buckskin, parched wild rice, and the like, were odors that carried far and could not be mistaken.

All these early experiences of mine led to a more or less intimate acquaintance with the pioneer country and the pioneers themselves: and my father, as I grew older, began to trust me more and more to make trips alone into the up-country. I have been astonished, when I have thought of it since, at the responsibilities far beyond my years that he placed upon me. I recall in particular a trip I made just before I was fifteen years old (I think in January, 1885) to help out during the taxpaying season. My father represented the ownership, or himself owned, large tracts of land scattered over two or three counties, chiefly Polk and Burnett, and in order to save certain penalties, taxes had to be paid before the town treasurers made their returns to the county treasurer. This meant that some one must visit a dozen or more remote settlements, find the treasurers, who in those days were pioneer farmers, usually Scandinavians who spoke little English, see that the proper tax receipts were made out, and the money paid over.

I had previously made such visits with my father, so that I knew exactly what to do, but the trip itself in midwinter in that wild country was never an easy one. It was the coldest part of the year and often the roads, none too good at best, were blocked with snow. I drove my father's team of spirited horses hitched to an old-fashioned light bobsleigh. On one of these trips a deer, bounding out into the road startled my team so that they rushed aside into the bushes and I had the greatest difficulty in getting them out of the deep snow. More than once I got lost, and since the country was so sparsely settled and many of the settlers spoke no English, I sometimes had trouble finding my man. Once I thought I was about to be eaten alive by a pair of ugly dogs such as most of the settlers kept.

On the trip I speak of I arrived just at dark at Erickson's in the town of Bone Lake (or was it West Sweden?)—the substantial log house back from the road with a welcome light in the frosty windows. The door opened and Erickson himself stood framed in the glowing doorway. I heard his shout of greeting. I was so stiff with the cold that I could hardly get out from under the buffalo robes and my fingers were too numb to unbuckle the harness from the steaming horses. Erickson led the horses into his low, warm log barn;

21

I heard the whinnying welcome of one of his own team, the stirring of the cattle in their low stalls, the sharp smell of hay and milk and manure, most pleasant. When we went out Erickson closed the door after pushing aside the gathered snow with his felt shoe-pack.

"Now," said Erickson, "ve vill go in."

I felt the grateful gush of warm air when the house door was opened. I stamped off the snow, and unwrapped my immense woolen scarf. There was only one large room in the cabin with a storage and woodshed behind. At one end stood an iron cook-stove, the pride of the household, decorated with shiny nickel, and spotlessly clean. A glowing smile of welcome from the open hearth greeted me; and from various pots and pans rose the ravishing odors of the cooking supper—infinitely appetizing to a cold and hungry boy. I met Mrs. Erickson, a large, beaming red-faced Danish woman, the personification of hospitality, full of half-guttural exclamations of solicitude. Six or seven little Ericksons, towheaded and awe-stricken, stood in the background watching me shed my overcoat and fur cap.

The delicious warmth of the room stirred through my numbed hands and feet, crept into my shivering body. I watched the bustle of activity that now began, in which every one had a part—setting the dishes on the table with its oilcloth top, cutting off enormous slices of snowy bread, piling every plate high with steaming potatoes, pork, beans, and putting on, I could see, for this particular occasion, various kinds of sausage, pickles, and even a pitcher of home-made maple syrup. And finally a heaping plate of doughnuts and a great pot of coffee!

My Adventures on the Frontier

I may in my life have eaten better meals, more delicately served, but few certainly I ever enjoyed as much, for I had been driving all day long in that cold weather, with nothing to eat since breakfast. The bountiful hostess kept filling up my plate—volubly explaining how she had made this or that prized delicacy—and I kept accepting until I could literally eat not another morsel. Everything was good, clean, plain—and so plentiful that the entire family, including all the children, glowed with health.

After supper, sitting by the kitchen stove, talking as wisely with Erickson as though I had been a farmer for at least thirty years, I grew desperately sleepy. The boy in me wanted nothing in the world but to crawl in anywhere and drop into dreamless slumber. Three of the younger children were already lying prone on a rag rug that partly covered the smooth swept dirt floor, fast asleep. But the man in me had to get up, reach for his bag and take out the lists of lands on which the taxes were to be paid. The treasurer, now all business, put his books, with a pen and a bottle of ink, on the kitchen table, which Mrs. Erickson had wiped clean. We both sat ourselves down and I soon found, as often before, that the farmer with his great, clumsy hands and his slow brain, would be all night working on my receipts. He wrote a fairly good hand and he would be accurate enough—but slow, slow! So I offered to write out the receipts and as I completed the lists and tore off the duplicates he checked them off ponderously and signed them. He took my own footings of the money totals, for my father was well known and trusted in all that country—and I was "Baker's son." When we had finished I filled out checks for the necessary amounts and the business was done. It had taken more than three hours of hard work.

By this time three of the younger children—I had watched the process out of the corner of my eyes—had been put into a plump trundlebed which had been drawn out from under the huge square family bed with its foreign-looking corner-posts and canopy, just such as the family had probably used in the old home in Denmark, which occupied the entire end of the room opposite the stove. I had wondered a little where I was to sleep and I was soon to find out. I was to have the big bed: but where was I to undress? I had had, fortunately, some previous experience with one-room log houses and I lost no time in getting off my coat and boots and stockings and trousers—which Mrs. Erickson immediately gathered up and hung on a line over the stove to dry out. She and Erickson sat by the stove with their backs to me but the three older children, including two girls about my own age, stood watching every move I made. I kept on my shirt and under-wear and climbed the little steps into the bed. It was an enormous affair, swelling upward and outward like a great flowering dumpling, but as clean as any bed could possibly have been, and infinitely inviting to a tired and sleepy boy. There was a fat straw mattress below and a feather bed above covered with a gay pieced counterpane. I slipped under the feather bed which was deliciously soft and warm and lay there for a moment dreamily watching the three older children who, having shed their clothes, or most of them, climbed a ladder to the loose-boarded attic where they had a bed on the floor just above the kitchen stove—quite the warmest place in the house. I wondered vaguely where Erickson and his wife were to sleep, since I was in the only bed. Soon stout Erickson threw off his outer clothing and climbing the little stairs got into the bed, under the feathers, next to me. A moment later Mrs. Erickson, having blown out the kerosene lamp, joined him. There we were all three, quite warm and comfortable. For a moment or so I watched the light from the hearth flickering on the rafters above me and then sank into a deep and dreamless slumber —the sleep of youth and weariness and perfect health.

When I awoke the sun was shining in at the windows. Erickson and his wife must have been up for an hour or hours earlier, for a pail of foaming new milk stood at the doorway, and breakfast was almost ready. I think it was the delicious odor of coffee and frying pork that awakened me. I dressed with a full gallery of admirers, for the youngest of the family, up and out of their trundle-bed, now joined the older ones in watching me.

What a breakfast, and what a morning!—crisp, sharp cold, with the smoke from the chimney rising straight to the blue of the sky. My heart sang as I helped Erickson harness and hook up the horses. The horses themselves, well-rested and well-fed, were eager for the road. All the family, smiling with good-byes and invitations to come again, stood around the doorway waving their hands. I was off to my next treasurer—glad of the morning, proud of my work, happy to be alive.

☆ 5 ☆

My Father's Way with His Sons

MY FATHER had a great affection, based upon a true understanding, for his sons. There were six of us, of whom I was the oldest. His discipline was absolute and sometimes even harsh, for he had been a cavalry officer in the Civil War, and the first article in his manual of conduct was obedience. He had a piercing eye and when he looked at a boy that boy knew that nothing he had done or thought could be covered up. I say that we respected him: it was something far more than that: we adored him. He was not only a man of unusual physical strength, but he was strikingly handsome and carried himself always like the cavalry officer he had been—erect, alert, vigorous.

He had an acute sense of obligation concerning boys brought up there on the frontier where the only school was hopelessly bad. He began early to read aloud to us or to encourage us to read for ourselves. How well I remember the little gatherings just before bedtime, the lamp in the middle of the table, the book, whatever it was, open before him and the small audience, tousle-headed, with grimy legs drawn up under them, sitting with mouths open and eyes fixed upon the reader's face! Whatever Father did, he did with gusto. What rolling zest he put into the adjectives: how

My Father's Way with His Sons

he dramatized the questions and replies. He was best with the Old Testament stories: the escape of Moses from Egypt and the stirring battles of Joshua. Nothing could have been made more exciting than the attack upon Jericho with the priests of Israel, each blowing his trumpet of ram's horn as he marched. If the narrative as presented by the biblical writer lacked thrilling details my father never hesitated to put them in and he was full of questions to make sure that we really understood. In the midst of the account of the capture of Ai he turned upon me suddenly and asked:

"Ray, how do you spell Ai?"

I was flustrated. It was a terrific thing to make a mistake in answering Father's questions. I concluded at once that it must be a peculiarly difficult word or I should not have been tested.

"Aighi," I spelled.

How my father laughed, throwing his head back; but I never afterward forgot Ai or anything concerning it.

I learned much Sunday afternoons or evenings, lying full on Father's bed with him, while he lay propped up on several pillows and read aloud the Norse legends of Thor and Wodin and the Frost Giants—I learned the Deception of Appearance, Thor drinking all unwitting from the sea, or wrestling with Time, the Old Woman. Nothing was what it seemed; everything was something else.

Somewhere Father had also found a metrical rendering of certain of the tales of Valhalla. Some parts of them were difficult and Father would stop to explain, especially if there was a battle or a hand-to-hand conflict—and when was there not?—and would often make his own interpretation more

27

thrilling than the narrative itself. How I remember the beat of those heroic meters, the wild and free adventure:

> "And lo! cloven in twain at a stroke
> Fell King Helge's gold shield from its pillar of oak.
> At the clang of the blow,
> The live started above, the dead started below."

My gentle mother did not approve of these readings. She appeared once in the doorway, standing there slim, small, white—we rough ones piled on the bed listening to the roaring verse of those old sagas.

"Stan, I think you should not read such terrible bloody stories to those boys, especially on Sunday."

"Oh, now," I can hear my father's reply, "these stories won't hurt the boys. They're good for them. They're full of fight."

But he was exceedingly attentive to my mother, whose judgment he greatly respected, and that evening at bedtime, or another evening, he was quite likely to read to us the parable of a certain rich man, or of the house built on the sand, or of the prodigal son.

One day my father came back from St. Paul with a large roll or package under his arm of which he made a great mystery.

"Now you are going to see where you came from," he told us.

"From Michigan?"

"No, no—farther back than that—thousands of years farther back."

We could not imagine what it could be. When our curiosity

had been sufficiently whetted my father remarked one evening:

"Now we'll get at it."

He made the ceremony dramatic by lighting three or four of our largest lamps and setting them around the room. We were in a high state of excitement. I was deputized to strip off the coverings of the mysterious package. It proved to be a large roll with glossy cloth at the back and smelling of varnish. When unrolled it reached nearly across the room, from the stove into the bay window, and it was covered with the strangest pictures, printed comments and figures, all in dazzling colors, and all attached to what appeared to be a river, beginning quite small at one end of the scroll, near the stove, and gradually with many tributary rivulets, enlarging until upon reaching the bay window it filled the entire width of the parchment.

We could not at first imagine what it was, so we all, including my father, went down on our hands and knees, or on our stomachs, and began to study it. It was a graphic representation of the stream of history. It began, as a good Presbyterian record ought to do, in the Garden of Eden with Adam and Eve quite naked except for fig-leaves, a tremendous serpent with glittering eyes curving down out of the apple tree—all quite proper. Babylon was there with its hanging gardens, sending a tributary into the stream, which afterward grew still more complicated by the great rivers of Greece and of Rome. Away up toward the end where the pictures were small and crowded and the print confusing, we found America joining the current, and a funny little picture of George Washington on a rearing horse. It was a shock to find that we occupied such an insignificant part in the stream. The years were charted at the margin so that it was easy to see how far after Julius Cæsar or Jesus or Charlemagne we were living.

That great evening and many of those that followed were devoted to our wonderful new map. My father seemed quite as excited as we were and told stories as he followed out this or that tributary or explained many things of which the scroll said nothing. It gave me my first sense of the immense sweep of history; whenever I have thought of Charlemagne in later years I remember him first of all placed near one leg of our old settee. I don't know what the scroll was called: I have never seen one since just like it, but it was tremendously interesting to that family of half-wild boys.

☆ 6 ☆

My Father and God

As I LOOK back along the years to my boyhood—mindful always of my resolution to tell only of those events which increased my life and those men and women who really changed it, I always think first of my chief hero—my father. My father and God, not then altogether distinguishable from each other, filled the largest place in my boyhood.

Sunday morning "prayers" were an institution in our Presbyterian household. I can hear my father talking with God; I can somehow *see*, as though I now stood aside with no real right to possession, I can see the little boy who was myself kneeling there on the carpet with his nose buried in the queer musty-smelling upholstery of the living-room chair, listening intently to what Father said to God. All the things I remember!—my father's broad back as he also knelt by his chair, his stiff white hair, his great beetling eyebrows with the eyelids under them trembling and sometimes partly opening, as seen by the little boy through the cracks between his fingers; the thin ankles and worn shoes of Aunt Amanda, and my mother's beautiful bent head with her delicate fingers thrust up into her soft hair, and the row of other little boys who were my brothers, kneeling more or less restlessly, each by his chair. I can see the house-plants in the warm window and our old cat curled in the Sunday

31

morning sunshine on the sill just outside, and the rows of battered books in the cases, and the picture of Beatrice Cenci, beautiful but sad, in its golden frame, just above the stove. It was wrong, of course, to look through one's fingers when Father was talking with God, but I had already learned that one often did what he disapproved because it was so interesting or so delightful.

"Consider, oh God, that we are dust. We have sinned, oh God, and deserve nothing at Thy hands. Be merciful to us, and punish us not according to our manifold transgressions."

The Presbyterian preacher always told God exactly what was what and never allowed any back talk: but my father, even when he really warmed up and did most of the talking himself, was a just man and strove to give God His chance. When he paused, apparently listening for God's response, I was always worried. Could there be any doubt as to God's intentions? How could He punish any one as wonderful as my father, or a poor, good, little boy like me—or the Baker family generally? And yet—it was terrifyingly uncomfortable to remember certain things that I had done. If God was anything like my father and found me out He might consider some of my sins quite punishable. And it might hurt.

One sin I had committed gave me a great deal of anxiety. Whenever there was a pause in my father's prayers it came storming into my memory and made me shiver as I knelt there by the living-room chair. A worsted-worked motto over the door in our dining room with the words "Thou God Seest Me" came to me with tormenting frequency. I had smelled the cookies that Annie Christianson, our "girl," had made, and with well-founded knowledge of what several little boys, if tempted, might do, had hidden in a jar in the china closet. Being the oldest of the children, I was naturally the wisest, and I knew, by instinct, to say nothing of smell, where those cookies were. So I tiptoed into the quiet dining room. All the doors were closed. I was very hungry and I could smell the cookies. But when I looked up there was the motto:

"Thou God Seest Me."

The torment of that moment! God or cookies! I walked across the floor, set the high chair near the closet door, and climbed up. I reached my hand over into the cookie-jar and paused. Sapphira was struck dead! Would God strike me dead? Or was He a nice kindly God who would understand how hungry a little boy could be, and how good the cookies smelled, and let him have just one or two? There I stood with one hand in the cookie-jar considering the theological problems of the ages. I hesitated, however, only a moment. The cookies got the better of God: I took not one or two, but as many as I could hold in my hand, and darted in terror out of the room.

Nothing happened. I was not struck dead: but I did not know what else God might do—He might be like Father, who didn't always punish promptly—and for many a week, at the pauses in the morning prayer, I trembled lest God speak out in a deep bass voice and point His finger at me.

These prayers made a powerful impression upon me, though I doubted whether Father was dust even when he told God so. I thought how really tremendous and wonderful God must be when my father was willing to bow down before Him. When I thought how much Father admired God, I had a high opinion of Him.

33

☆ 7 ☆

My First Lesson in Astronomy

MY FATHER was always plumping surprising questions at all of us—questions about our work, and our play, and especially about what happened at school, after we began to go. He often asked these questions at the table, sometimes greatly to our confusion. Once he turned upon me suddenly:

"Ray, who is President of the United States?"

I think I could not have been more than seven years old. I began searching desperately in my mind. My father at that time was devoted to *The Christian Union* and read and quoted the sermons of Henry Ward Beecher. I thought Henry Ward Beecher the greatest man in the world next to my father. So I piped up:

"Henry Ward Beecher."

I shall never forget the roar of laughter from the older people, nor the fact learned at that moment that a man of whom I had never before heard—Rutherford B. Hayes—was President. It was, I think, my first morsel of political information.

Father's questioning more often related to my school work, with which, plainly, he was much dissatisfied. One day I volunteered the information that the teacher had been telling us about astronomy. My father immediately pounced upon me and began a cross-examination to find out what I really knew, which was next to nothing at all. After supper my father called me into the sitting room.

"Ray, light the lantern and go out into the garden. Bring in one large round turnip—the largest you can find. Get another small one—the smallest you can find. Cut off the tops and tails, wash them up and bring them in here."

This was exactly like my father, the mystery of such an errand! What could he want with turnips in the sitting room? I knew that something exciting was afoot. When I came in with the turnips my father laid aside his paper and with his large pocket-knife began trimming and rounding them off.

"This little one," he said, "we must make much smaller—and still it will not be small enough."

I had not the remotest idea of what was afoot. We stood there, three or four of us, open-mouthed. Presently my father went into the parlor and dramatically brought out the largest lamp in the house, one with a big round globe of a chimney, lighted it and set it in the middle of the center table.

"Now come here," said he. "This lamp is the sun, this big round turnip is the earth: this little one is the moon."

I can recall the sudden thrill of surprise and astonishment that this announcement caused, and the way my heart began to beat.

Holding the turnips one in each hand he showed us how the earth revolved around the sun, and the moon, at the same time, around the earth. He stood away from the lamp as far as the room would permit in order to exhibit the immense distances. Incidently, while he was trying to get his elbow 93,000,000 million miles away from the sun, I heard my mother cry out in alarm:

"Look out, Stan—the vase, the vase."

It was, however, too late, the earth had collided with mother's favorite pedestal and the vase with its dry pampas plumes had gone crashing to the floor.

"You see," cried my father instantly and triumphantly, "the force of the momentum of the heavenly bodies"—which did not in the least assuage either my mother or my Aunt Amanda.

This small interlude did not disturb the course of nature: my father illustrated the shadow of the moon on the earth and explained about eclipses. It was as fascinating as any story, and could never be forgotten. To this day I think sometimes of astronomical wonders in the terms of turnips —perhaps as good a way as any.

Afterward came the invariably alarming part of such experiences, with which we were well acquainted.

"Now, Ray, you take the turnips and explain the eclipse."

An awkward little boy, not quite sure he understood!

"Hold them up there. No, no, not *there*. Here."

I was trembling, and my father, reddening in the face, grew testier and testier. He explained again, and asked my next brother Charlie to demonstrate. Charlie was worse than I was. At last, growing angry at our stupidity, my father tossed the turnips into the wastebasket and went back to his paper. Strangely, we accepted it all without resentment: for this was Father, always interesting, always exciting, always right.

When I tried a few days later to explain the wonders of

the heavenly bodies to two of the neighbor boys by a similar use of turnips I came to share my father's irritation. They *would* not understand. I had an inclination to pound one of them, who was my best friend, on the head with the earth, but we soon made up and compromised by cutting up both the earth and the moon and eating them raw.

☆ 8 ☆

I Make the Acquaintance
of Books

OURS WAS a house of books. I believe my father at that
time had the only collection of books—and it was by no
means a large one—that could be called a library in all
of that part of Wisconsin, certainly in all Polk County.

He was especially fond of controversial books; he enjoyed
the battles he found in them, and felt perfectly safe, since
none of them ever changed him. He read not so much for
enlargement as for confirmation, adding not to the breadth
but to the depth of his convictions. Those assertions with
which he agreed, or which substantiated his own views, he
scored down the margin of the page with a stout pencil,
sometimes adding "True" or "Excellent." When he found
anything that displeased him or went contrary to the truth,
as he knew it to be, I have heard him bring his foot em-
phatically down upon the floor and cry out, "Bah!" Sometimes he would write "Absurd" in the margin. Not long ago
I found among a package of his papers a characteristic
memorandum written on paper now faded and torn, in his
own strikingly individual hand, a definition of Truth:

"The Truth is that which has gotten itself believed by
me."

I Make the Acquaintance of Books

All this reading, to a lonely man marooned on the frontier, whose deafness prevented easy human contacts, furnished the metal of controversy out of which he could fashion his assurances of truth, and weapons with which to scatter his opponents.

I think it was more satisfying to him than actual conversation, for in argument he himself soon became angry, at least testy, if his opponent showed any signs of being unwilling to admit defeat, and accept the law as he laid it down. Many a stormy controversy he had with a stern old Presbyterian minister named Crozier, who was given to setting forth what he called "the law and the prophets," one in particular, long to be remembered, on the question as to whether an unregenerate man could do a worthy act. But his fiercest combats took place with a cousin by marriage, whom good ladies, whispering behind their hands, called an atheist. He never attended church and he dared to criticize the accepted religious beliefs. As a matter of fact, he was a man of no broad intellectual foundations; but he had been one of those single-book men sometimes found on the frontier, as prodigiously addicted to one author as other men were to the Bible. In his case it was Herbert Spencer. He had a formidable arsenal of Spencerian criticism and comment, and he was dangerous indeed, if met on his own ground. He was such a devotee that he named his oldest son Herbert Spencer.

He came occasionally to talk with my father and both, at first, by common consent, steered away from religious topics. It never, however, lasted long: they inevitably drifted nearer and nearer the whirlpool. It began usually with some quotation from Herbert Spencer which George Ely could not keep to himself—and the waters began to rush and boil.

In those years my father was able to hear through a flexible speaking tube which he wore around his neck. When any one approached he thrust one end of the tube into his ear and presented the other like an aimed blunderbuss at his visitor. He was so prompt and vigorous that only a hardy spirit—the first time at least—could help quailing.

My father would listen to the Spencerian arguments of his friend with patient dignity for some little time. While he considered them "balderdash" or "buncombe"—two of his favorite words—he would respond in measured but wearied forbearance. These meetings always had a fascination for the little boy curled up in the corner: I awaited with a kind of solemn joy and complete confidence the onset of the storm—and the invariable victory of my father. I could see him growing more and more restless; his face beginning to redden: his replies quicker and higher in tone. At some more than usually preposterous argument from Herbert Spencer, he would withdraw the end of the tube which went into his ear and lay down the law once and for all, occasionally emphasizing his remarks by pounding the arm of his chair. In vain would his visitor talk with rising and sometimes angry voice into the blunderbuss: nothing could go through. When my father had set forth the truth, all in an orderly manner, he would roll up his tube and put it into his pocket. That was the end of Herbert Spencer.

It was inevitable, in such an atmosphere of books, that I should soon become a reader on my own account. The first book I remember reading through, except possibly certain forgotten children's books, was *Pilgrim's Progress*. I should not myself have thought of reading it, although several pictures in it were thrilling enough, particularly the fight of Christian with Apollyon, but my father told me something about it, and remarked:

"Ray, if you will read that book straight through I will give you a dollar."

A dollar in those days to a boy there on the frontier was as good as a million. I started in at once, and being fully aware of my father's uncomfortable habit of finding out, when a boy said he knew anything, whether or not he really did know it, I read carefully and thoroughly—and finally with tremendous interest in the story if not in the simple and realistic theology. I cannot now remember whether I was cross-examined after I finished the book, but I do recall, vividly, getting my first silver dollar.

Once started as a reader I found it a great joy—a joy that has lasted me all my life: one of the few joys as keen at fifty or sixty or seventy as at twelve or fourteen, keener perhaps. Of what other appetite in the entire range of human desire can this be said? Time satiates all the appetites but this.

At fourteen or fifteen when I got into a book that really interested me I could scarcely lay it down. My father was a great reader in bed—I can see him now lying there, his great head, with its unruly grizzled hair, propped up on the pillows, one hand holding a partly shaded kerosene lamp on his breast, the other his book—and I soon began to follow his example. This was likely to keep the other boys, my younger brothers, awake, and was finally forbidden. Nevertheless I would put the lamp on the chair at the head of my bed and when I heard Father's step on the stairs—he was likely to make a round of inspection after the boys were in bed—I would quickly blow out the lamp and when he appeared be quite serenely asleep with my book hidden between my knees, deep down in the bedclothes. I waited usually until my brothers were asleep and then got up quickly, lit my lamp, and went at my book again. My actual early schooling, as I look back, amounted to little: my reading and my father's talk were everything.

As it was, I was much too much inclined to galloping and romantic poetry—Scott, Byron, Longfellow, and later Tennyson. I have wondered since what it was that lured me so powerfully to romantic poetry, save the madness of youth: but it was there. One great day I shall never forget. While foraging among my father's books I found an old leather-clad volume with one of the corners worn down until the brown board within was plainly visible. It looked as though it had been gnawed. In this old book I came across the *Spanish Ballads* by a worthy author now mostly forgotten save as the biographer of Walter Scott—John Gibson Lockhart. In those days I knew nothing and cared nothing for the accomplishments of authors. Smith was as full of significance for me as Milton. I knew what I wanted: that was literature: and all the world of writing else was trash.

In the *Spanish Ballads,* I came across, quite by accident, "The Wandering Knight's Song," which begins:

> "My ornaments are arms,
>   My pastime is in war,
> My bed is cold upon the wold,
>   My lamp yon star."

I Make the Acquaintance of Books

It was one evening after supper I read it, and it went straight to my head. After finishing it in one delicious draught I shut the book with a snap, seized my cap and dashed out of doors. A young moon hung in the clear autumn sky: the silence of evening lay deep upon the earth. Cool airs had followed the warmth of the day. So I ran wildly down the hill waving my arms and chanting to myself:

> "My ornaments are arms,
> My pastime is in war,
> My bed is cold upon the wold,
> My lamp yon star."

I don't think I knew what "wold" meant, but it was an advantage at that age not to be too knowing! Worlds were thus opened to a word.

And as I ran, I chanted also the last stanza:

> "I ride from land to land,
> I sail from sea to sea,—
> Some day more kind I fate may find,
> Some night kiss thee!"

I was gloriously, ineffably mad!

My mother, I think, deliberately encouraged me in "good literature" as a counterpoise to the stories my father read to us or told us. I have among my most prized possessions a book of poems, edited by Duyckinck and illustrated with exquisitely engraved woodcuts, bearing these words on the

43

flyleaf written in my mother's beautiful and delicate hand-writing:

Presented to
Ray S. Baker
By his parents upon his ninth birthday
April 17, 1879

Turning over the leaves sixty years afterward I can tell by the worn or loose or soiled pages the very poems I loved best. One was by Thomas Percy with a thrilling picture of an armed horseman, axe in hand, facing a charging company of Moors with spears, and the verse under it read:

> "Like a lion turns the warrior,
>   Back he sends an angry glare
> Whizzing came the Moorish javelin,
>   Vainly whizzing through the air."

Another—and these pages are in tatters—was "The Burning of Rokeby," by Walter Scott, others Tennyson's "The May Queen" and "Morte D'Arthur," another still "A Dream of Fairies," by a poet now probably forgotten—S. S. Conant—but that, I think, was because of the entrancing pictures.

I had a gift in my boyhood—now unfortunately quite lost —of being able to commit easily to memory poetry and even prose that delighted me. At one time in my boyhood I was able to repeat considerable portions of "The Lady of the Lake," "Marmion," the "Prisoner of Chillon," "Locksley Hall" and many other poems. During a severe illness at Baltimore several years ago I comforted weary hours by

44

turning over this ancient treasure. Quite unexpectedly I found I could remember passages I had not thought of, certainly, for fifty years. Where had they been concealed all that time? In what dusty attics of the mind? And how was it that when I had turned up a verse or a stanza of some old poem, wearing it bright with many repetitions, it would suddenly begin to glow and bring with it other long-forgotten stanzas? Where were they? And if one had the time and the persistence could he restore everything that had gone into his mind in times past? Is anything of experience or emotion or thought ever entirely lost? I have told of these experiences more fully in *Adventures in Solitude,* by David Grayson.

In the attic of our house were several barrels of old books left there by an aunt of mine who was breaking up housekeeping. Digging into them one day I found a book called *Uncle Tom's Cabin.* I don't think I had ever heard of it before but I dipped into it and was soon absorbed, sitting there by the little window in the quiet attic with my legs curled up under me. Never shall I forget the acquaintance then made with Uncle Tom and Topsy, and Mr. St. Clair and Miss Felie—and how deeply I entered into the lives and sorrows and joys of them all. It was like a new world opening around me. When I got to the end of the book, however, I was dreadfully disappointed. The story seemed to break off right at the most exciting point. What became of Uncle Tom? I made the astonishing discovery that this was only Volume I, and that I had another whole volume yet to come. What joy! It was as though a feast snatched from my hands was suddenly returned to me. But where was the other volume? I went at my poor aunt's barrels like a terrier at a woodchuck hole. I turned them all out, but Volume II was not to be found. I confided in my mother. She too looked: it was not there. She attempted to satisfy me by telling me what happened in the missing volume. This was terrible: I put my fingers in my ears and ran out of the house. There was no library in those days nearer to us than St. Paul, and my father finally promised to get me the book the next time he went into the city—a long trip in those days. I can recall my acute impatience. Would he forget? At length he came back with the complete book—a fat volume in green covers. How I gobbled it down—took a long breath, and gobbled it all again.

When I was about twelve or thirteen years old my father bought a complete new edition of Shakespeare, edited by Hudson, in twenty-two volumes and began to read it himself. He also tried reading certain of the plays aloud to me —I remember "The Tempest"—but I did not at that time take to them. The language was too difficult and the poetry, or much of it, too subtle. I know from the experience of my friend Norman Hapgood that Shakespeare can be read by children or to them with real pleasure (he wrote a book about it called *Janet Reads Shakespeare*), but it was years before I entered this domain of magic and wonder and beauty.

My father also presented to me one Christmas an edition of Milton's *Paradise Lost*. It was of large size and illustrated by Doré, pictures I greatly enjoyed studying, with their captions, but I could not read the poem then or since, although one of the pictures, that of Satan falling out of

I Make the Acquaintance of Books

Paradise—"From morn to noon he fell, from noon to dewy eve, a summer's day"—was so alluring that I did look up the text relating to it and found it unexpectedly interesting.

I fear in re-reading these pages that I have made too great a point of my reading, for I am not now and never was a "thoroughly read" man. My reading was always a kind of living: not so many books, not so much facts or history or philosophy or even stories, but a longing to know some man or men stronger, braver, wiser, wittier, more amusing, or more desperately wicked, than I was, whom I could come to know well and sometimes be friends with.

☆ 9 ☆

My Father's Stories

My FATHER was a prodigious story-teller, the best I ever knew, judging at least by the fresh interest of those who heard him. We teased incessantly for stories and it was not unusual, in the earlier days, for my father to have a roomful of people for his audience, all the family and often several friends or visitors. He had the gift of creating an atmosphere; he liked night stories with a shudder of mystery or horror in them. He liked battlefields and charging ranks of men and the smoke of battle. He had many a graphic phrase which fermented in a boy's memory. "Hands up, or I'll let the daylight through you." He had been a cavalry officer during the war, as ranking major commanding the First District of Columbia Cavalry in some of the fiercest raids and battles along the Virginia front. Before that he had been in the Secret Service, stationed at Washington, his cousin General Lafayette C. Baker having been its chief. Lincoln once spoke to him, an experience memorable to the end of his life, of which I shall write later.

After the battle of Sycamore Church, while defending the rear of General Kautz's command in its withdrawal northward, his regiment, dismounted in a little wood for more effective resistance, was cut to pieces by an overwhelming force of Confederate cavalry under the command

48

of General Wade Hampton. He himself was struck down by a saber cut across the head and left for dead on the field of battle. Such a wound, by a saber, I have understood, is one of the rarest known in modern warfare, since it was unusual even in the Civil War for cavalry to charge near enough to dismounted men to cut them down. I have seen my father toss aside his heavy growth of hair, thick and white to the end of his life, to show the long scar across his head.

On the morning after the battle he was aroused to consciousness by the attempt of some one to pull off his heavy cavalry boots. When he began faintly to resist, he heard a voice saying:

"He's alive. Bring him along."

He was too weak from loss of blood and exposure to walk so that two of his own men who had also been captured made a stretcher out of a blanket and carried him into the Confederate camp. He demanded at once, bloody and weak though he was, to be taken to the headquarters of the commanding officer: and his men, after considerable protest, put him down in front of General Hampton's tent. I shall never forget Father's report of the military courtesies that followed—his own extremely formal address as he lay there on the ground covered with blood, and the General's elaborate Southern courtesies in response. What Father had come to demand was his boots.

"One of your men, sir, has taken my boots."

I heard that story with exquisite delight many times and my father never failed to get a beautiful, sympathetic, congratulatory laugh by remarking:

49

"I wanted those boots. They were brand new and had cost me $125."

(This amount varied: when he was in his best form it was often $150, and it never went under $100.)

He made us *see* the elaborate courtesy of General Hampton's response.

"You shall have them, suh."

Not long afterward they were returned by the ragged Southerner who had pulled them off, thinking that Father was dead.

A sequel to this story happened long years afterward. When the passions of the war had died down and the old Southern leaders began to reappear in national affairs General Wade Hampton was appointed a Railroad Commissioner of the United States—as I recall he was one of the earliest Confederate leaders to hold an important office in the Union. My father told the news at the table one day and recalled the old story of his capture.

"I believe I will write to the General and ask him if he remembers the Federal officer who was carried to his headquarters after the raid at Sycamore Church and demanded the return of his boots."

A few weeks later he came in smiling with a letter in his hand. It was General Hampton's response, saying with the utmost friendliness and circumambulatory courtesy that he remembered perfectly, and paying my father many compliments not only for the hard fight his men put up in the woods below Sycamore Church but for his pertinacity in demanding the return of his boots.

"I hope," wrote the General (I am quoting from memory), "that the boots continued to give you service long after the battle."

"That rebel," said my father, using the term he always used, "that rebel was a perfect gentleman."

My father kept General Hampton's letter for years, but I cannot now find it among his papers.

After his capture Father was taken to Libby Prison at Richmond—with his boots on!—where he was confined for a terrible five months. He nearly died of his wound and of malaria and exposure, but was finally exchanged for a Confederate officer of the same rank. His later deafness was attributed to the exposure he endured at that time and the illness that followed it.

After a few months' rest he was able to return to the front and commanded his regiment during the final struggle around Richmond and along the Appomattox.

All these incidents and a thousand more remained with incomparable vividness in his memory. He could tell stories for hours and never tire even a restless crowd of boys. He had fire, drama, passion: he even had, in some of the stories relating to the Southern Negroes who came into the Northern camps, a broad, rough humor. I have often wished that I could have heard these stories in later years when my critical faculties had become more active. Possibly my judgments might be different, but as the matter now stands in my mind, I can truthfully say that I never knew another such story-teller: one who could make a boy's hair rise on the back of his tousled head, set his heart to thumping wildly, make him terrified going up the long stairs alone to bed, or bring a lump in his throat or hot tears behind blinking eyelids—or roars of laughter wherein a boy could roll over backwards and punch a younger brother in the stomach as an evidence of his delight.

Sometimes we boys would agree beforehand as to what we wanted.

"Tell us a war-story—when you were in Libby Prison. Tell us a story of the time when you were travelling in Iowa. (This was before the war, when Father was a youth trying to earn his college expenses first at Oberlin, then at the University of Wisconsin, by selling maps through the sparsely settled pioneer territory of Iowa.) Tell us a story about when you were a boy."

They were all good, all sharp with detail, all exciting. Some even gave us pictures of historical events connected with the war that are unforgettable. One of these latter in particular has always stood out in my memory with unusual clarity. My father told it with something in his voice and in the look in his eyes which indicated how deeply he treasured the experience. This was the story, already referred to, of his one meeting with President Lincoln—or "Old Abe," as he called him invariably, with a kind of reverent affection. Father had often spoken of seeing Old Abe riding horseback along the dusty road to the Soldiers' Home, where he was spending part of the torrid summer, but this was the first time he had met him face to face.

Curiously enough, when I have thought of the story in later years one single expression in it springs first into my memory, probably because of the feeling in my father's voice when he repeated it.

"But the Major has only 350 men."

My Father's Stories

It has seemed to me that there was much of the considerate Lincoln in those few words.

The circumstances were these. It was on the 9th (or 10th) of July, 1864, and Early's bold raiders were already in Maryland just north of Washington, preparing to swoop down and take the capital. Grant, fully occupied in front of Richmond, had been dilatory in sending troops for defense. Hunter had been left far behind, and Early had broken through the small but valiantly resisting forces of Lew Wallace. Washington lay quite defenseless before him.

Both Lincoln and Stanton were greatly alarmed. Stanton called in General Baker, the head of the Secret Service, whose men had been bringing in reports regarding Early's advances, and asked him to get together every possible man of the First District of Columbia cavalry, a part of which was temporarily encamped in Washington. He wanted to make a reconnaissance in force. My father, being the ranking officer of that command, was ordered to report at once to Secretary Stanton.

Father had several descriptive phrases regarding Stanton, with whom his earlier connection with the Secret Service had occasionally brought him into contact. He did not like Stanton: "a sharp, hard man with a long white beard."

Stanton took the young officer with him across the street to the White House.

"Lincoln was sitting at his desk," my father used to say. "It was evening, but he was sitting at his desk, still working. When he leaned back I could see how worn and anxious he looked. There were deep lines around his eyes, and I remember how his hair stood up, as if he had just run his fin-

53

gers through it. He was wearing loose carpet slippers. He knew that Early might at that moment be galloping down the Seventh Street road with all his men."

Lincoln did not say a word to Stanton. Stanton sat down in the chair near the desk; the young officer remained standing. Save for the light on Lincoln's desk it was nearly dark in the room. Stanton spoke rapidly and with irritation.

"What he wanted," related my father, "was to send my companies—all the men that were left in Washington—immediately to Rockville, there to strike at Early's outposts to find out whether he was advancing in force."

"But the Major has only 350 men," said Lincoln, looking for the first time at the young officer.

"He can strike at Early; he can help delay him," urged Stanton.

"But he has only 350 men," said Lincoln.

"Delay is what we must have," said Stanton.

"Major," said Lincoln, "can you go up to Rockville and find out exactly what is happening there?"

"Yes, sir."

"And go at once?"

"Yes, sir."

"Well, go," said Lincoln, "but don't try to fight all of Early's army. Come back and tell us where they are and what they are doing."

Father often went on to tell us the story of that reconnaissance, the hard, hot riding through the dusty night, and how he deployed his men to get information, and how he had a sharp engagement at one point with a detachment of Early's soldiers. All this was exciting enough as he told it,

54

My Father's Stories

but there was something in his voice, in the look of his eyes, that made his meeting with Old Abe the supreme moment in the story. Whenever, in later years, I have thought of Lincoln it was the weary President, leaning back in his chair, whom my father had seen, an impression deeply surcharged with his own feeling.

Such were my father's stories. When I was about twelve years old I was so excited by a narrative that dealt with his Secret Service period that I tried to write it out. I remember the confusion I encountered in dealing with direct and indirect discourse, the mystery of quotation marks, and the problem of spelling some of the words Father used—such as minié-ball, ambuscade, chevaux-de-frise and the like. But the problem of all problems I discovered at twelve, as I was destined to do many times later, was to get Father into the story—the look in his eyes, the sound of his voice, the vigor and urgency of his personality. Father's stories with Father left out always seemed tame!

Many years later when I was struggling for a foothold as a magazine writer I thought of some of Father's old stories and wrote out a number of them, as nearly as I could remember them. When they were finished they fell so far short, in graphic power, of the stories that lay warm in my mind, that I was completely discouraged. To my surprise they were eagerly accepted by the editor of *McClure's Magazine* (then a new and brilliant adventure) and more were demanded. They were bloody yarns! One called "Walt Bowie" was published in December, 1898, and several others afterward. I am giving one of them in full, as a sample, in the following chapter. I was also much indebted to my

55

uncle, Lieutenant L. B. Baker, who had been quartermaster of my father's regiment. I used his account of the capture of John Wilkes Booth, he having been in charge of the expedition, in an article I wrote for *McClure's Magazine,* May, 1897.

It was my father's stories that helped me on my way, however faint reproductions of his fire and force and drama and power my narratives were.

☆ 10 ☆

A Story of the Secret Service

I AM HERE setting down one of my father's innumerable war-stories. I wrote it long ago, as nearly as possible in his own words: but I knew then, and know better now, how poorly the written words convey the fire and gusto of his telling: the dramatic gestures, the modulation of his voice, and the pauses—the petrifying pauses! But the story, save for one or two fictitious names, is all here.

In the spring of 1862 I was comparatively new in the work of the Secret Service. I had joined the force at the request of my cousin, Colonel L. C. Baker, the organizer and chief of the Bureau, and he was anxious that I become at once familiar with its workings. Perhaps that is why he soon sent me out with Traill for a tutor. Traill was a close-knit, swarthy-faced Virginian, with thin lips and a sharp nose of singularly delicate cut. On his left cheek there was a puckered white spot the size of a flattened Minié ball. Under excitement it sometimes twitched slightly and reddened— the only evidence of emotion that I ever knew him to show. Traill had made a reputation in the service. If there was a particularly desperate undertaking in hand, the Colonel had a way of calling off his force on his fingers, man by man, as if he felt uncertain which to send—and then always

57

sending Traill. He knew every by-path and ford and ravine in the Potomac Valley, and he possessed an aptitude, that fell only a little short of a passion, for slipping back and forth through the Confederate lines. In all my experience with him I never saw him frightened, or even ruffled; and, to the best of my knowledge, he never was hungry or tired —although I have seen him amazingly thirsty.

I had been lounging in the waiting room one night for upwards of an hour, when Traill came out of the Colonel's private office and closed the door gently behind him.

"You are going with me," he drawled; "I have ordered up the horses."

One thing a military man learns early in his career—not to ask questions until there is a fair likelihood of having them answered—and I followed Traill's preparations in silence. He selected three revolvers, and twirled the chambers of each of them and clicked the triggers to make sure that they were in good working order. Two of them he loaded, thrust deftly into the holsters of his belt, and buckled the leather flaps down over them; the third he slid into the slack of his cavalry boot. Then he rolled a blue army blanket inside of his poncho, and drew the bundle into wrinkled ridges with thongs of leather. A certain silent swiftness and gentleness marked everything that Traill did.

It was a dark night. We crossed the Long Bridge at a sharp trot, and climbed the Virginia hills. The road was soggy with moist sand that slipped and clogged under the hoofs of our horses—like riding in an oats bin, Traill said. The road crooked through the pine woods, and, as we moved, the trees seemed to march up out of the darkness, present themselves like soldiers on parade, then wheel backwards again, and give place to other companies and battalions. The spring air was heavy and pungent with the smell of moist mold, and in the hollows almost sharp with the lingering coolness of winter. I had no idea where we were going. Traill galloped steadily at my side, saying nothing. A man of few words, he was by no means sullen.

"I haven't heard the nature of our mission," I said to him: I felt that the auspicious moment for asking questions had come.

"We're going out to get Captain Cameron," he answered shortly.

I had heard much of Captain Cameron even during the short time I had been in Washington. He was a young Southern officer, born of a well-known Virginia family. Early in the war he became a violent Confederate, and, from his intimate knowledge of the country about Washington, he was assigned to the work of spy and blockade-runner. He was related by ties of blood more or less direct to half the aristocracy of Virginia and Maryland, and when we went out after him, we found that he had as many holes as a gopher. Ever since the opening of hostilities the authorities at Washington had sought to capture him; but a year of the war had passed, and he was still spreading terror along the Potomac. His finger, so said common fame, was always crooked to the trigger of his pistol, and more than once his reckless daring had cost the lives of Northern soldiers sent out to trap him. Report added to his reputation for bravado by arming him always with a bowie-knife, which he had used on several occasions with bloody effect.

Native American

Beyond Alexandria, where we halted a moment while our horses plunged their noses into a watering-trough, the country grew more desolate and forbidding. Many of the plantation buildings had been deserted, and they loomed up black and forlorn in the darkness. Sometimes a dog howled from the Negro quarters in the rear, and dismal echoes responded from plantation to plantation as we passed.

The first incident of the night worth mentioning—and it nearly cost the success of our expedition—occurred just after we tightened our saddle-girths for the third time, about midnight, as I judged. We knew that the country swarmed with Confederate guerrillas, but it was never the custom of the secret service to give them even the passing compliment of anxiety. We had stopped at a cross-roads, and Traill had thrown his bridle-rein to me while he went down on his knees and crept across the road, feeling for the wagon tracks: he was not quite certain in the darkness which road to take. In a moment there came a voice so sudden and sharp that it seemed to split the darkness: "Halt! Who comes there?"

Traill leaped to his saddle without a word. We drove the spurs into our horses' flanks, hugged close to their reeking necks, and galloped up the road. We heard a sharp command, then the sound of beating hoofs behind us. A revolver shot rang out sharply in the night air, and we heard the wailing cry of the bullet as it passed over our heads.

We were riding up a long hill. At the top, cut in silhouette against the sky, I saw the form of a horseman sitting statue-like at his post. We were evidently surrounded. Before I could speak, Traill laid his hand on my bridle-arm.

"Turn in here," he said.

We swerved wildly to the right, into what seemed an impenetrable forest, and rode a hundred yards or more in imminent danger of being brushed from our saddles by the down-sweeping limbs of the trees. Then the horses came to an abrupt standstill, and we narrowly escaped pitching headlong into a deep ravine that yawned before us. As we paused, we could hear the sound of hoofs in the road, then the sudden fierce challenge of the vedette, then voices in conversation. Traill grasped the nose of his horse, to prevent a telltale whinny.

A moment only we waited; then we scrambled down into the ravine, our horses sliding after us, and made our way around the vedette, striking the road again less than a mile farther to the south.

"A narrow escape," I commented, as our horses' hoofs again beat the steady music of the gallop.

Traill laughed. "There was only a handful of 'em or they would have given us a harder rub," he said.

Once more we hitched our saddle-girths, for time was precious, and rode in silence for an hour or more. At length Traill drew rein near a high-arched gateway of the kind so familiar in the ante-bellum South. Then he swung from his saddle and knelt close to one of the ghostly white columns, parted the weeds about its base, and struck a match. It lit up his face for a single instant, and then went out.

"This is the place," he said; "I have found O'Dell's mark."

To this day I do not know the exact location of the plantation, but of this I am certain: it was in Prince William

County, not far from the Potomac River. It took upwards of four hours of hard riding to reach it.

The gate was locked, but I wrenched loose two of the boards from the dilapidated fence, and we rode up the long, winding lane, guiding our horses to the grass at the edge of the drive, that they might make no noise.

It was a beautiful old place, even as we saw it, by dead of night. Great spreading trees covered the knoll on which it stood, and their branches, reaching out over the wide verandas, swept the gutter eaves.

The building had every appearance of being deserted— a great, black, silent block of uncertain shadows. The blinds were drawn, and not a ray of light gleamed anywhere from its windows, or from the Negro quarters, which we could see dimly huddled together half a hundred yards to the rear. There was not even a dog to bark, nor a sleeping Negro to waken and cry out.

"The house is vacant," I said to Traill, as we tossed our reins over the pegs on the hitching-bar.

"No, it isn't," he answered with some positiveness.

We stood under a syringa bush that half hid the wide front door.

"Have you got your pistols?"

"Yes," I said, drawing one of them from its holster and feeling for the loads.

"Go round to the rear of the house. Take care to make no noise. You will find a wide back porch. Go up and stand on the steps, near the back door, so that you can cover all the windows. If any one tries to leave the building, shoot 'em." Traill said it softly, almost gently.

"That man Cameron," he cautioned, as I was starting, "is a good deal of a fighter; he's quick on the trigger."

I went to the rear. I remember I was lame and moist from riding, and that my fingers clutched the revolver handle until my wrist throbbed with pain. It was the hour of night when a man's blood doesn't run the bravest, especially if he isn't sure what odds he may have to meet, or whether a shot from a darkened window may not drop him in his tracks.

My sense of hearing was painfully acute. I distinctly heard the squeaking of Traill's boots and the metallic tinkle of his spurs as he mounted the front porch, and then the resonant echo of his summons on the iron knocker. Like many Southern mansions, the house was built with a wide hall running straight through from the front to the back door. For a moment I fancied I heard the cautious squeak of steps on the stairs within, and then all was still again. I edged farther up on the porch, that I might better command a wide, shutterless window at the right of the door. There is this terror in a dark window: those within may see out, while those without cannot see in; but you don't appreciate it until you imagine a desperate man inside, waiting to put a bullet through your jacket.

There came a second and much louder knock on the front door. I knew that Traill was using his pistol butt. The sound echoed and re-echoed through the big, silent building. Presently I heard a shutter creak somewhere at the front of the house, and I set the hammer of my other revolver. A woman's voice spoke; I could not catch the words.

"Never mind, come down here and open the door," I heard Traill reply.

There was another parley, and then the shutter creaked again in closing. A moment later I saw through the glass of the side light the glimmer of a candle, with its sharp shadows creeping in huge angles along the ceiling of the hall.

"Who is there?" asked a frightened, feminine voice.

I heard a chain jingle and the sliding of a bar, and then voices in low conversation. Traill was speaking:

"I tell you he's here, and I'm going to have him. He can't get away."

"He is not here; I tell you he is not here. You have come to the wrong place."

The woman's voice was wonderfully calm and clear, and I mentally decided that Traill had made a mistake. Then I heard a sharp whistle, the signal agreed upon, and I ran around to the front door.

"All quiet out there?" asked Traill, speaking in a loud voice. "Are the men all stationed?"

"Yes, sir; the sergeant has every window covered."

As I said this, I fancied I saw the corners of the woman's mouth twitch just a little, and she drew herself together as if she felt the cold. She was past middle age, with the beauty of the South yet clear in her face, and a cold, fearless black eye. In spite of her hurried toilet, she carried herself proudly as if accustomed to be obeyed.

"I must search this house," Traill drawled gently.

"There is nothing here," she answered; "you can search it if you care to."

As she threw open the door of the drawing room she was as calm and dignified as if ushering a company of guests to some grand dinner.

64

A Story of the Secret Service

The house was much dismantled, but it still showed traces of its former estate. There yet remained a few fine old paintings on the walls, and the furniture—what was left of it—was of carved mahogany. Traill examined the desks and wall cases, and peered into the fireplace and up the chimney. From the kitchen we stooped our way down a narrow passage into the cellar. The woman led, holding a candle high, and I covered the rear, revolver in hand. We found butter-tubs, apple-barrels, and wine-cases, long since empty, but there was no trace of our quarry.

"What is in here?" asked Traill, when we again reached the wide hall.

"That is the chapel; there is nothing in there that you want. Surely you will not desecrate the chapel?"

"I'll see," said Traill.

As the woman threw open the door, I remember thinking how easy it would be for a man hidden within to kill us both as we stood there with our arms down and the candlelight in our eyes.

It was the only room in the house that had not been dismantled—a high, somber room with Gothic furnishings and all the fittings of a private chapel. Traill searched every nook and corner. At the altar he paused, and poked his pistol under the embroidered curtain. I saw the woman's face flame red and then fade swiftly away. Traill laughed softly. Hanging to the altar sides in regular rows were twenty carbines.

"You can have them," said the woman coldly.

"I am here for Captain Cameron," was Traill's response.

The search went on uninterrupted. In one of the upper

rooms—the room occupied by the mistress of the house—we found a terrified mulatto girl crouching and praying.

"Is Captain Cameron here?" Traill asked her suddenly, his face glaring close to hers.

She glanced at her mistress fearfully.

"Fo' de Lawd, he ain't yere. He done gone 'way las' week. Fo' de Lawd, I ain't seen nothin' ob him——"

"So he has been here," said Traill quietly.

"Yes, he has," was the woman's response, her voice still clear and steady; "but, as the girl says, he has gone away."

Traill paused in the upper hallway. I knew he was perplexed.

"Do you mean to tell me that you are the only person in this house?"

"The only white person, and this girl is the only Negro—the others have all been stolen by your army," and the fire of the South blazed up in her eyes, and died away again as swiftly as it came.

Just then I caught the outlines of a square trap-door in the high ceiling at the farther end of the hall. I touched Traill's shoulder and pointed it out. His eyes flashed, and I saw the jagged white scar on his cheek twitch and color.

"How do you get up there?" he asked, fixing his eyes on the woman's face.

"We don't get up," she answered steadily; "we haven't had the place open for years."

Traill turned to me.

"Get that table out of the bedroom."

I pulled it out, taking care to make no noise, and placed it under the trap. Traill jumped up on it, but he could not reach the ceiling. The woman had followed us as if fascinated. She leaned against the wall, with a sarcastic smile curling her lips.

"Do you intend to go up there?" she asked.

"Certainly," said Traill.

"If Cameron was in that attic, do you suppose you would come down alive? You evidently have not made the acquaintance of Captain Cameron."

She spoke steadily, but her fingers were knotted and twisted together, and I remember observing that the nails were blue.

I brought another table—a smaller one—and placed it on top of the first.

"Jump up here," said Traill. "Hand up the candle."

I climbed up beside him. I remember observing, with the minuteness of attention that comes with moments of great intensity, that Traill's cavalry spurs were scratching the polish of the mahogany. We were now both standing on the narrow top table, stooping over, with our heads close to the ceiling. The woman's lips had dropped open, and there was such a look of horrified interest in her face as I hope I may never see again. Traill handed me the candle.

"Is your pistol ready?" he asked quietly. "That man is up here. He is probably awake and ready for us. When I open the trap-door, you thrust the candle up as far as you can. If he shoots me, you kill him."

"What if there are other men with him?"

Traill shrugged. "Ready?" he asked.

"Ready," I answered.

Traill straightened upward, and threw back the trap-door. Both of us rose through the opening together. As I raised the candle, my hand grazed the shaggy face of a man in Confederate uniform, who was leaning almost over us. By the stare of his eyes, he had just wakened from a heavy sleep.

Within a breath I was looking into a black hole with a gleaming rim around it. Traill had not time to raise his pistol. I heard the click-clack of a hammer drawn sharply back. Traill bent forward, and grasped the handle of a bowie-knife sheathed at the other man's belt. A flash of steel in the candlelight, a swift lunge of the arm, and I felt the hot blood spatter in my face. The pistol rattled to the loose boards of the attic. With a sobbing in-drawing breath, the man lurched forward, quivered convulsively, and then lay quite still. I saw the useless fingers loosen their clutch, and a little dark fountain playing about the knife-handle and spreading on the white shirt-bosom. The blade had reached the heart. While this happened no one spoke.

"Now we will get down," said Traill almost gently.

The woman leaned stiffly against the wall. Her face was a ghastly blank, neither interest, nor fear, nor hatred in its lines. "What have you done?" she whispered. Traill glanced upward. On the dingy plastering, near the gaping trap-door, a red spot was slowly widening. There was no outcry, no confusion. "No use in staying here," said Traill.

We went down the stairway, and left the woman leaning against the wall, looking up. Ten miles we rode without saying a word, and then, just as the dawn was breaking through the scrubby pines, we drew rein on our gaunt and lather-gray horses. There was a little creek at the roadside, and we stooped to drink. I looked at Traill's face. It was studded with black blotches; so was his gray coat. "Am I bloody?" I asked.

"Yes," he answered.

And then my knees gave way under me, and I shook with the horror of my first killing. I could not control the trembling of my hand when I tried to wash away the blood. Traill looked at me.

"Never mind," he said quietly, "it could not be helped; it was death to him or death to us. We took the only course."

"Was that woman Cameron's mother?"

"She said she wasn't."

"But she was?"

"Yes." Traill dabbled his hands in the water, in his peculiar deft way, but his face showed no emotion.

At noon we reached Washington. I followed Traill into the Colonel's private office, weary of body and wretched of soul.

"Well?" questioned the Colonel.

"We got Captain Cameron," drawled Traill.

More than ten years afterward, although I had seen more than one bloody battlefield later in the war, I woke up sometimes with the picture of that woman standing there alone, looking up, still distinct in my mind.

☆ 11 ☆

My Father's Mottoes

Now THAT I have begun telling about my father it is with difficulty that I relinquish that inexhaustible subject. It is, indeed, an indispensable foundation for any account of my own life: since his character and example and instruction were primary influences in my early development.

My father had two mottoes, founded I think upon his experience as a soldier. I heard him often in the earlier years—not so much later—repeat both of them. The first served him well in many a difficulty, especially during the hard, barren years after he first went west to the frontier. It was: "Admit nothing to be a hardship." It guided him always. Nothing ever seemed to discourage him, or make him afraid. He never grumbled, though he was often angry. He would not complain, but he would fight on the slightest provocation. What feuds he had, what unnecessary lawsuits! His motto applied to all sorts of difficulties. His deafness was certainly a major hardship, interfering with his work, cutting him off from human contacts he would have enjoyed, but never once in all the years did I hear him make complaint, not one expression of self-pity. On the contrary he often referred to his deafness as a great blessing.

My Father's Mottoes

"Too much talk in the world! Think how much of it I escape—and all the bores!"

The other motto was even bolder, and while it carried him over many a rough place—indeed, it lay at the foundation of his success—it also did him many a disservice. He was by nature overimpetuous, given to jumping at conclusions and then, setting his teeth, hanging to them with grim constancy. This was the motto—I remember the look in his eyes and the very inflection of his voice when he said it, like a flag flung in air:

"When in doubt, CHARGE."

Charge he did: he was charging the whole of General Wade Hampton's army when he was cut down by a Confederate saber. After the war he charged into various business enterprises, losing all he had: but he finally charged into the wilderness and made it all back again. The frontier was never favorable to doubters: its prizes went to the fearless ones. It is a grand motto when a man knows when *not* to charge, a truth my father never quite understood, at least in his earlier years.

My father, in short, was an individual, and there are not so many left in this age of machinery in social organization as well as in industry. He was never afraid to be different. When he had convictions he never hesitated to let them be known, anywhere, at any time—if the occasion demanded it. Owing to his deafness his voice, naturally strong, was somewhat unmodulated and often when he became interested, talking to some friend of an evening on the broad pillared porch of our home, he could be heard halfway to the village.

Native American

Every one in that country knew my father: his erect, vigorous military bearing, his flowing side whiskers, the white hair that stood straight up from his high forehead—and the speaking tube which he so readily thrust at any one who wished to speak to him. He was known always, to everybody, as Major Baker.

There were never any half-shades in people's attitude toward my father: they liked him or they did not like him —and it seemed all the same to him. Men who hated him, and at one time they were not few, also feared him, and some of them had good reason to. When he had made up his mind that a man was a cheat or a liar he never minced his words. "A scoundrel." "An unmitigated liar." There was the angry explosion and that was the end of it.

But he was trusted: all his life he was trusted. In that country in the earlier days there were no banks nearer than the cities of St. Paul and Minneapolis. My father carried accounts in a bank in New York—the Importers and Traders—and in banks at St. Paul and Stillwater. He did a good deal of the simple banking business of the countryside: sold drafts and gave checks for cash which were often held for months as certificates of deposit.

One evening a wild young character of the valley, a lumberjack and log driver who had just come down river after a winter's work, came into the office. He was drunk.

"Where's Major Baker?"

When my father appeared his visitor pulled off his woodsman's cap.

"Major, I'm drunk. Can't you shee? I'm drunk. I got my money here. Go'ne lose it. Wansh you keep it."

72

My Father's Mottoes

Whereupon he went into his pockets and emptied out several hundred dollars in bills and silver—his entire wages for many months.

"You keep it," he said and turned to go.

"Wait," said my father, "we'll count it and I'll give you a memorandum."

"No, you keep it."

It was months later that N—— came for his money, looking sheepish enough.

A beautiful relationship existed in ancient times, before education became institutionalized, of Master and Follower, Scholar and Pupil; it was enough to walk with Socrates: to talk with Epictetus.

Something of this beautiful old relationship existed between my father and me. He was my Master, I was his Pupil. I looked up to him, I obeyed him, I followed him. He did not ask his sons to avoid evil, but he infected us with something, a kind of individual pride, a stout belief in certain rules of conduct, a *personal standard* that was not easily diverted by other people or by their habits or customs, either good or bad. This is what *I* do: this is right for *me*. However poorly we may have practiced what he taught, it was there, we knew what it was.

Even more than this, I think, Father had the gift of making the current of life so interesting, he set us so often on fire with his own enthusiasms, that the ordinary rough excesses of that time and place which were considered amusement seemed poor and thin and silly.

Once when we were ten or twelve years old my brother Charlie and I got into the drawer where my father kept his cigars, took two of them and went out back of the smoke-house where we lighted them up. My father had taken up smoking in the army and had become a devotee of good tobacco. I think it gave him great comfort.

While my brother and I were puffing exultantly at our cigars we were suddenly petrified—the word is none too strong—by the appearance of Father, looking around the corner of the smoke-house. How he found us out I never knew, but there he was. Knowing well his explosive temper we expected the worst; but beyond the keen straight glance of his gray eyes he said no word and presently disappeared. This was terrible! We knew the enormity of our offense— we had *stolen* Father's cigars. We knew well that the incident was not closed. As to the smoking itself he had never advised us not to smoke, much less forbidden it: and he never afterward, although our formidable aunts considered smoking a sin only one degree short of getting drunk, advised any of us not to smoke.

Two contrite little boys appeared shortly afterward for supper. Father seemed just as usual, in no way disturbed. No sooner, however, had we begun to eat than we both found ourselves growing deathly sick. I presume Father saw exactly what was happening—and offered us some more of the pudding. I remember the desperation with which I shook my head.

"You two boys," said he, "may be excused."

We bolted from the table, scarcely in time, but our apprehension of what might happen in the future was far worse than our immediate woes. What did it all mean? What would he do next? When would he call us in, as he usually did in such cases, for a talk—and that which usually followed the talk?

Nothing happened. How we wondered and suffered! I don't know how long this continued—a week, possibly two or three—but one day we made the astonishing discovery that Father did not go out on the porch as usual after supper to smoke his cigar. What did this mean? My brother and I kept watch and discussed it anxiously. Father said nothing: he said nothing then, or ever afterward, so far as I know, about the incident, or the reason why he stopped smoking. He never, indeed, smoked again. These facts sank into us gradually, but with tremendous power. They rankled, they hurt, but there they were for two small boys to think about.

My Old Aunts

I HAVE had much to say of my father, who was the greatest influence and joy of my boyhood, and something of my delicate and sensitive mother. I must speak of certain other members of our family, because, as I grew older, and my mother's strength began to wane, they exercised more and more influence upon my life.

These were my old aunts, Aunt Hill and Aunt Amanda, both older sisters of my father, and Aunt Em, a sister of my mother. Although none of them knew it, each was a product, in her own way, of the disappearance of the frontier and the passing of the pioneer stage in American development. We were all that, indeed, but the women seemed far more vitally affected than the men.

One of the chief characteristics of pioneer life, for two hundred years, had been the large families of children. It persisted because it was useful and profitable, not only to the family itself, but to society in general. At an early age children began to do the "chores" and to contribute to the welfare of the entire family. There were nine children in my grandfather Baker's family, six girls and three boys. My own father finally had a family of ten children, eight boys and two girls.

The changes came with astonishing swiftness and subtlety. The farms, having been laboriously hewn out of the forest, no longer needed so many hands. The little towns grew rapidly into cities. Household necessities and conveniences began to be made in factories far more cheaply than they could be made at home. Farm machines began to be widely used. A surplus of women, having been overworked for generations, now found too little to occupy them, at least within the somewhat narrow scope of what was considered "woman's work." They had no longer any spinning and weaving to do, no making of butternut trousers—nor dyeing the cloth in the first place—no butter to churn, and even, a little later, no bread to bake. Readjustments came hard. Thousands of women, well-born and well-trained, could not seem to get into the main tide of life. They were not more hampered by their skirts than by the common taboos as to what was proper and improper. A few began agitating for "women's rights," but in my early boyhood it was still the age of the "unattached woman," the "old maid." Even as I write, I reflect upon the fact, as a symbol of the momentous revolution in American life, that the term "old maid" has almost disappeared from the American language. There aren't any more "old maids" as I knew them when I was a boy. And I think the world, in some ways, is the poorer for it! For I remember many of "those beautiful souls who were gentle when I was a child."

Not a few of the unattached women had been widowed during the sanguinary Civil War that had so recently been fought; uncounted thousands of others were "old maids" because the men whom they might have married had died

on southern battlefields. They were familiar presences in
many of the family homes I knew, sometimes deeply loved,
sometimes a care and a problem, always more or less bonds-
women among their married relatives. Having little life
or joy of their own, they often contributed largely to the
life and joy of other people, most of whom did not appreciate it, at least at the time. Here and now, after many years,
I pay humble tribute to the "unattached women," and the
"old maids" of my boyhood.

Since they had to do *something,* and the time had not
yet come when they could take part in most of the vital
work of the world, many of them turned eagerly to "art"
or "gave music lessons." For a generation or so they largely
dominated the intellectual life of the country, as my friend,
Fred Louis Pattee, has shown in his delightful book, *The
Feminine Fifties.* In our home, when I was a boy, we had
on the wall several little pictures made by ardent feminine
artists whom we knew, "plaques" some of them were called,
thickly painted with roses and violets, sparkling snow scenes,
shapeless little cottages, and dogs and birds. On the book-
shelves, if not on the marble-top table, we had *Fern-leaves
from Fanny's Portfolio,* the *Poems of Alice and Phœbe
Cary,* and *American Female Poets,* to say nothing of *Godey's
Lady's Book.* My father did not care for them, nor read
them, but there they were, the irrepressible evidence of the
popular taste.

My old aunts, all of them, belonged to the clan of "unattached women." So did Miss Field and Mrs. Gwynne, those
exquisite ladies to whom I was sent for painful lessons in
"art"; so did many another woman among the families we

knew. Of all of them I remember, none seems a more perfect example than my Aunt Mandy. She was the soul of gentleness—loving, uncritical, often irritating. I have never known a more unselfish human being or a more complete Christian. She was so good, so self-forgetful, with such a passion for helping everybody, whether she knew how or not, that she was sometimes a grievance. In the earlier years, she lived in a little dormered room in our house. I can see her now, sitting pleasantly at the low window, reading her Bible, or looking at the pictures in Fox's *Book of Martyrs* with a kind of gentle horror. I think of her as a veritable pattern of serenity. In her earlier life she had been ill and had taken the water-cure, so that special provision had always to be made for her at meals: the indispensable pot of hot water and well-toasted Graham bread. We all liked her, yes, loved her; for she read us stories and took the little ones to walk; and in her goodness let us do many things that my mother had forbidden. I don't know how or where she could have obtained her supplies, but she was rarely without an unexpected cookie in her pocket, or an apple, or a stick of black licorice, which she herself liked. My mother protested against eating between meals, which she considered a cardinal offense, but it never did any good.

Other inevitable sources of friction caused my father to build Aunt Mandy a neat little cottage in a grove of oaks down the road and there she lived, busily and happily, for many years. We all delighted to visit her there and sometimes came home with the stomach-ache.

She had no money of her own, and I think she never had had any. So far as I know she never earned a dollar in her life. When her father died and his farm was sold, she inherited a few hundred dollars—I think three hundred. This she placed at once in my father's hands and began to draw on it from time to time to meet her small requirements. On these important business occasions she always came dressed a little more carefully than usual: she put on her fingerless lace gloves, perhaps, and carried her best black bag.

"Stan," she would say, "I'd like to draw a little of my money."

Years and years this went on, long after her small inheritance had disappeared, and my father, saying not a word and keeping up the fiction, always paid her what she asked. Except once: and then his rebellion was short-lived. It grew out of Aunt Mandy's passionate devotion to her church, the Ladies Aid Society, and especially to a certain missionary group that supported a representative in China whose life and work down to the last hungry details were most intimately known to every good lady in the society. He wrote them a monthly letter, a lugubrious narrative concerning the diseases contracted by his numerous family, or the necessitous woes of the Chinese. My aunt believed firmly in "tithing," in setting aside ten per cent of her income. And how she did enjoy giving!—even though it might cost her the usual allowance of tea which she loved. I don't know just how my father found out, but one day when he came home from the office he said with a laugh:

"I've learned Amanda's method of keeping books with the Lord."

It seems that when she had $3.00 and there was a good cause to serve she gave thirty cents. This left her $2.70. A day or two later if there happened to be an urgent letter from the missionary in China, she would contribute twenty-seven cents to what she called her "China fund." This would leave her with $2.43. An appeal that very week from the Ladies Aid would take twenty-four cents more. And so on until she had almost nothing left to live on.

"But, Amanda," my father argued, "you are not tithing ten per cent; you are tithing fifty or sixty per cent."

"Stan," replied my aunt firmly, "I never give more than ten per cent."

It was in vain that my father argued. Along with her gentleness and meekness she had a persistence that would wear away the hardest rock. When my father hinted, however vaguely, that there must be some new arrangement that he called by the terrifying name of a budget, she wiped her eyes.

"But, *Stan,* how can I get along?"

He knew well that it would destroy the greatest joy of her life—which was to give—and again the old practice went on, year after year. She kept coming in her fingerless lace gloves, with her black bag, to get her money. She did it until she died.

My father had the strong feeling of family solidarity, so common among the pioneers, and difficult and expensive as he must have found many of the problems presented to him, he never wavered. Our weak and futile old Aunt Em gave both him and my mother many difficult hours of anxiety and distress.

My Aunt Hill, on the other hand, was one of the great characters of my boyhood. She was a personage, dominant, independent, often quite overwhelming. She was much older than my father, anyway sixteen years, but she strongly resembled him both in character and in physical appearance. She was as erect as he and in her earlier years quite as fine-looking. She also had immense vigor and gusto. While my father had indeed been a Major, and had fought in the Civil War, she was the Brigadier who often forgot that he was not still a little boy to be vigorously admonished and instructed. She had been named Luthera after her father, who was Luther, and some of the family called her or tried to call her Aunt Luthera: but we all knew her as Aunt Hill, or Auntie Hill, after her married name. She had had a stormy and, indeed, tragic career, having lost both her husband and her only child, to whom she was passionately devoted. She had taught in several old-fashioned academies and at first had always been brilliantly successful, but sooner or later, her personality having overflowed in all directions until even the headmaster was awash, she "stepped aside," as she called it, with her head up.

She was a large woman and, like my father, very strong. She dressed commonly in rather stiff black clothes, I think poplin, or was it alpaca?—and there seemed something utterly permanent, complete, indestructible about her. She walked with a firm step and spoke with a strong, clear voice. When she was amused she could laugh until the tears ran down her face.

Aunt Hill, like my father, was a wonderful story-teller, but while his stories were chronicles of actual experience, hers were made up, as we used to say, "out of her own head." She had a tale for us every evening before we went to bed, often continued with the same characters night after night.

My Old Aunts

She usually left her characters hanging by a thread over some bottomless pit, about to be scalped by Indians, or ambushed by "rebels"—for she was still fighting the Civil War—so that when she stopped we all roared out,

"What happened next?"

Once in a great while, knowing the value of surprise, she would yield, only to leave her hero in even greater jeopardy of life or limb—or soul! For my aunt was always especially concerned with souls and when she didn't frighten us out of our wits with the physical dangers confronting her characters she would melt us down with pity over the hopeless state of their souls—if they did not accept salvation, and join the church. In such cases we would call out when she stopped, "Was he saved?" "Tell us, was he saved?" "Oh, please, Aunt Hill." On such occasions she would close her lips and shake her head mournfully, and we'd have to wait another whole twenty-four hours to learn whether or not he was still in sin.

My aunt knew well, also, how to use the discipline of suspense to enforce order among her unruly subjects: she had only to threaten to stop the story to send us all off quietly to bed—which was a miracle in itself.

Ever since the Civil War had ended and the "rebels" had surrendered, my Brigadier aunt, still thirsting for battle, had been looking about for another cause. In the years before the war she had been a valiant supporter and conspirer in the Underground Railroad, by which fugitive slaves from the South were smuggled into Canada, and afterward she was interested in the Freedmen's Schools, in which two of her aunts were actually at work.

My father, who had been through four bloody years of

conflict, wanted no new cause; he was content with peace; but my aunt presently took up a new campaign which looked really promising from the point of view of carnage. This was the fight on Demon Rum, which she, as a woman, could get into on equal terms with the men. She wore the insignia of the new crusade, a bow of white ribbon, on her broad breast and read every week in *The Union Signal* the account of the travels of her general, Frances E. Willard, who was then campaigning through the country. She had a picture of Miss Willard on the wall of her room, and near it a lithograph of a group of women in hoopskirts and bustles, kneeling in the snow before a door marked "Sample Room." It was labelled "Locked Out—The Praying Band in the Street before a Saloon." I was often thrilled by the thought that my militant aunt might almost any snowy night decide to go across the river and pray before Bill Mullen's saloon. It abashed and embarrassed me, and yet I determined to be on the spot to see what happened. I had no doubt whatever that my aunt would win out even if the road in front of the saloon were strewn with the dead and wounded. It would be horrible, but it would be exciting. Later she was to write a play for us on the subject of Demon Rum, which we acted with great éclat—as I shall narrate in another chapter.

☆ 13 ☆

Sundays in Our Town

SUNDAYS in our home in my boyhood were sometimes dreadful days. It was a Presbyterian household with an ingrained rule: "Remember the Sabbath day to keep it holy." We were to attend public worship and study the scriptures. My old aunts, of whom I have already spoken, were veritable gorgons of the faith. They knew all of the shalt-nots in the Bible. My mother was, I think, equally certain regarding what boys should not do, but she, poor creature, worn out with bearing six hardy boys in ten years' time, was content to leave the compulsions to my aunts and to my father.

To regulate and suppress six wild young Indians like us was no easy task. It was not so bad to go to Sunday school and to church, as I shall presently acknowledge, for we met other hapless boys and girls, but when it came to "studying the scriptures" on a fine Sunday afternoon in spring and going to "evening service," it was beyond human endurance— almost as bad as Thursday evening prayer meeting. "You mustn't, you can't. Remember the Sabbath day."

If it had not been for my father I think we should have exploded. He was, I know, as convinced as his sisters or my mother of the necessity of religious observance, but he knew boys. I have already referred to his reading aloud on Sunday

afternoons or evenings: but that was not all. I can still hear
his voice, on a Sunday afternoon when inaction was growing
all but unendurable, booming out lustily:

"Come on, boys, let's go for a tramp."

Those tramps! Down by the river, up along the rapids,
climbing the rocky cliffs, back through the woods quite regardless of roads or trails. A part of the ritual was for each
of us to cut a cane of kinikinick, the Indian name for a kind
of red willow, if we could find it, each using his own jackknife, which was supposed to lie quiet on the Sabbath day.

My father seemed to enjoy the tramps as much as we did.
He was inexhaustibly interesting. Sitting on the rocks on the
hilltop above the river he would tell how the early French
voyageurs had come down from Lake Superior by way of
our own St. Croix to reach the Mississippi. Our falls were
too rough and swift for them to shoot in their canoes so they
had to carry around. When I was a boy we knew of a trail
through the woods, along the hillsides, which was supposed
to have been taken from time immemorial by the Indians
and later by voyageurs, priests and traders. I remember the
thrill I had when Father told of these bold men and their
Indian guides struggling through the wilderness so many
years ago.

"One of the earliest French forts in all the Northwest was
built right here," he would say, "and Le Sueur and Duluth
and other explorers may all have passed this way."

We could then trace out considerable stretches of the trail
and even locate the places where the camps had probably
been made. We spent some time poking around at one of
these camp-sites and found a copper seal with a bell on it

and an inscription in old French which had plainly been lost by some early French explorer. My brother still has it. At a later time a beautiful silver spoon bearing the fleur-de-lis of France upon it came to light—and is still preserved.

Our valley was also extremely interesting geologically and my father used to stop by the riverside and show us how the strata ages ago had been tipped up by some mighty convulsion of nature. Just at our falls the rock was of the lowest order, hard brittle trap-rock, through which our plunging river in the course of uncounted years had worn a smooth channel. Farther down there were strata of sandstone, and at Osceola, nine miles away, outcroppings of limestone, representing the most recent of geological deposits. Many years later college classes from the Universities came frequently to our Dalles, since the geological structure of the earth could be seen there in small compass. It was these fascinating geological facts, as related by my father, that led to one of the most interesting experiences of my boyhood, of which I shall speak later.

In this description of the Sundays of my boyhood I can see how incomplete the picture is, how far less than just I have been. While I have said nothing not true of the weariness of our repressive Sabbaths and the joy of our walks and talks with Father, I shall never forget some of the morning services in the stiff little wooden church on the hillside that my father had been largely instrumental in promoting and building.

Something in those morning services, dreary as they often were, deeply stirred the Other Boy I had hidden within me. I cannot now at all fix the dates, but it must have been at an early age, during the ministry, I think the temporary ministry, of an old preacher whose health was poor and who, in his humility, looked upon himself as a failure. He told my father once:

"My days have been long, and I have failed. It was not given to me to reach men's hearts."

But one towheaded boy sitting there in a front row dreaming dreams, if the sermons reached him not at all, was yet thrilled to the depths of his being by that tall preacher. By some instinct he chose his reading mostly from the Old Testament—those splendid, marching passages, full of oriental imagery. As he read there would creep into his voice a certain resonance that lifted him suddenly above his gray surroundings.

How vividly I recall his reading of the twenty-third Psalm —a particular reading. I suppose I had heard the passage many times before, but upon this certain morning——

The windows were open, for it was May, and a boy could look out on the hillside and see with longing eyes the inviting grass and trees. A soft wind blew in across the church; it was full of the very essence of spring. On the pulpit stood a bunch of crocuses crowded into a vase: some Mary's offering. An old man named Johnson who sat near us was already beginning to breathe heavily, preparatory to sinking into his regular Sunday snore. Then those words from the preacher, bringing me suddenly out of some formless void, to intense consciousness:

"Yea though I walk through the valley of the shadow of death, I will fear no evil: for thou art with me; thy rod and thy staff they comfort me."

Sundays in Our Town

Well, I saw the way to the place of death that morning; far more sharply I saw it than any natural scene I knew: and myself walking therein. I shall know it again when I come to pass that way; the tall, dark, rocky cliffs, the shadowy path within, the overhanging, dark branches, even the whitened, dead bones by the way—and as one of the phantasms of boyhood, cloaked figures I saw, lurking mysteriously in deep recesses, fearsome for their very silence. And yet I with magic rod and staff walking within—boldly, fearing no evil, full of faith, hope, courage, love, invoking images of terror only for the joy of braving them.

So that great morning went away. I heard nothing of singing or sermon and did not come to myself until my mother, touching my arm, asked me if I had been asleep. I looked up at the sad face of the old preacher with a new interest and friendliness. I felt, somehow, that he too knew about my secret valley. I should have liked to ask him, but I did not dare. So I followed my mother when she went to speak to him, and when he did not see, I touched his coat.

That tall, lank preacher, who thought himself a failure: how long I shall remember him and the words he read and the mournful yet resonant cadences of his voice!

☆ 14 ☆

Religion in My Youth

I FIND IT most difficult of all, I think, to make comprehensible the immense power of religion upon the lives of most of the people I knew best as a boy, and the authority of the Bible as its symbol.

I used to see my great old Aunt Hill, when in doubt, solemnly take down her larger Bible, the one with leather covers and a woodcut of God on His throne for a frontispiece, and seating herself in a chair, open it at random upon her knees. There she would sit for a moment in complete silence. Her eyes would close, a look of complete devotion and surrender would come into her face. Presently she would lift her hand, like one in a trance—a shudder of awe would run down the back of the little boy who was watching her with reverential eyes—and she would slowly lower one finger to the open pages of the Book. There she would hold it firmly for a moment and then, slowly opening her eyes, read the verse that her finger rested upon, to find there, by the guidance of God, the advice or the decision she was seeking. It was a powerful and dramatic performance; it brought the veritable voice of God into the quiet room: for my aunt's faith in it as a reality was profound.

I was only a small boy, and not critical as to interpretations, and some of the answers she found seemed amazing in their applicability. I believed as faithfully in the process as she did—even when I might be the culprit about whom she was consulting God. On one occasion, after I had committed some deadly crime, the verse under my aunt's finger read:

"Be kindly affectionate one to another in brotherly love."

My aunt's eyes looked at me with piercing intentness. The words did not seem even to my struggling intelligence to apply exactly to the crime under consideration—I think it was hooking a quarter of a custard pie from the kitchen cupboard—but my aunt knew, from this divine guidance, that something mattered far more than pie. This troubled me, since I had recently been scrapping with my brother Charlie. How could my aunt know this? It must have come direct from God. I shivered and trembled, and came away with the words, "Be kindly affectionate one to another," ringing in my ears—the veritable command of God Himself.

All those whom I loved or revered believed, or seemed to believe, absolutely, in the Bible, in the church, in religion. They all seemed to know what God would have them do, and where they were going after death. Their lives there on the frontier were often hard and barren; all this would be changed; all finally would be rest, peace, joy—if they had faith! It was compensation and assuagement for their struggling lives. My old aunts seemed to have no doubts; neither did my mother, nor the Preacher nor many of the people we knew best. As for my father, I remember sometimes looking at him sharply and thinking of questions I should like to ask him, but did not dare.

And I, a small boy, also believed utterly—until certain incidents which, in the afterlook, may seem ridiculous, set me to wondering. I am here setting them down just as I remember them.

There was a town character I used sometimes to meet—a frontier type he was, argumentative, assertive, especially when partly intoxicated. I can see him now, his little gimlet-like eyes: I can hear his rasping voice.

"Ye say God can do anything. Tell me, can He make a two-year-old heifer between now and sundown?"

I suppose it was a hoary frontier jest—a rude familiar challenge to the revivalism of the times—but I had never heard it before, and I bit hard. Of course God could make a heifer—any kind of a heifer He wanted to.

"And do it before sundown?"

"He surely could, if He *wanted* to"—stoutly.

"Can ye tell me, perhaps—jes sensibly now—if that ther' heifer was made before sundown how it could be two years old?"

I must have shown how hard I was hit: God, then, could not do everything! I do not remember arguing at all, but it made me anxious. I could not get it out of my mind.

A little later I had another shock, this time from my father himself. It went even deeper than the first.

My father had been telling the story of the battle of Sycamore Church, to which I have referred elsewhere. The "rebel" cavalrymen were riding him down in the little wood. He was dismounted and had no ammunition left. One of the mounted men raised his saber to strike——

How my breath came and the tears in my eyes when I *saw* him falling there, the blood spurting from his head, and the cavalrymen riding on over his body. Nothing I ever saw with my own eyes was clearer to me than that scene. I can also hear the remark he always made, that if the saber had not caught in the branch of a little tree on its way down he would not have been there to tell the tale.

At this point in the narrative, one evening, he introduced an unexpected variation. Turning suddenly upon me, sitting there before him tense with emotion, he asked:

"Ray, suppose that tree had not been there: suppose the full blow of that rebel saber had been delivered"—I remember acutely the pause and the look in his eyes—"where would you be?"

I did not answer: I did not at the moment, I think, grasp the full significance of the question. But that night, in bed, I found myself broad awake, trembling. Where would I be? It seemed as if a great emptiness had opened around me: I felt a paralyzing insecurity, so that I grasped at the bedclothes. I had always seemed so real to myself, so certain, so necessary—and I was a mere accident. The accident of a twig on a little tree in Virginia! Was my father also an accident? And my mother? And my tremendous and overwhelming aunt?

My mind struggled with the problem—not only that first night but many times afterward. Once on a sunny afternoon, on the river-bank where I was tramping or fishing—I don't remember what—it came over me with a shock as though I had been struck: was all this also an accident? These rocks and trees? These birds and flowers? Were they all accidents? I had a sense of the unreality of everything I saw—and I alone in the emptiness——

Another thing that disturbed me, a youngster bursting

with life, fascinated with everything he saw and heard, was the constant talk of death—and what would happen after death. It was, indeed, a melancholy generation, soaked in tears—thinking of its sins, fearing the vengeance of God, often singing dolefully about death.

"Hark from the tombs a mournful sound."

I have recently been looking over the voluminous diaries left by my aunt, written mostly in the fifties and sixties. It is unbelievable that any human being—especially a lively, robust, energetic young woman such as my aunt must have been—could have written hundreds of lugubrious pages, bemoaning her sad state and the imminence of death. But she did! Here is a single paragraph:

"But why should I indulge in vain regrets for the departure of earthly joys when a few fleeting days will convey us beyond these changeful scenes? Why should I allow my heart to be captivated by these fascinating scenes that so *soon* will fade and disappear? Oh, when compared with the high and holy joys and hopes unfolded in the book of revelation how insignificant do they appear. Why can I suffer myself to grieve over the sorrows and disappointments of this world when such prospects are before me beyond the grave?"

One Christmas the good minister, no doubt wishing to impress upon me the seriousness of the Great Judgment, presented me with one of those curious old prints representing Heaven with God the Father, near the top of the picture, sitting on His great white throne. The archangels were around and above Him. At one side crowded the angelic throng in long white robes, with tremendous wings on their shoulders. And there were harps, or I supposed they were, though I had never yet seen one. On the other side, the dark side, were the damned, with their agonized faces, their contorted and suffering bodies, on their way to be cast down into Hell.

It made a tremendous impression upon me, that picture. Often when I went up to bed I took it out of the drawer where I kept my treasures and looked long and earnestly at it. And curiously, the more I looked at the picture the more I became fascinated by the throng of the wicked who were on their way to Hell. I began to be sorry for them. As for the angels, they were all alike and they had nothing more to do through eternity except to sit about and sing.

I picked out various of the most fearful of the devil-ridden horde and while I did not like the looks of them, and they even frightened me, I began to tell myself little stories about them—chiefly how, being so strong and fierce, they escaped the rather sleepy-looking and benevolent God who sat up there on His throne. As a boy not unaccustomed to the process of disobedience and punishment, I knew there were usually ways of getting out of trouble. In time I had devised a method for every single one of the unrepentant sinners in that chromo: that is, all of them I could definitely pick out from the somewhat confused jumble of arms, legs, wings and the like.

In some of the starchy, unused parlors of the homes I knew I remember the huge old family Bibles on the marble-top tables. Our own Bible was surreptitiously used by me for pressing autumn leaves, and one of our neighbors was said to hide his money among the pages of the Apocalypse, knowing that no one would ever find it there. For the Bible was a kind of household god to be worshipped, a magic talisman that protected the family, and, as much as anything, a warrant of respectability. Even if there was no place of enthronement, the attitude of worshipful awe persisted. Once, long afterward, I saw a huge black Negro come into a country store to buy a fifteen-cent Testament. He opened the collar of his shirt and having taken out an old, torn, greasy copy which he wore tied by a string around his neck, he replaced it with the new copy. Whether he could read I do not know, but it was plain that he regarded it as a sure fetish for his protection. Something of the same spirit existed among his betters.

Even in families of intelligence, the very act of reading was considered a virtue, a kind of magical process for securing divine approval. One of my progenitors, two or three greats removed (Ezra Stiles of Yale University), wrote in his diary on July 21, 1793:

"My D. Ruth from 1775 to 1793 or in 18 y. has read her Bible fourteen times through; and my Gr. D. Eliza aet 11 has read it thro' five times. Emilia has lost her minutes, but has prob^y read it a dozen times & more for she read it once a year for several y. after 1775. My other Child. have read it sundry times. May G^d bless the Read^g of this Holy Book to them.

"My Wife died 1775. She read thro' the Bible five times the last four years of her Life, once in about 9 or 10 months. Kezia died 1785; she read it thro' five times the last five years of her Life.

"Besides read^g in course privately in my Study, I read thro' the Bible in my Fam^y at family Morning Prayers from 1760 to 1791, Eight times, or once in 4 years. My Fam^y have had full opport^y of being acquainted with the sacred Contents of the Bible."

In my own youth I did everything in the world with this mighty book except to read it—I mean *really* read it—and yet I was scarcely less Bible-ridden than my ancestors. The poor little lads I remember, itching with new woolen underclothing, eager to escape to the snowy hills, being examined as to the size of Solomon's temple! I learned the order of the books of the Old and New Testaments. I studied the geography of the Holy Land. I learned how much a cubit was, and a shekel, and the meaning of Shekinah, and what an ephod looked like. One thing alone I cherish warmly, and this is the store of short passages and a few complete chapters that I was required to commit to memory. These and the reading of some of the resounding and poetic chapters of the Old Testament by one of the early preachers in our town have been priceless possessions all my life.

It was years later that I began to rediscover the Bible, and by quite the simplest of all processes—by reading it. One of the first books to awaken me in this respect was the so-called *Jefferson Bible*—an early copy of which my father received as a gift from the congressman in our district. It had been issued, of all things, as a government document! Jefferson called his Bible "The Morals of Jesus." He made it up by cutting out passages from Greek, Latin, French and English versions of the New Testament, selecting "the very words only of Jesus, paring off the amphiboligisms" and printing them side by side in his book.

"There will be found remaining," he said in his introduc-

97

tion, "the most sublime and benevolent code of morals which has ever been offered to man."

This book wonderfully interested and stimulated me in a further reading of the Book, trying at every point to understand what was meant as well as what was said. I have wished many times that I could have come at it *ab initio* without recalling at every turn the mystifications and obfuscations of the gentle, earnest, ignorant old women and the storming pulpit orators of my youth. For it is a Book that goes to the roots of human nature.

☆ 15 ☆

The School I Went to, and What I Learned in Spite of It

THE SCHOOL I went to was typically pioneer: a barren, weather-beaten building with one large room. An iron stove stood near the middle of it, into which in wintry weather the teacher, who was also the janitor, heaved great chunks of wood. During the winter term, farm work being light, boys and girls from eighteen to twenty years old came in to complete their education—with mere children of six or seven. I did not understand it at the time, of course, but the pioneer school was not the real source of education in the community: that was in the life itself, the complete and self-sufficient life of the frontier, in which every boy and girl played a part and learned of life by hard experience such sound and practical lessons as no school could have taught them. One rough but vigorous and able man in our village, said that it "didn't make no difference what they taught in school s'long's them boys got a little readin', writin', and 'rithmetic." All that was needed was enough "book-l'arnin'" for "gettin' on with." And for that purpose·many of the frontier schools were not at all bad: not half as bad as many a later critic, looking alone at the school and not at the complete life of the neighborhood, has glibly pronounced.

Native American

So far as books were concerned I learned extremely little in that school. At the beginning of a term when I got a new reading book I proceeded at once to read it straight through and afterward paid no attention to it, and this applied also, in less degree, to the geographies and the "language lessons." I used my spare time drawing pictures on my slate—mostly locomotives—shooting paper wads with a bit of whalebone from one of my mother's old corsets, or pulling the pigtails of the little girls. When the teacher caught me at it I was snaked out of my seat by a powerful rough hand and shaken until my teeth rattled.

Arithmetic was the one subject I could not read: and I was not easy or ready in it. We had for one winter—perhaps two—an unusually good teacher, who thought that the most necessary accomplishment for every boy was to know how to "figger in his head." In this he agreed wholly with the pioneers: and he made such a game of it that it was a pleasure to the entire school when he was drilling his classes. He had a large number of homely problems—how many cords of wood a man, working so many hours a day, could cut in a week, and so on and so on—which stimulated competition and established many a small hero in a little place. He would write on the blackboard long problems full of plus and minus signs, with here and there a multiplication or division, and his eager class of great hulking farm boys would pant after him to see which could come first to the answer. It was the real thing!

Probably my school was not different from hundreds that dotted the frontier save, perhaps, in having, when I was a small boy, quite a number of Indian or half-breed pupils from the settlement at Quailtown which I have already described. One of them was named Josephine Squires, a daughter or granddaughter of Old Mindy, a strong and well-developed girl of fifteen or sixteen years. The remarkable thing about her—I recall the intensity of my fascination when I first saw her—was that she had no nose. It was said that in a drunken row among her people, when she was a child, a hatchet or axe thrown in a fight had clipped it off. She was stupid and intractable, but she seemed to like to come to school.

We had a new teacher one fall, a powerfully built young fellow, who attempted stiff discipline. He soon ran afoul of Josephine. When he told her one day to do something or not to do something, whether from stupidity or perversity she did not obey; he strode down the long aisle to where she sat. The school held its breath. As he approached, Josephine seized a large slate that lay on her desk and rising quickly struck at him. He threw up his elbow to ward off the blow and the slate was shivered into fragments, so that the frame confined his arm. While he was thus handicapped Josephine attacked him like a tigress. We sat transfixed. After fierce wrestling in the narrow aisle the two finally went down with a crash upon the floor. While the teacher was no stronger than the Indian girl he was much nimbler. There was a dreadful instant when he had his knee on her breast and his hand throttling her. I remember her strangled shrieks and oaths——

That was the graduation day of Josephine: her education in the white man's school was completed. She never came again.

Native American

Of the two groups of pupils in our school, one was of the old American or French-Canadian stock, mostly town boys, hardy fellows who loved fishing and hunting and liked to pattern themselves after the loggers and river-drivers: often profane and obscene, but not "bad." The others were mostly Scandinavians from the farms or the village, some of whom at first spoke English with difficulty. They were quieter and more studious than the American boys, less given to practical jokes and horseplay.

Never was there a fiercer democracy than the school of the frontier even if one had sometimes to fight to get into it. In later years it seems to be one of the weaknesses of democracy that one can get into it without fighting. And lean on it, and expect it to support him!

I had one real rough-and-tumble fight. A boy slightly older than I was but no larger took to playing jokes on me, knocking off my hat, tripping me up, and worse. Probably I well deserved it, for I think I played the little prig in some of my classes, presuming on what I had read, or on what my father had told me. This boy, after some new joke, would square off and raising his fists in quite a professional fashion, dare me to fight. And when I wouldn't he and his friends jeered me. I had never fought in my life, though I had "scrapped" wildly and desperately with my brothers and other boys. If he had dared me to "wrestle" I should have gone in for it with joy. But to get mad and fight over nothing! However I remember resolving that if ever that boy played a certain dirty trick on me again I'd go for him whether it was silly or not. Only a day or two later the moment came. A kind of light flashed before my eyes: I grew hot all over, and went at him. He hit me one hard blow on the nose that brought the blood. The Marquis of Queensbury would not have recognized that battle! We punched and scratched and kicked and bit and cried—and finally I found myself down in the dusty road—but he was under me. I kept pounding him in the face until some of the older boys pulled me off. That fight did me no end of good inside: I knew now that I belonged: and the other boys also knew it.

I soon began to make warm friends of my own age, outside of my family. I remember well a little club we formed. I must have been twelve or thirteen years old, and it was a secret club, the first meeting of which was held in the dusky haymow of my father's barn. Will Harvey, who was to be my friend for many years, a boy of far more than usual gifts, was one of the members. August Elmquist was another: I think there were five of us altogether. The only important rule I can remember was that we were not to let in any "little snoots"—that is, our younger brothers.

Somewhere in my romantic reading I had seen an account of a secret order which "swore on the cross." So we made a wooden cross out of lath, and carved upon it a cabalistic sign—a star and a sword. Each of us then in turn, with great solemnity, and a few mumbo-jumbo words invented I think by Will Harvey, whose father was a Mason, held up a grimy hand to swear our undying allegiance. Afterward, and with equal solemnity, we pricked our thumbs, looked into one another's eyes and mingled our blood upon the wood.

How vividly it all comes back to me now, the scene there in the dusky hayloft, the low earnest voices, the thrill of the vision we had of being bound together in inseparable friendship, generously growing up together, going to war together, even growing old together. How beautiful and endless, in the light of that boyish faith, it all seemed!

I forget now what happened to our secret society. We soon disagreed, I think, as to which of us should be Supreme General of the order, and there was always some boy's mother who would not let him get out, or some other who had to play town-ball.

At any rate, the cross of our loyalty was only lath! Will Harvey grew up to be the president of a great flour-milling company in Minnesota; August Elmquist became a cunning cabinetmaker and died in the West.

Since then, to how many a cabalistic sign of eternal friendship have I lifted an eager, and never quite unrewarded, hand!

It was decreed that my education must also include Art. My mother, who used to draw, in pencil, little soft shapeless pictures of houses and trees, sent me down to Mrs. Gwynne and Miss Mary Field, of whom I have already spoken. These were the unattached daughters of an old politician who had come into our wild country as Registrar of the Government Land Office, which then did a lively business, giving away land. They were somewhat exotic, never quite fitted into the frontier life; and they gave lessons in Art.

It was an ordeal for me! I had to be cleaned up, and put on my best clothes as if I were going to church, so that I felt, in that prim, neat, quiet home, with the prim, neat Miss Field, intensely uncomfortable. I perspired and could not take off my coat. And I was asked to draw pictures of roses from other pictures of roses. A red-blooded boy who wanted, on a hot afternoon, to go swimming! It was intolerable. If only I had had some robust artist—some one like my father—to take me out on the hills or down by the river, in my old clothes, barefooted, where we could pick tablets out of our pockets and, when excited and self-forgetful, set to drawing a river-driver "cuffing" a log, it might have been different. But probably, for me, the real passion could never have been well kindled, for, when I began to be interested in expression, I thought not in lines or in colors, but in words. I had found to my delight one word that seemed exactly to fit our grandly curving river where it swept through the rocky gorge of the Dalles. It was the word "annular." Not angular—annular. I don't know where I could have heard it, but it somehow sounded right: it expressed what I felt when I looked down the rocky valley from the top of Mt. Pisgah, and I never afterward thought of that grand sweeping curve of the river without thinking also of my precious word. I even made sorry work of verses in which I referred to our "annular river" and how it "flowed on forever."

But all these direct assaults upon the citadel of education, as I have already remarked, were as nothing compared with the indirect schooling I had. To read about a thing in a book was nothing compared with the doing of it day by day.

Although not a farmer, my father had, and had to have, all the equipment for an independent life. Animals we had, horses, cows, pigs, hens: we kept a large garden, almost a farm, in which we grew nearly everything necessary for the family table and part of the feed for the stock. We made our own butter and part of the cheese we used: what sunny days I spent miserably in the cellar working the plunger in the old stone churn when the butter would not "come"! In the spring there was the soapmaking, an outdoor process I always enjoyed. The lye had first to be made, in two huge empty sugar hogsheads set up by the stone wall near the barn, slightly tilted, so that the lye would run out of the holes bored at the bottom. I helped put in the clean chips and straw and lime and finally the accumulated ashes from the wood fires of the winter until the hogsheads were filled. Water had then to be carried in pails from the well or the cistern and poured in at the top—a laborious process. Presently the lye began to ooze out at the bottom, dark and strong, to be tested by floating an egg in it. The great iron kettle had been made ready in the yard with a fire under it. The hired man rolled out the barrels of grease, trimmings of pork, beef, sheep, hen, that had slowly collected during the long winter. Sometimes they were still partially frozen and had to be loosened with an axe. The lye was poured in to "cut" the grease, and there were always great discussions as to how long the boiling should go on and when the soap was "ripe."

Every fall we butchered our own hogs: days of excitement for all the family. A square-shouldered, round-faced Swede came with his son to do the work. Water was boiling in the big, black kettle in the yard: barrels for sousing were rolled out of the barn and set under the maple tree, where, on a firm crossbar among the branches, there was a hoisting pulley.

"Now," said the powerful Swede, "I tank ve are retty."

It was with bated breath and a kind of tremulous and yet

106

absorbed horror I saw him take up his axe and start for the
pigpen. The unsuspecting pigs were there behind the barn
by the strawstack. I had myself helped to feed them: they
had names, like friends of ours, that expressed some individual characteristic. I knew how to scratch their sides with
a lath until they grunted their satisfaction.

"Coi, coi, coi," called the Swede.

The pigs came running, thinking they were to be fed.
Could I bear it? It was terrible, and yet for what other purpose had we kept and fed them? The powerful Swede put
one leg over the low fence, poised himself and called again
seductively:

"Coi, coi, coi."

I saw him raising his axe, blade edge up, for he intended
to stun them with a single blow. I could bear it no longer:
I plunged for the doorway of the barn, plugging my ears
and, I think, crying a little. But I could not help hearing the
dull thud and the sharp squealing of the pig. I peeked out,
quivering, terrified, and yet intensely fascinated. The Swede
was setting aside his axe quite deliberately. His son was
handing him his knife. I remember exactly how it looked: a
long-bladed butcher knife ground down until the end was
sharp and narrow like a dagger. It shone in the sunshine.
The Swede stepped into the pen. I waited long enough to see
him thrust his knife deep into the pig's throat—then I dashed
again, dazed and half sick, into the barn. How I struggled
with myself—the passion to see and know and not be afraid,
with the sick terror and revulsion that was near to overcoming me.

When I came out of the barn again the younger Swede

was just lifting a large dishpan over the fence. It contained the pig's blood which these people always saved to make into their famous blood sausages. They had it as part of their perquisite, since the lordly American usually let it go to waste. A little later I saw the dishpan in the hands of a Swedish woman who had suddenly appeared from nowhere, and I watched her stir the blood rapidly with a bundle of whisks from a new broom to make it coagulate while it cooled, a part of the process of the sausage making.

They inserted the spreader between the pig's hind legs and by use of the pulley in the tree lifted the heavy body, until it was suspended high above the ground. One of the barrels was now half-filled with scalding water from the great kettle and the pig was soused down into it to loosen the bristles. I watched the cupping or scraping which followed, both Swedes working swiftly and deftly until the pig's body was clean and white. I helped tug on the pulley rope to lift the pig again into the air, where the powerful Swede swiftly opened the body with his long knife. I saw the great, round, soft entrails pouring out—the steaming wonder of the heart, the lungs, the liver, the bladder, each handled with the deftness and knowledge of long experience.

Some time later, some cool evening, I went down into the cellar with my father to help cut up the pig. I held the lamp so that he could see while he worked. He stood there coatless by the great round meat block, his sturdy figure erect and strong, while he sharpened his butcher knife. The steel rang on the whetstone, there was a merry look in my father's eye, a zest in all his actions, as he set about his task, talking as he worked like a surgeon to his class. He told me the names of everything and why he cut here and sawed there. He made the trimming of a ham a fascinating experience for the little boy with the lamp.

A little later the hams and shoulders and "sides" were hung in the stone smokehouse near the barn and my brother Charlie and I had the interminable task of keeping up a smudge of corncobs and chips to smoke them. But how good that ham and bacon, and that sausage and headcheese, on cold mornings later in the winter!

☆ 16 ☆

My Boyhood Diaries

SINCE I am speaking here of my early education I must not omit a reference to my boyhood diaries which I have been reading with amusement for the first time in more than half a century. "Vol. I," as I marked it at the time, was opened on January 7, 1880, when I was in my tenth year, and I have continued it, with numerous lapses, for sixty years. I am now writing "Vol. LV."

Here are extracts from the entries of the first weeks— spelling and all:

"Wednesday Jan. 7, 1880. I went to school to-day. My Geography lesson was aboyt the western states. I think it is fun to study Geography. Pa and I plaid dominoes to-night and I beat him three or four times. I think it is a nice game to play. My Papa bought me a new pair of boots this morning. Boots are not bad things to have in cold weather.

"January 9, 1880. Tonight we cracked nuts and had a good time eating them. Pa read me about one of his old battles. I think war storries are nice things to hear but they are not so nice when you are their."

I am reminded freshly in looking over these old diaries of the tremendous part my father played in my early life. Hardly a day passed when I did not chronicle his doings, or his stories, or the games I played with him. He instructed

110

me in the use of his printing press, helped me with my collections of minerals and the like, and went fishing and camping every summer with me and my brothers. More precious than anything else were the long trips I took with him into the "up-country." I find this entry regarding one of them we made to Grantsburg in June, 1883:

"I talked with Papa all the way. He told me about the banking system. It is very interesting."

He was constantly talking about various public and political questions, luring me to keep myself informed. I find references on September 21, 1881, to the assassination of President Garfield:

"The *President* is *DEAD*. Am very sorry. Mourning all over the U. S. Arthur will now be President. He died Sep 19 at 10 minutes past ten."

On January 18, 1883, I wrote:

"The case of Giteau has not been given to the jury yet, though when they do get it I think they will deside to hang him directly. I hope they will. I believe I will get all the papers I can tell about the President's assassination."

On May 12, 1883, I note:

"Guiteau will be (hanged) on the 30th of June" and I drew a little picture of a gallows to illustrate the entry.

In rereading these old diaries I find them for the most part mere chronicles of the tumultuous daily happenings in our large and active family, with little or no reference to the life going on within the boy himself, which now remains so clear in my memory. I must myself have felt that I was not reporting the really interesting events of my life, for on April 28, 1883, I find this entry:

"I am a-going to add something new to the interest of my diary. I am going to tell each evening what I have learned during the day. This will drill me and also add to the interest of the diary if I should happen to read it hereafter. This new part shall be abbreviated by this mark or letters— Int. Par. (Interesting Part)."

I started off bravely the next day:

"Int. Par.—I read in *Lippincott's Magazine* (Aug. No. 1880) of Mormonism. How it was started by Joseph Smith. The revelations baptisms, etc. it is very novel and int. Learned some important facts in religion in S.S. [Sunday School] I learned the ans. to the question which has long puzzled me. Why does God create men when he knows they will turn out bad? I found the answer to be he creates all men for some good purpose and if there were no bad men there would be no good. As in the case of Judus the betrayer of Christ. If it was not for this *bad* man our sins would have remained unforgiven.

"Read something concerning ballooning—Learned about the great warrior Tamberlain who subdued all Persia and Turkey. He died in 1405. Learned of a coal mine in Penn. burning 50 years & still kindled. I will try to read slower & think of & remember what I read that is one of my besetting faults—absentmindedness—I will sometimes read a long time without knowing what I do."

On "Monday the 30th," after chronicling the fact that the weather was "warm and pleasant" and that I "got my hair cut," I go on:

"Int. Par. I got Cube Root through my scull today. It is

a very hard subject. My trouble came in getting new divisors. But I mastered it. Learned about the climate of Africa. Am studing of the 'Respiration & Voice' in Physiology. Am in division in Algebra. Learned something of Japan from a book by Bayard Taylor. Something of history of it also of the effect of Perry fleet on it in 1852."

By May 1 my grand new scheme evidently began to peter out. Here is the complete entry:

"Tuesday the 1—Did not go to school. Helped to make garden. Cow did not come home. Went over the river and got the horses shod. Fred and Auntie Annie came today. Went down to the river with Fred and got cornelians. Had an orange. Very nice and warm today. Int. Part.—I did not learn anything today."

On May 2 the "Int. Par." reads as follows: "I did not learn anything to-day except usual school knowledge."

On May 4: "Int. Par. Nothing."

May 5: "Int. Par. Nothing."

May 6: "Int. Par. Learned about Frank H. Cushing, Zuni tribes. It is very interesting about the old priests. Took a [horseback] ride."

May 7: "Int. Par. Read some of [Washington] Irving stories."

May 8. "Int. Par. Not anything."

That was the end of it. Spring was coming on: the entries on the following days will be sufficiently explanatory:

May 9: "Went down to fish & caught 8 fish, 6 red horse & buffaloes & sucker & 2 pike."

May 10: "Went fishing & caught a buffaloe & pike. Beautiful day sunny and warm."

May 11: "Went fishing & caught 1 pike. Lots of fun. River lower."

May 12: "I went fishing & caught 3 red-horses and a shiner."

Sometime later I evidently resolved again to start the department called "Int. Par." but after two or three entries I find this remark on May 27, 1883:

"Int. Par. I begin to see I dont know much. I thought I did but I find I dont."

Some years ago, I found among my boyhood papers a chart which I could not at first remember. It contained a list of virtues down one side: industry, cleanliness, temperance, chastity, and the like, with various crosses on the squares I had drawn opposite them. Presently the entire incident flashed into my memory.

Some one had called my attention to Benjamin Franklin's *Autobiography*, especially to his method of achieving virtue, with the remark:

"If you want to be a great man, you can see how Ben Franklin did it."

Well, I did want to be a great man, and I studied with some eagerness Franklin's method. I secured a little book and drew up a chart like Franklin's wherein I could record daily my imperfections—as to whether I was temperate, industrious, clean, orderly, and the like. But I could not keep it up. Days when I was so busy every moment with things that deeply interested me I could not stop to find out whether I had been industrious, and silent, and orderly, and temperate, and chaste. I considered that it must be a defect in me, and that I should never be a great man, but this daily self-examination as a duty became intensely distasteful. It was something like the prohibitions of my old aunts, and I knew even as a little boy that it was not my father's way. Why should I be clean and orderly and silent if I did not know what it was for? And I presently discovered that B. Franklin himself found his method unworkable!

☆ 17 ☆

I Decide to Become a Geologist

I HAVE spoken of my father's description of the geological interest of the St. Croix Valley. It scarcely needed such an incentive, but it helped to lure me, as it lured many another boy of our town, to the exploration of the wild gorge through which the turbulent waters dropped in foaming rapids from the broad and placid river above the town to the rock-guarded Dalles below. Day or night, all my boyhood, the sound of roaring water was rarely absent from my ears. I can remember awakening in the dark of the night to listen to the thunder of the rapids. I listened to them during the wearisome church services on Sunday. I knew every one of the strange potholes worn in the solid trap rock through the action, during uncounted millions of years, of the swirling waters. I knew every by-pass among the rocks in the rapids themselves where the migratory fish—great rock sturgeon, shovel-nose sturgeon, buffalo, suckers and sheepshead—could be found by thousands during the right weeks in spring, struggling northward to hundreds of lesser rivers and little lakes to spawn. We used to spear or "snag" these great hurrying fishes: and one notable day, after a hand-to-hand struggle in the water, we landed a rock sturgeon as big as we were. We carried it between us on a pole—taking turns

I Decide to Become a Geologist

—up into the town where Thompson's scales proved that it weighed fifty-seven pounds.

Today the Dalles are included in the Interstate Park, visited for its labelled beauties and worn wonders by thousands of automobile excursionists, but in my boyhood its wilderness had scarcely been intruded upon: it was not only little known, but largely unexplored. I used often to climb a rocky cliff above the Dalles. It was a wild and silent spot. A few stunted pines grew along the rough hillside, and I could look down into the swirling water of the river, brown and deep, and in spring often flecked with streamers of white foam from the rapids above. I sat in an opening at the top of the cliff called the Embrasure, and I could look across the river to a pinnacle of rock, curiously formed, called the Devil's Chair and farther down, the Devil's Pulpit and the Devil's Oven. The Devil had much to do with the chaos of our rocky cliffs!

Long before the white man came to that country, our river had been the boundary line between two great nations of the Indians, the Sioux to the westward in what was later known as Minnesota and the Dakotas, and the Chippewas to the eastward in Wisconsin. I had heard many a traditional story of the bitter wars between these neighbors, as bitter as any known to our own age and supposedly higher civilization. The last great battle, said to have been won by the Sioux, took place in this very valley, among these very rocks. The bodies of the dead, after the conflict, were supposed to have been thrown into the Devil's wells or potholes, so that the Indians called the place the Valley of the Bones. In my boyhood these wells were full of water, dark, still, and deep, and some of them, as we firmly believed, were bottomless. When we shouted into them, our voices came back in sepulchral echoes, and occasionally if we dared to lean over far enough, we could see the phantomlike reflections of our faces.

Sitting in that high Embrasure, looking down upon the scene of the ancient battleground, I often fought it all over again in my imagination, watching the half-naked Sioux, in buckskins and feathers, with their great bows, creeping up behind the rocks to attack the Chippewas, who were landing from their birch-bark canoes in the river. I made me strange Indian names of the leaders on both sides. I caused prodigies of valor to be performed, until presently the battle grew so vivid there before my eyes that I could literally see Sioux and Chippewa warriors struggling at the edge of the precipice and falling finally, knives in hand, into the dark waters below. I made me a scene in which an infuriated Sioux plunged into the river and, swimming deep in the water, came up beside a boatload of Chippewas and after knifing all he could reach and being knifed in return, succeeded in overturning the canoe, so that all were swept downward into the whirling waters. I had bands of Chippewas crouching on the cliffs of the eastern shore, as indeed actually happened, awaiting the landing of canoe-loads of the Sioux, and then rolling off great rocks to crush them. I conjured up every form of death by arrow and knife that could be imagined; and once or twice, I recall, it became so real to me that I ran and jumped down the rocks myself, half-terrified at my own visions.

And what times I spent wondering whether there were

any of the bones of that old battle still in the Devil's wells! Once while we were fishing in the Dalles, a boy friend of mine and I tried letting down stones tied to our fishlines to see how deep the holes were, and even big hooks on which, I firmly believe, we expected to pull up some remnants of a dead Indian.

Nothing in my boyhood fascinated me more than these rocky gorges, mysterious wells, and the wild rapids above them. One day when I was thirteen or fourteen years old I was exploring and dreaming on the river bank, I saw there a strange and unfamiliar figure. I do not remember that I was at all surprised. I had seen so many strange figures, real and imagined, in that river gorge—log-drivers with their canthooks, lumbermen in their great wannigans and bateaux, and our own blanketed Indians with fish spears, to say nothing of unshaven, knee-booted surveyors and prospectors—that if it had been a half-naked Sioux Indian warrior, I think I should have considered it nothing unexpected or unusual.

I looked at the new visitor with keen interest. He was roughly clad in leather leggings and wore an old cloth cap. On his back, attached to a shoulder strap, he carried a canvas bag. What interested me most was the short-handled hammer he had in his hand. Instead of a claw on the opposite side it had a blunt pick. I watched him intently for some time. From time to time he would climb up the cliffs, chip away bits of rock, examine them with great care, sometimes with a small glass fitted into his eye, like a jeweller. Often he would split the pieces apart with his pick and sometimes slip a specimen into the bag on his shoulder. I was as curious as any young crow and presently, when I had sidled quite near, the man spoke to me. I had thought at first that he was a prospector, for in those days it was generally believed that there were rich copper deposits in our valley, like those along Lake Superior—if only one could find them.

"Are you looking for copper?" I asked.

"Oh, no," he responded, "these strata are not copper-bearing."

I considered at once that he was entirely wrong, that he did not know what he was talking about. I knew perfectly well that there was plenty of copper in our hills! Didn't we find worn lumps of native copper on our river shores, and at that very time, wasn't Jake Berger sinking a shaft deep into the barren trap-rock, quite certain of striking a rich vein of it? But I wanted to keep up the conversation.

"I know," I said, "where there are some curious, smooth, shiny rocks."

"Do you?" he asked, and there was a pleasant look in his eye. "Will you show me?"

I led him up a little ravine, and there in an outcropping of stone I exhibited a treasure I had found while exploring some weeks before.

"Well," said he, "this *is* interesting. I have not seen any of it just here before."

"What is it?" I asked eagerly.

"Calc-spar," he replied and with that he deftly picked and hammered out a number of the specimens, finally washing them off in the river to show how beautiful the crystals were. Then he explained to me what calc was and how the "spar" had been formed, and why the deposits were in that

I Decide to Become a Geologist

place. I was completely fascinated and must have listened with both eyes and mouth wide open.

"Do you know what fossils are?" he asked me presently, seeing that I was an eager pupil.

"No, sir," I said.

With that we scrambled along a steep bank lower down the river where there was an outcropping of sandstone. Here he broke off quite a chunk and with his pick split it into flat slabs.

"Do you see those little white shells?"

I was filled with wonder. I had walked the river bank and climbed those very cliffs many a time but had never found any such treasures. Standing there that sunny afternoon in our own wonderful valley, he let me deep into a new mystery. He told me of the great lake which had once covered all this smiling land before there was any St. Croix River, or any Dalles, or any devil's handiwork of potholes and bottomless wells, and how finally this lake, far greater even than Lake Superior, wore a channel southward through the rock, and that was the beginning of our river. It was a rich discovery for me, enough to live on for many a week afterward. I thought of the waves deep above our ledges and the long sandy beaches where they rose and fell through countless years: and finally of the great flood there must have been when the waters broke their bounds, and formed the channel that was to become the St. Croix.

My friend told me how these little shellfish, probably long before there were any men on earth at all or even any animals or birds, had lived in the waters of that lake, and had left their remains for us to find, millions of years afterward.

"Would you like to know the name of these little shells?" he asked.

"Have they names?" I asked in utter amazement.

"Why yes," he answered, laughing. "Don't you see that they look a little like fingernails?"

They did indeed.

"The geologist who found them first," he said, "thought so too and called them *pinnaformis,* which in Latin means formed like a fingernail. That's their given name. But they also belong to a family, just as you do, and their family name is *Lingulepis.* So we call them *Lingulepis pinnaformis* —and they are to be found by thousands in your cliff."

What an afternoon that was! How the hours slipped by: how eagerly I followed and listened to my new friend. When I got home that night my pockets were bulging with wonderful specimens to show my father: a bit of calc-spar, a broken geode, several specimens of *Lingulepis pinnaformis* and many other fascinating bits.

I had found that my friend was to spend part of another day on the river and I joined him again. When he finally left he asked my name and put it down in his little book. Two or three weeks later I was astonished by the arrival of a large package addressed to me. When I opened it I found it contained two large volumes of the *Wisconsin Geological Survey* filled with maps and colored plates. It was accompanied by a letter from my friend telling me how to find an account of the various fossils of the St. Croix Valley. It was signed T. C. Chamberlain, who was then, my father discovered to his surprise, state geologist and professor at the University at Madison, of which he afterward became president. My father was vastly pleased and interested and joined me in a thorough examination of the books. We even found a plate representing, exactly, the fossil specimens we had discovered.

For a time I was all on fire to become a geologist and with a bag on my shoulder, a little hammer with a pick in my hand—and leggings!—go about the country revealing wonders that no one knew about. I began at once to tell myself long stories of my adventures in which I accomplished the most extraordinary feats and made the most astonishing discoveries, including copper deposits that completely outshone the Calumet and Hecla in the Lake Superior country north of us. In order to develop them it would be necessary to realize the dream of our valley and build a great dam at our falls, and a mighty copper smelter in the shallows of the river below—a locality I could easily stake out. Of course all this would cost millions upon millions of dollars, but that was a small matter! With a mother-lode in sight—I think I was not clear whether "mother-lodes" were of copper or gold, or both—with a mother-lode known to nobody but me, millions could be had for the digging. For good measure, in my spare moments, I located several excellent gold mines, but never had time to dig them.

I began at once making a collection of minerals wherein our country was unusually rich, getting all sorts of bits and strays, including two real prizes, a lump of native copper as big as my fist, found on the river shore, and an unusually large carnelian which I ground down on one side to show the beautiful markings. But I had no instruction and no further visitors from Heaven, and the world was so full of other strange and interesting things that my ardor gradually cooled.

It was perhaps just here that I began a process, worked out a pattern, that was to be repeated again and again in my later life. So many things I have longed passionately to do: so many things to be: and there has never been time enough. There was never time enough even after I learned that I was really a writer, and could relieve some of the urgency of my enthusiasm by writing it off. Somewhere, quite early, I came across a book or an article on the theosophical belief in the transmigration or reincarnation of souls, whereby men were given future lives on earth in which to work out their destiny. While I cannot say that I believed the doctrine to be true, the idea took hold upon my imagination. I never wanted to go to the Heaven currently described by the revivalists and lay preachers who came to our town: it resembled, suspiciously, one long Sunday. But the theosophical idea suited me exactly. I could put over into future lives all the enthusiasms, the hopes, the adventures, I did not have time to work out in this one. One whole life I could devote to geology, travelling about the world with a little hammer in my hand—and leggings—visiting unknown mountains in China and South America, and growing fabulously rich and famous as a result of my discoveries. There were also lives I could devote to the study of strange languages and visits to outlandish peoples. There were innumerable books to read, and when I made a new friend and began to love him very much, why, I could plan a whole future life to be lived in his company!

My adventure with my geological friend there on the

I Decide to Become a Geologist

bank of the St. Croix River was to have an interesting sequel. Many years later when I had attained a certain not altogether enviable reputation on account of the so-called "exposure" articles I was writing for *McClure's Magazine,* I attended a dinner at Chicago and was placed next to a fine-looking old man with a white beard. I was introduced to him: Professor Chamberlain of the University of Chicago. A few questions served to identify him as my friend of the fossils of the St. Croix.

"Were *you* that boy?" he exclaimed, incredulously.

"I was," I said, "and I am glad at last to have an opportunity of telling you how much I am indebted to you."

I remember the half-quizzical look he gave me.

"I thought," he said, "I had inspired a coming geologist."

He did not say it, but I knew, as well as though he had, what he was thinking!

☆ 18 ☆

The Death of My Mother

MY MOTHER'S death was a strange and deep experience, the reverberations of which, both direct and indirect, continued long in my innermost parts. I was thirteen years old and there were so many things I could not understand.

I was awakened in the night.

"Do you want to come down and see your mother?"

Something in the voice I understood immediately. I sat up paralyzed with fear. My aunt evidently thought I was not yet awake.

"You may not see her again: would you like to kiss her good-bye?"

"No, no," I cried out, "no, no."

I was terrified. The scene in the sick room, my mother lying there, the shaded lamp, the medicine-glasses on the chair, the doctor standing helpless—and my father—arose as vividly in my imagination as though I were already in the room.

"No, no."

I buried my face in the pillow. I would not go down.

It is strange that I can recall nothing whatever about the funeral service itself, not one incident, but the funeral procession comes back to me as though it happened yester-

126

The Death of My Mother

day—the slow-moving, horse-driven vehicles, the coffin in an open platform-wagon draped with black, for there was then no hearse in all that northern country. We were just behind it in an open three-seated carriage: my father, my aunts, my uncle and his wife, and my five brothers. It was mid-November, cold and raw.

I was full of wonder and a kind of terror. I remember the thoughts that raced through my mind.

"My mother is dead. What shall I do? Ought I to cry? My mother is dead."

I wondered how people acted when their mothers died. I was afraid: was it the same to be sorrowful as it was to be afraid? I knew deep down that I did not love my mother as much as I did my father, and yet the loss of her was terrible beyond anything I had ever known. Why was it? How could it happen to us? Without any warning?

My mind was keyed to a high pitch. I looked at my father sitting there ahead of me with the driver—his great square head, his powerful shoulders—sitting immovable. What did he feel? I looked at my aunts and my brothers: why were they not crying? Ought they to cry? I knew I should not do it but I turned to look back at the long procession of carriages and wagons behind us. I found myself counting them: there were fifteen. I saw the people in them, looking sober. Did they feel sorry? I ought to feel sorrier than they did. It was *my* mother who had died. *Did* I feel sorry? What was it to feel sorry?

I could not help having an interest in everything that was happening, the horses, the drivers, the long bleak hill up to the cemetery, a little later two men climbing out of the sandy grave—a terrible thing from which I shaded my eyes. The minister was there with his book, and my father twisting his hands in a hard knot behind his back.

Something was wrong. I should feel sorrier: probably I should cry, but all I could feel was terror—and a kind of irresistible, fascinated interest. Another strange feeling intruded: a kind of pride. It was *our* funeral, and we had ridden at the head of the procession: a long procession, too, for our town. I felt that it was wrong to be proud at such a time, when I should be sorry, when I should probably be crying. But there it was: it was what I felt.

The first thing I did when we got home was to look for my father. What was he doing? How did he feel? I finally found him alone, and quite unaware, in our living room. He was sitting in his own armchair. His hands were over his eyes, his shoulders shook with strongly suppressed sobs. It went through me like the thrust of a sharp knife: it was more terrible than anything else that had happened. My father, that strong man, that refuge of safety and fearlessness, my father shaken with weeping: I shall never forget the hurt of it in my own heart. I must have glanced about the strange, familiar room where so many interesting things had happened. Here we had our morning prayers, here Father told us great stories or read aloud to us, and here at one side stood the reed organ where my mother used to play, "Wait for the Wagon" or "Tenting on the Old Camp Ground," or "Just before the Battle, Mother." It came over me with a flash, the memory of my father standing near the end of the organ watching us singing—for he could not hear

The Death of My Mother

us—and the sudden swift glance my mother gave him, and the flood of tears in her eyes.

My poor, gentle, beautiful, sensitive mother! My father loved the frontier, loved the adventure of it, loved to build, had a passion for opening roads, clearing and smoothing rough land, damming streams for power—but she mourned for the sweetness and light of life. She longed for old friends, old dear places.

I must have paused only a moment there in the open doorway watching my father. I remember brushing off my own tears and running up the stairs to my refuge in the attic where I flung myself down on the floor, weeping resistlessly.

"I am sorry, I am sorry, I am sorry," I said over and over —thinking most of all of my father.

So I lay for a long time and presently I felt a curious sense of satisfaction stealing over me. I was glad I knew what it was to be sorry, not merely afraid. I knew now what it was to be terribly sorry, to have my heart ache all through. I could not think of my father sitting alone there in his chair, or of my mother, without crying again.

What strange things had happened—strange and different and new. I found myself absorbed in thinking about all that had happened. I felt that I ought to *stay* sorry, but I couldn't.

After that, for days, I watched my father secretly, for I loved him. He was sad and silent: I think he was never quite the same afterward. While he lived happily for many years, something of the joy of living that I knew seemed never quite to return.

129

☆ 19 ☆

We Celebrate Christmas

COMPARED with the Christmases of today, the celebrations of the Baker family there on the frontier were simple affairs—but I cannot remember that we enjoyed them any the less. We never had a Christmas tree, nor a sprig of holly, nor any mistletoe; we sang no carols nor ever burned a candle. As for a plum-pudding, I think I had never heard of one—except perhaps in the books of Charles Dickens. Our old aunts had inherited the puritan tradition and were suspicious of "pagan ceremonial," to say nothing of "pagan indulgence." Even the gifts were few and simple, and if possible practical, like a pair of mittens or a new cap—and, of course, books. Each child, as he grew up, was presented with a Bible with his name in it. And yet, after all the years, I cannot look back without a strange warmth and pressure about the heart as I recall those days.

"For none will ever know the gleam there used to be
About the feast-days freshly kept by me."

How they all troop before me as I write, my father, erect, handsome, strong—the very personification of zestful vigor —and in the earlier Christmases my delicate, graceful, thoughtful mother, far too gentle for the rough world she lived in; and my great old aunts, Aunt Hill, Aunt Amanda, and even Aunt Em, of whom I have already spoken. I can see the eager, adventurous, pugnacious, imaginative, fun-loving brothers of our family; and the long succession of Presbyterian ministers and their families who were often guests in our home; and finally the Annies and Idas and Helgas, who presided in the kitchen.

One Christmas, the one that so soon followed the death of my mother, I recall with especial clearness. I think an effort was made by my father and by our old aunts to make it seem cheerful and usual. We began to think of it several weeks in advance largely because of an odd problem presented by the youngest of the tribe, Fred, who was then nearly four years old. Some one had found out that no one in the family knew the exact date of Fred's birth. At the time he came, another boy more or less in the family when there were already five, seemed to have awakened so little interest—Mother being ill—that the usual entry in the family Bible either had not been made or was incorrect. The discovery led to excited discussion. At first Fred himself was enormously proud of the distinction. He went about telling any one who happened to come in, "I've lost my birthday. I'm the only one who hasn't any birthday." After a time his loving older brothers began to explain to him that having no birthday he could not, of course, ever have any birthday parties, nor any cake, nor any presents. When he fully realized these terrible consequences he abruptly changed his tune.

"I want a birthday. I want a birthday," he wailed, and was so noisy about it that my father finally said:

Native American

"Now, Fred, be quiet. I'll see that you get a birthday just as good as any of the boys has got: and I'll give it to you for a Christmas present."

The effect upon Fred was as instantaneous as it was surprising. Knowing that he was now sure of it—we always believed implicitly in what Father said—he returned to his boast, which he evidently considered a great distinction:

"I'm the only one who hasn't any birthday: and I'm goin' to get one for Christmas."

On Christmas eve my father, as usual in the past, gathered the entire family around him and read aloud the poem by Clement C. Moore which begins:

" 'Twas the night before Christmas, when all through the
   house
Not a creature was stirring, not even a mouse."

My father sitting there in his big chair with the book held high in his hand (I have that very book here before me as I write) and reading with zest those rolling lines—and my aunts not far away in their rocking chairs, smiling and nodding their heads to the cadence of the verse, and all those eager little boys, tousle-headed, red-faced from the cold they played in, fresh from the hills they slid upon in our bright northern winter days—all gathered there to listen to that matchless classic of the American Christmas:

"The stockings were hung by the chimney with care
In hopes that St. Nicholas soon would be there."

My father was not at his best, however, until he reached the passage describing the oncoming reindeer. It was then, literally, that "he whistled, and shouted, and called them by name."

> "Now, *Dasher!* now, *Dancer!* now, *Prancer!* and *Vixen!*
> On, *Comet!* on, *Cupid!* on, *Donder* and *Blitzen!*
> To the top of the porch! to the top of the wall!
> Now dash away! dash away! dash away all!"

As soon as it was over all the younger members of the family demanded to see the picture that went with the verses: a fine old wood-cut showing Santa Claus sitting astride the chimney, his pipe in his mouth and a great pack of toys on his back. A round winter moon, rising behind a church spire, filled the sky and near at hand the champing reindeer awaited their master's return from his visit to the little boys and girls in the rooms below. It was a wonderful picture and I can remember seeing two of the little boys, Clarence and Hugh, lying flat on their stomachs, the book open before them, studying every line of it. It gave rise to scores of questions. Clarence, who was known as the Regular Roarer, proved highly skeptical. He went out into the snow and looked up at our chimney. How was Santa Claus to get down into any such hole? Especially if he had a big pack? And how was he to get out into the room? Wouldn't he get all blackened with soot? For in those days we had no fireplace at all, only a great hot iron stove.

While we were hanging up the stockings along the moulding where the fireplace should have been and wasn't, there was a steady fire of questions. Charlie and I, as mature older brothers, seasoned by experience, took it upon ourselves to defend the legend in its entirety. I suspect, in our earnestness, we made certain assertions that could not be literally defended, and I think we entirely satisfied the two younger brothers, Hugh and Fred, but the Regular Roarer seemed still unconvinced. He just wouldn't see how St. Nicholas could get down our chimney and into the boys' room.

Charlie and I were delighted when my aunt, assuring us of our elderliness, asked us to help fill the stockings, after the younger boys were dragged off to bed. This we did with many circumlocutions and much discussion, wondering at the same time what there could be in the remaining packages which were evidently designed for our limp stockings after we also had gone to bed. When we could not delay a moment longer—for we had heard our father's imperative voice, "Ray, Charlie—off to bed"—we crept reluctantly up the stairs. While we were undressing we made the astonishing discovery that Clarence was not in his bed. We made a hasty search, since the Regular Roarer enjoyed his jokes, but he was not to be found. Hugh and Fred, awakened from sound sleep, said they had not seen him. We called downstairs but Aunt Hill knew as little as Hugh and Fred.

"I know," cried Charlie, "he's gone out to watch for Santa Claus."

Great excitement. This was exactly what the Regular Roarer might well do. We all came tumbling down the stairs and dashed out into the darkness and the snow. My aunt, grown anxious, followed us. No Clarence!

"He'd be in the barn where it's warm," suggested the imaginative Charlie.

We all rushed through the snow to the barn, Charlie calling at the top of his voice, "Bring a light, bring a light." But no Clarence.

We Celebrate Christmas

By this time my father, who had as usual been quietly reading in bed, his peace fortified by his deafness, appeared on the stairs.

"What's the trouble?"

Our excitement made us so inarticulate that we had some difficulty in explaining—through his speaking tube.

"Bosh!" said my father good-naturedly.

We were now in the boys' room, where the stockings were hanging.

"Bosh!" said my father.

I never knew whether it was by calculation or by accident, or whether he was about to replenish the fire, but at that moment he raised the lid of the huge wood box.

"Huh!" said my father.

We all looked in. There was the Regular Roarer fast asleep on the woodpile. He had determined to watch, through a crack in the box, the coming of Santa Claus, and nature had been too much for him. He was not going, any longer, to take the word of his older brothers.

The morning brought tremendous excitement. Two of the gifts were a total surprise—two hairy cocoanuts, such as we had never before seen in the flesh. I remember yet the wonder of the business of boring a hole in the "eye" and pouring off the "milk."

The gifts, as I have said, were few and simple, but how we did gloat over them. The strangest of all, for every one including the recipient, was Fred's birthday. He had come pounding downstairs all expectancy, crying out,

"Where's my birthday? I want my birthday."

When this commotion was explained to Father, he began

slapping his breast pockets. "That's so," he said, and drew out a bit of paper on which appeared the date, "April 23, 1880." Father had evidently forgotten all about it—even though he had considerable difficulty in getting the information. Poor little Fred took the paper and turned it over in his hand, and then, suddenly, began to roar—and roar—and roar. A scrap of paper when he expected a birthday! There must have been some glorified vision in the little chap's mind of what a birthday would be like—a cake? gifts? a party? And this was only a bit of paper.

My warm-hearted aunt understood instantly and gathered him into her arms. We all passed our candy boxes, and some one brought him his bulging stocking—but it was long before he could be comforted.

Charlie and I each had a new jackknife—quite the most valuable of possessions. Mine was a "hunting-clasp"—enough of a woodsman's knife to produce a thrill, and Charlie's had four blades. The little boys each had some small gift. I remember a box of jackstraws, and any amount of candy and a large orange—in those days oranges were a rare treat to us—in each stocking.

The last I remember of that particular Christmas was the sight of Aunt Hill holding the Regular Roarer firmly by the nose while she fed him a tablespoonful of dark medicine out of a dark bottle.

☆ 20 ☆

The Baker Family Stages a Play

OUR AUNT HILL had decided that the Baker family was to present a play. At first she had considered a Christmas play with wise men and angels in it, but when she looked over the actor-material, consisting mainly of the six Baker boys, and considered presenting them on any stage as angels, even she was daunted. As for a Christ child, Fred, who was a chubby, red-faced boy with pugilistic tendencies, was a hopeless impossibility.

Anyway, a manger-play with wise men and angels in it would have been too tame for my aunt, however strongly she may have approved it on religious grounds. My aunt wanted action.

As I have already related she had long been engaged with all the urgency and ardor of her nature in the battle against the Demon Rum, and it was quite in character that she should give up the Christmas play and stage the cause in which she was most of all interested. A play on the subject would not only afford the opportunity for action and climax, but it would not be cluttered up with ineffectual angels, when something real was to be done. What could be more instructive to the tender youth, all boys, who were growing up around her and might soon be tempted by the Demon himself?

Native American

My aunt wrote the play with delight and I recall the gusto with which she read the last of several versions aloud to Charlie and me, who as the oldest brothers were to play the principal parts. When we discovered to our astonishment and satisfaction that the Demon was to appear on the stage in person, my brother cried out—such is the weakness of human nature—"That's the part I want," and I answered instantly, "No, I'm older than you are, and I'm going to have it." My brother, who was also my inseparable friend, immediately tried to hit me on the nose, but my powerful aunt held us apart. She seemed somewhat surprised at the popularity of the Demon: and at the unwillingness of either Charlie or me to be the Minister in the play, which she considered the most important part. I remember we had a tremendous set-to and finally agreed to resign the Demon because he appeared in only one act and had nothing to hiss except "So-o-o, you would escape; s-s-sinner, come along now," and I was cast for the Drunkard, who was to have delirium tremens on the stage, and my brother was to be the Drunkard's wife. Charlie objected violently until he learned that he was to be dressed up in women's clothes, at the thought of which he went off into spasms of laughter. The third brother, Harry, having gone, after mother's death, to live with our uncle and aunt at Hudson, did not have a part in the play, but the three younger boys, Clarence, Hugh and Fred, were to be the children of the Drunkard's family. They were delighted with the prospect. Clarence had overheard some older member of the family say of him sometime before that he had "the loudest voice of anybody," that he was "a regular roarer," which was entirely true. It seemed to him a great compliment and he would go about remarking "I've got the loudest voice of anybody." When he heard that he was to be an actor in the play, and that the Demon himself was to be on the stage, he was so pleased that he immediately demonstrated his prowess—and roared so that he could be heard across the road. Hugh, who was the sedate one of the tribe, and grew up to be a college president, was less noisily excited, but Fred, a faithful follower and imitator of Clarence, began to jump up and down and add to the best of his ability to the noise that Clarence was making.

What excitement and hilarity we had in setting up the scenery and learning our parts! For the time being our aunt was the most popular person in the St. Croix Valley. She was infinitely inventive in keeping every one happily at work, and when we began to rehearse she would sit in the middle of the room and laugh at our efforts—especially at the Demon and at me, the Drunkard—until the tears rolled down her face.

We youngsters had for our own the largest room in the house. It had windows on three fronts, a great stove at one side with a capacious wood box with a hinged cover, near it, and not much else save a few battered chairs, a heavy deal table and, I think, two settees. Oh yes, and a battered bookcase stuffed with battered books.

We strung the curtain across one end of the room, after many discussions as to the mechanism for pulling it aside. We worked out two complete scenes, one the Drunkard's pathetic home—a ragged carpet, broken furniture, torn curtains and even a picture or two on the wall that were hung at a disorderly angle. Our attic proved unexpectedly resourceful and how we did enjoy rushing up and down the stairs, whenever a new inspiration struck us—usually as the result of sly prompting upon the part of our aunt—with broken furniture to try. One of the most important properties was a disreputable old bed with a torn mattress which protruded its hair stuffing with utter shamelessness. My aunt insisted upon calling it a "pallet of straw."

The other scene we were not so sure about, but we gave wings to our imagination. It was a Bar-Room—the well-known resort of Demon Rum. We must have collected and tested at least twenty bottles for the shelves of this sink of iniquity. I think my aunt could not have told a whiskey bottle from a paregoric bottle but she instructed us gaily in making ostentatious labels and pasting them on: "Rum"—which she considered the greatest villain of the Demon Family—and "Gin," "Whiskey," "Wine," "Beer." Incidentally we learned a good deal about those various intoxicants that might prove of value to us in the future.

Scene One was to be the Drunkard's home: Scene Two, the Bar-Room, and Scene Three, the Drunkard's home again.

When the great evening came, we had an enthusiastic audience, mostly boys and girls, for my aunt wanted as many of them as possible to see the play and be instructed as to the evils of "the Traffic," as she usually called it.

The first act went off beautifully. There the poor Drunkard sat in a broken-down chair, ragged of clothes, with unkempt hair, his face pale with powdered starch, and there his wife in skirts too long for her, pretending that uncontrollable spasms of laughter—my brother Charlie was the champion laugher of the neighborhood—were in reality sobs of distress. The Regular Roarer and the two younger brothers were enough awed by the excitement to act their sad parts at least in this act with tolerable authenticity. Our aunt stood at one side, just behind the curtain, to prompt and encourage us.

The Drunkard's family, having been discovered in this deplorable condition of poverty and hunger (all due to drink) and having accepted the roar of applause from the front of the room, the Minister appeared on the stage, clad all in black with a worn Bible under his arm. He was a neighbor boy and so frightened that Aunt Hill had fairly to push him out on the stage. To make matters worse, just as he began to speak, a voice in the audience, sharp and clear and choking with laughter, called out:

"Look at Charlie Baker. *He* don't know how to wear skirts."

Charlie was, I think, about to rise from his grief and make a remark or so not in the script, but he caught Aunt Hill's eye and settled back again after casting a withering glance at the audience.

My aunt was nothing if not edifying, and the Minister's tremulous voice stripped the last rag of respectability from old Demon Rum, and the Traffic in which he was engaged. My aunt had tempered the ordeal which confronted the Minister by providing him with frequent opportunities of referring to his Bible to prove what he said. He sometimes had difficulty in finding his place—his hands shook so violently—but he seemed relieved when he could read instead of speak:

"Wine is a mocker, strong drink is raging: and whosoever is deceived thereby is not wise."

Everything considered, the first act went off pretty well. Every one present knew the arguments already, and approved the climax in which the Minister solemnly drew from his pocket the Pledge and asked the poor old Drunkard —which was me—to sign it. If only he would sign it, everything would be bright and cheery again. There would be beefsteak on the stove, and a pitcher of milk for these poor little starving innocents—upon which the Minister dramatically placed his hand on little Fred, who looked, in spite of his rags, like a stuffed cherub. But the Demon had got his grip on the Drunkard and he shook his head sorrowfully but obstinately. Even after all these perfectly good arguments, which everybody knew to be true, he would not sign! When I had earlier raised the ethical problem of this refusal, my aunt had explained it clearly to me, that if the Drunkard signed in the first act of course there couldn't be any play. It didn't quite satisfy me—but the show went on.

I should have explained earlier that our entire audience, from the beginning, had been eagerly expecting the entry of the Demon: and was somewhat disappointed by his failure to appear in the first act. While every detail of our play was supposed to be a "dead secret" every boy and girl in town knew that Albert Christopher, who was as agile as a monkey, was to appear as a devil—with a red hat on his head and a long red tail with a spike in the end of it. My artful aunt had added to the suspense and expectancy in her introductory remarks by explaining that she hoped any of the younger children who were present would not be alarmed by the appearance on the stage of a Certain Apparition. She called it a Certain Apparition, she said, because it was supposed not to be seen by any one on the stage except the Poor Victim of the Rum Traffic. And anything that this Apparition might say could not of course be heard by any one else on the stage. This delightful mystification my aunt had adopted entire from an explanation that my father, who had recently been reading a new edition of Shakespeare, had made regarding the problem of the subjectivity of the ghost in Hamlet. The very thought that there might be a Demon on the stage who couldn't be seen must have sent a delicious thrill down the backs of all the little boys and girls: and even some of the older ones. I, the Drunkard, who had his eye fixed to a hole in the curtain, saw them all looking questioningly at one another. What was an Apparition anyway? And how could He or It be on the stage and act a part without being seen or heard?

The second Act was awaited with great expectancy, all the more because in the excitement of setting up the scenery of the Bar-Room some one let fall a whole box of gin and whiskey bottles. One of them broke with a resounding crash and the liquor spilled across the floor. It was of a reddish color and some of it ran out under the curtain, to the vast diversion of the audience.

I forgot to say that we had two colors of liquor, one red and one black. In the beginning we had contented ourselves with plain water, but as our imaginations took fire we complained to our aunt:

"But Aunt Hill, they'll know this isn't whiskey or beer or wine or *anything*. It'll look just like water."

Native American

"That's so," said my aunt, and with evident pleasure led us down, mysteriously, into the basement, where we were entrusted with several jars of canned raspberries and blackberries to carry upstairs. The juice was poured off, diluted, and used to fill the bottles. It was really most effective, but not altogether durable. On the morning after this great dramatic innovation had been made, several of the bottles were found to be empty. My aunt looked sharply at my brother Charlie and me and locked up all of those that remained in the china closet—until the great night.

In all the lore of the stage, I doubt if there is a record of a more effective second act than ours. It was indeed a simple Bar-Room, but no one could have doubted its purpose. There was the shelf with the essential mirror over it, and the bottles in full display. The labels were so large that the audience could be in no doubt as to what they contained. Every one was on the outlook for Demon Rum himself, but he, knowing well, as our aunt explained, that the Lure he had to display was quite sufficient, kept himself cannily in the background.

The action at first was somewhat constrained, but when the barkeeper poured out the liquor and two or three citizens who were present began to sip from their glasses and smack their lips as hardened old topers were supposed to do, things began to liven up.

When this lamentable scene had been given time to soak in, the Drunkard was seen to come slowly staggering into the Bar. The more he staggered and fell over chairs the more delighted the audience became. Presently he approached the Bar and demanded, in a loud, rough voice:

144

The Baker Family Stages a Play

"Give me the hardest drink you have on your shelves."

My aunt had trained me thoroughly in this startling speech and it made a profound impression on the audience.

While the Drunkard was in the very act of getting drunker, however, who should appear but the Poor Wife with her three Innocent Little Ones clinging to her skirts. Let me draw a veil over this pathetic scene: it is beyond my eloquence. Suffice it to say that the Drunkard, who was, after all, not really Bad but only Weak, and who would have been all right if Demon Rum had let him alone, suffice it to say that he staggered out of the room on the arm of his devoted wife.

This act was a great success, loudly cheered by the audience, but it was nothing compared with what followed. We changed the scenery back to the poverty-stricken home of the Drunkard with only one unfortunate mishap. One of the necessary properties of the Drunkard in Act III was a bottle of liquor which he was supposed to have brought home from the Bar, but when I looked around for it, none was to be found. The fact was, that the moment the Bar-Room scene had been removed, the Minister, the Demon, the Drunkard's Wife and all three of her hapless little ones had been on hand and every bottle had speedily been emptied. Could the Drunkard, who really needed his bottle, be blamed for being angry? The Minister, a good friend of mine, had apparently been the chief offender—he was the oldest one of us and could hold the most—and if it hadn't been for the immediate presence of my aunt we should probably have gone down together in mortal combat on the Bar-Room floor. I cried out:

"How do you expect me to get delirium tremens on a bottle of water?"

This perfectly reasonable exclamation was heard by some of the delighted audience outside: and was quoted to me too many times afterward.

Act III opened with the same scene as Act I, except that the Drunkard was seen upon his pallet of straw in terrible agony of body and of soul. He had the bottle still in his hand, and it was half empty, which made it evident to every one that he was still unredeemed. No one in our family, before the play was put on, could tell what a Drunkard with delirium tremens would do. My Aunt Hill and I looked the subject up in *Zell's Encyclopedia,* but the information was hopelessly vague.

"You will have to use your imagination," said my aunt to me with much good sense.

Well, I did use my imagination and I am certain that no Drunkard could have done a more competent job than I did. I wriggled and gurgled, groaned and roared. I tore my hair, I ripped the bed-clothes to pieces, and finally fell off the pallet and was boosted back on again by my loving Wife who was literally choking with laughter. The audience was uproarious.

Just at the moment when it seemed impossible that the Drunkard could any longer bear such agony and was about to expire, the Minister was seen walking into the room. He was plainly horrified by what he discovered, but his words of wisdom and beauty, mingled with the tears of the Wife, began soon to calm the Drunkard down. After moaning effectively several times he began to revive, and finally admitted that he had made a great mistake in not signing the Pledge.

These words had no sooner come from his lips, than Demon Rum himself, no doubt suspecting that his prey was about to escape him, came bounding into the room. Never was there such a dramatic sensation! The audience gasped and cheered—and, I regret to say, laughed. The Demon leaped in the air, switched his spiked tail, and threw out his red-clad arms as though he intended to seize the poor Drunkard and carry him off.

"S-s-so, you would es-s-scape me," he hissed, "come along, s-s-sinner, you belong to me."

Of course the Minister and the family were not supposed to know that there was any Demon present but nevertheless they seemed deeply affected, indeed quite desperate. The Minister and the Wife both fell upon the poor Drunkard and held him firm and fast so that he could not be carried off. This scene continued with tremendous excitement and applause for several minutes. The Demon fairly outdid himself: his rage was without bounds. The oldest of the Drunkard's poor little boys, indeed, became so excited that he forgot he was on the stage and began to jump up and down, and seemed about to cry out that he had the loudest voice of anybody, when my aunt's long arm reached out on the stage and pulled him off into oblivion.

When every one was at the point of exhaustion in this struggle between Good and Evil, the Drunkard rose feebly but nobly from his pallet of straw, and "with the light shining in his eyes"—as the script had it—cried out:

"I'll sign the Pledge. I'll sign."

The Baker Family Stages a Play

Hearing these heroic words, and seeing the Pledge being actually drawn from the Minister's pocket, the Demon gave one last despairing yelp and bounded from the room.

Curtain.

It was a grand success, even though I did hear a rumor that the Presbyterian minister who was there with his wife did not give it his entire approval. He thought it somewhat undignified: and he was not certain whether the message, in that form, had gone home to the hearts of the audience. But he was a newcomer, and did not know my aunt.

☆ 21 ☆

The Vision of the Frontier

As I LOOK BACK, it seems to me that the predominant quality or virtue of the frontier was hope, and that corollary of hope—faith. The past had been hard, and the present was hazardous, but what a future we had! A dream in every square foot of land, hope in every tumbling river, and in many a waterfall a vision of a city with mills!

How I recall the hope—yes, the certainty—of every man in the little settlement on the St. Croix where I grew up, of the glory that would be "when they build the dam," "when they improve our falls." I know men who held on to their meager plots of land in the village, paid taxes and often interest for half a century, waiting for the rise of the city that was to be and that never was. When the great dam was finally built—the irony of it!—the power was not used locally but carried away by high tension to St. Paul. How could we pioneers, who knew not electricity, have dreamed of such a perverse destiny?

Next to God my father believed in the land. He came from a line of pioneer ancestors each of whom in his generation had worshipped the land and suffered for it—John of Connecticut, Remember and Ozi of Vermont, Luther of Western New York. To him it was the only solid, material reality. It was there. Everything else shifted, dissolved,

might easily be tricked away by the cunning of men; everything else might be stolen, burned, destroyed. The land remained. My father had one infallible rule for investing
money: "Put everything you have close to the land." No
stocks or bonds for him, but good land held in fee simple,
or first mortgages (payable in gold) upon good land. As
soon as he himself accumulated any surplus he followed his
own rule—he bought more and more land until he groaned
under the weight of the taxes. At one time he owned or
partly owned many thousands of acres, and controlled even
larger tracts. But if he groaned in the present, if his holdings
made him "land-poor," he had also the promise, as vital to
him as the comforts of his religion, that his acres would presently mount in value, he would be richly repaid for his fore-
sight and his sacrifice of present comfort for future profit.
One had only to hang on, to be steadfast. Farmers would
come in to clear and till the valleys, engineers to dam the
rivers and purchase the otherwise worthless flowage properties, and there would be towns with corner lots rising to
values inconceivable to the weak imagination of mankind—
like streets paved with gold and thronging with shimmering
harpists—and all would at last be happiness.

My father died before the disillusionment was far advanced. He died in the faith. He would not have known,
much less respected, a world in which the value of land went
steadily downward, when a mortgage was a liability, when
sober farmers revolted against the payment of interest and
taxes. He would have been as much shocked by its perfidy
as by the questioning of his faith in God.

Another aspect of the hope of the pioneer, his complete

faith in progress, was his love of building, development, of seeing things grow—of making them grow himself. My father had this passion developed to a high degree. He loved all kinds of road building, "opening new country," he called it; he liked to make plans for dams and the development of water powers. Fences interested him; he often built them where they were not really needed, for they were convincing evidences of ownership. He designed a new kind of picket-fence which in early days he built around his home place, and painted white. It was as contagious in that country as measles. The first sidewalk in our town he considered a triumph.

My father loved tools of all kinds. He had wonderfully complete sets of surveyors' instruments and carpenters' and plumbers' tools which he prized so highly that he burned his full name or his initials on the handles of every one of them. I never knew any one who could make inanimate objects more completely his own than he. In all his books he had a bookplate which he himself designed and printed made up of a monogram of his initials "J. S. B." with the added words: "The ungodly borroweth and payeth not again." The other day I had out the beautiful set of ivory chessmen with its graceful king and queen, which he used when he taught me to play, and I found that he had not only put his full name and address on the bottom of the box that held them and on the inside cover, but that every chessman, pawns and all, bore his initials in indelible ink. Upon everything in life that he touched he burned the symbols of his personality.

He had, at one time, a complete printing outfit, no amateur affair, on which he himself printed the stationery and the advertising material he used in his office. Here I learned how to set type, block it in, and run the press. I printed unnumbered thousands of letterheads and envelopes. Sometime later when my father had to take over, temporarily, the local newspaper, I helped the irresponsible, brilliant, interesting, drunken printer every Thursday to run off the edition. I was the devil and stood behind the old Washington (or "improved Washington") press and inked the type with a double-handed roller. I sometimes perched myself upon a high stool and set local items in type—"Mrs. Pike went to the Twin Cities on Monday. She reports a good time."—without bothering to write them first. I can remember the feel of the rounds of the tall stool on the soles of my bare feet. It was here that I got the first smell of printer's ink—said to be forever afterward irresistible. Some of my experiences at that time went into a novel called *Hempfield* that I wrote long afterward.

My father was also an excellent draftsman and had in his room a draftsman's table which he built himself, with a fine set of instruments. He superintended the rebuilding of our home place, making all the drawings carefully to scale. He built an elaborate cottage for one of our old aunts, he planned and built a system of waterworks—the first anywhere in that country—with a hydraulic ram on a stream in the valley below, the water being forced upward to a reservoir on the hill above the house and thence piped into the kitchen and garden.

But the thing that interested me most of all as a small boy was his invention of a new kind of privy.

The Vision of the Frontier

I have thought that sometime, though the subject is not ordinarily discussed, I should like to write an account of the pioneer privy, as I knew it. There it stood, as ours stood, some fifty or a hundred feet from the back door. A narrow boardwalk ran out to it which in winter had often to be shovelled clear, or swept, for our snows were frequent and deep. What an ordeal of a morning for the family when the thermometer registered twenty or thirty degrees below zero, as it often did in our country. I can see the women of the household with cloaks thrown over their heads rushing back and forth, shivering with the cold. The old, the young, the well, the ill—what heroes, what martyrs!—and they never even knew it.

To me, a small boy, our privy was quite an institution. I enjoyed it. It had two large seats and one little one, each with a leathern-hinged cover. There was a little moon-shaped opening in the door. Some one in the family, either to secure greater privacy, or to prevent the icy winds from blowing through the cracks, had pasted the walls with edifying pages, including many pictures, from *The Christian Union*, *Scribner's Monthly*, *The Advocate and Guardian*, *The Pioneer Press* of St. Paul and even from our own local paper, *The Valley Standard*. I suspect that our old aunts were responsible for the especially instructive reading on the back of the door where it could be most easily seen—but this I avoided, preferring the more secular matters higher up. I can remember standing on the seat and reading the articles and stories, which I found interesting even though they often had neither beginnings nor endings. A poem pasted sidewise, "An Old Dog," I committed to memory,

153

and can recall some of the lines of it to this day. I can see them yet, running up and down—and the little boy standing there in the dim light of that sequestered spot with his head crooked to one side to read them.

> "I am only a dog, and I've had my day,
> So idle and dreaming stretched out I lay
> In the welcome warmth of the summer sun,
> A poor old hunter whose work is done."

My father never liked such primitive arrangements, and early in my boyhood he built a grand new privy connected with the house, a substantial building with real windows, and instead of a hole dug in the earth he constructed a large wooden box which could be drawn out at intervals by a team of horses. The covers of the seats were so connected with a lever that when they were shut down they were supposed to empty a charge of clean sand from a large receptacle above and behind the seats—an excellent invention which did not work.

To cap the climax my father installed a small box-stove of cast iron which could be fed with chunks from a convenient wood box. Before breakfast on cold mornings in winter he would have a fire built so that the room was the most comfortable in the house. How many times of a Sunday morning I have seen him arrayed in his Sunday clothes—he wore usually a white vest, the only man in the northwestern states, I think, who did so—with his black-rimmed glasses on his great nose, going toward the back of the house. He always had *The Christian Union* under his arm and was gone a long time. It was an opportunity to read in complete comfort the latest sermon of Henry Ward Beecher.

The Vision of the Frontier

So far as I was concerned I missed the old privy with the poetry on the wall, and the portrait of Lydia Pinkham, and the recipes for floating island pudding—so early does tradition set its mark upon the human spirit.

What a sensation in that new country Baker's privy created! A privy in the house! Ho, ho! A stove in it! Ha, ha! But my father neither heard nor cared in the least what people said of him. He was going to have things the way he wanted them.

In the later years, after I left home, my father became greatly interested in forestry. Two of his sons, after courses at Yale and in Germany, became foresters. He had a fine tract of about one hundred acres on a beautiful lake a few miles from town which he lumbered according to the most approved methods, setting up his own sawmill and carefully burning all the tops and refuse to keep out fires. Afterward he planted it with pines, spruces, cedars, and with deciduous trees, oaks, maples and ash. It was a rather expensive business and some of the neighbors used to ask slyly when he expected a crop. He was already along in years and occasionally said to his sons: "I shall never live to see these trees grow up, but you will, and they will be beautiful and valuable."

And yet how they did grow while he still lived! I remember well walking with him, when he was an old man, in the forest which he had grown. He was still as erect as a major and light on his feet, though his hair was as white as snow. He put his hand vigorously and affectionately upon the bole of one of his tall pines, as another man might clap a friend on the shoulder, and said to me:

"Ray, there are many kinds of immortality. This is one of mine."

That forest still stands: towering pines and oaks and spruces: both the memorial and the immortality of a man who loved life and lived it greatly and deeply.

This, then, was the atmosphere in which my boyhood was spent: these were the people I knew and loved. I know better now than I could have known then what a stamp it put upon me.

☆ 22 ☆

What I Learned in College

I DID NOT realize it at the time, but I was most fortunate in the college I went to, for I learned in it, as I shall relate, the one thing that I needed most to know.

I was fifteen years old and as ill-prepared as any boy ever was. I had attended a frontier district school in my own town, with one year in a new high school at Taylor's Falls, just across the river in Minnesota, the first, I believe, in all that country. I can remember courses in Latin and primary Algebra—and unlimited horseplay and fist-fighting, with a pallid principal vainly trying to keep order. One thing, however, I had learned to do well, mostly by myself and with the example and encouragement of my father, and that was to read, *really* read, so that I could get out of a printed page at least a part of what the writer had put into it.

I was sent to the Michigan Agricultural College near Lansing, Michigan—my birthplace—for several good reasons. It was inexpensive, there being in those days no tuition charges whatever, and the entrance requirements were ridiculously low—scarcely equal to those of a good high school of today. Moreover, it was the only college we could find which would admit a boy of fifteen. My father, who had known of it for many years, liked it for another reason: it was practical: it trained, or was supposed to train, students in the actual processes of agriculture, horticulture, and engineering; and the economic application of the sciences, chemistry, botany, entomology and the like. It had even gone to the revolutionary point of reversing the school year so that the long vacation came in the winter, when operations on the land were at a minimum. While we had to sweat through the summers, the system, as I shall show later, was of great importance to many a boy, like me, who had to earn a considerable part of his expenses by teaching country schools in the winter.

When I entered as a student in 1885 the college still exhaled an atmosphere of self-conscious pride in being a new experiment in education. It was, I believe, the pioneer college of its kind in the United States, founded in 1857. It had institutionalized the heady faith, then new to the world, in SCIENCE as the supreme key of human endeavor. On every side marvellous advances were beginning to be made in the application of the new technique, that is, in invention and discovery. Darwin's revolutionary book *The Origin of Species* appeared in 1859, Spencer and Huxley were abroad in the world. The laboratory was becoming not only the hope of a new world, but the actual seat of its creation: at once the cathedral of its faith, and the shop of its Vulcan. The agricultural colleges of America—and they were soon scattered throughout the nation—were in certain ways the boldest, most imaginative institutional ventures in the entire movement, for they essayed the application of science and the laboratory to the oldest processes known to man—the cultivation of the earth—occupations indurated with tradition and superstition, devoted to methods that had scarcely changed in a thousand years.

Many of the prophets and evangelists of the new movement were still active when I entered the Michigan college —Miles, Kedzie, Beal, Cook, and others. I could not have told what it was, this invigorating air that blew across our campus, but I could feel it. It had much in it of the religious fervor of the time—with a new God; and much of the enthusiasm of the passing pioneers—with a new world that was not beyond the sunset but under a man's feet. It is difficult in these later days to recapture the exaltation of that time, still harder to express it. It had a colossal faith of its own: that man had now the key for unlocking every door that led to the Shekinah of his future happiness. I recall, sadly, words quoted from Pasteur, then one of the great prophets of the new faith:

"I believe without a shadow of doubt that science and peace will finally triumph over ignorance and war and that the nations of the earth will ultimately agree not to destroy but to build up."

My own first direct contact with the yeasty new ideas was in the laboratory of William J. Beal. Doctor Beal was then professor of botany, occupying the first laboratory devoted exclusively to that subject erected in the United States. He had a fine equipment of compound microscopes, one of the first, I believe, that any American teacher was able to place in the hands of all his students. He was a unique character, a Quaker brought up on the frontier in Michigan, and retaining to the end of his life many of the simple, all but

Spartan, habits of the frontier. He was a bearded man, somewhat stooping, with a plodding walk, slow speech, dry humor, utter indefatigability as a worker—and a hatred of alcohol and tobacco. He had "buck-sawed" his way through Michigan University, graduating in 1859, where he had acquired as sound a classical education as the West then afforded. But he had been set on fire by Alexander Winchell, the geologist, then one of the great scientific teachers of the country.

Three years later in 1862, when he had earned enough money to pay his expenses, he went down to Harvard College to study "natural science." It was a wonderful time— in some ways the most wonderful—in our history. It was a time when, in every field of the human spirit, there seemed a new impetus of life, a new blooming. The West was unrolling like a scroll, enlarging all the visions of men, gold had been discovered in California, Japan had opened to Perry— and now the country was at war over the most vital issue of its history.

In literature the New England poets and sages were at their zenith. Emerson, Lowell and Holmes were writing and lecturing—the young student from Michigan heard all of them. Thoreau was still alive.

In no field of the human spirit was there an intenser or more ardent awakening than in science. It was not yet a broad field and its devotees in America were few, but what they wanted in numbers they made up in enthusiasm. And in all America the center of that new interest was at Harvard College.

In the very year that the young Quaker from Michigan

entered Harvard Darwin published his second great book, *The Fertilization of Orchids.* Darwin's books and the European controversy which they aroused produced a reverberant storm in America. Louis Agassiz, probably then the most stimulating figure in American science, was at his prime. He was fifty-five years old and so devoted to the new fields of knowledge he saw unfolding before him that he had "no time to make money." He became at once a vigorous opponent of Darwin's theory.

Asa Gray, the botanist, also one of the pioneer figures in American science, was a few years younger than Agassiz and a stout supporter from the beginning of the doctrine of evolution. In 1861, the year before Beal became a student, he had published *A Free Examination of Darwin's Treatise* which, in that time of intense religious dogmatism, at once precipitated ardent controversy.

Into this vivifying atmosphere came the young Quaker student from Michigan: and began to take the courses of Agassiz and Gray and of the young and brilliant Charles W. Eliot (who was one year his junior), then professor in chemistry, afterward president of Harvard University.

On his first interview, Agassiz said to him:

"Why do you want to study zoölogy? There is no money in it. You must make up your mind to be poor as long as you live."

At that time only three men in the United States devoted their entire time to the teaching or study of botany: there were few textbooks and those of little value: and zoölogy was scarcely better served. The use of compound microscopes by students was practically unknown, and laboratory work in the sciences, outside of a few courses like that of Agassiz, was non-existent.

Agassiz was one of the greatest teachers America ever produced. He it was, more than any other man, who broke with the old traditions in education, set the minds of men free by making them investigators and discoverers of truth rather than mere receptacles into which traditional knowledge could be poured. He turned the student boldly back to nature herself—quite careless of the fact that he was placing in his hands a method, giving him an attitude of mind, which might demonstrate the truth of theories, such as that of Darwin, in which he himself did not believe.

Besides being an unequalled teacher, Agassiz was a warm, inspiring, radiant personality and the young student from Michigan accepted him at once as his master. To the last of his ninety-one years he kept a portrait of Agassiz in the principal position above the fireplace in his study; but in the matter of evolution he followed Gray. He accepted the doctrine from the beginning: and delighted throughout his whole life in every new demonstration of its truth.

When I entered Doctor Beal's classes, I knew nothing whatever of this background, I knew nothing of botany, I knew nothing of Darwin or the fierce controversy over the doctrine of evolution. I was one of the cleanest slates that ever education had to write upon!

I shall never forget the first weeks in Doctor Beal's laboratory—they were so different from any previous experience I had known as a student. I had already become accustomed to lectures, to learning from books, to returning to the teacher in quizzes and examinations all the information he had previously given me or directed me to get out of books.

Doctor Beal handed me a specimen of a plant he had just brought in fresh from the river bank—leaves, roots, flowers, everything complete—and told me to study it. But how? What was I to do? I had never seen the plant before, did not even know the name of it. I was told to look at it, make sketches of the various parts and write down what I saw. I was an impatient student, eager to get a task finished, and go on to something else. I may have spent fifteen minutes looking, sketching, writing. I showed what I had to the professor.

"Go on," he said, "you've only just begun."

I went back to my desk and used the little hand microscope that had been provided: and presently went up again with my notes.

"Go on," he said patiently, "you haven't begun to see all there is in that plant."

This continued for three or four days with almost no help from the professor. I remember it seemed to me at the moment a great folly, a great waste of time, when I could so easily read about the plant in a book, find out its name, and stand up and recite what I had learned.

In those days the conventional study of botany consisted first in being told by the professor the name of the plant, or finding it in a book, and then, after drying it, and perhaps learning the names of certain parts, mounting it on heavy white paper with the name written below. This collection was called an "herbarium": it was evidence that the student had "passed his botany."

While I was completely mystified by the problem set me,

there was something about it all, some communicated enthusiasm, which lured me along. Two or three of Doctor Beal's famous mottoes or sententious sayings which he wrote on the blackboard caught my attention:

"To be constantly giving information in science makes intellectual tramps, and not trained investigators."

"Merely learning the name of a plant or parts of a plant can no longer be palmed off as a valuable training."

"An eye trained to see is valuable in any kind of business."

"Details and facts before principles and conclusions."

These mottoes and the talk among the students about "old Beal's queer teaching" at least aroused my curiosity.

"Did you ever see the prof's definitions of a weed?" asked one of the older students.

I hadn't.

"Well, you will. Watch the blackboard."

A little later they appeared:

"A plant out of place or growing where it is not wanted."

"Tobacco."

"A plant whose virtues have not yet been discovered"— the latter quoted from Emerson.

Also he never failed to keep this warning posted on his blackboard.

"He who expectorates on the floor, need not expect-to-rate high in my classes."

Presently I began to get down to business, and to find, somewhat to my surprise, that the plant I was working on, which I had finally learned was the blue lupin, was far more interesting than I had dreamed. The veining of the leaves,

164

the arrangement of them on the stalk, the channels in the stems when cut across began to fascinate me, especially after I learned to use the little hand lens. Most of my discoveries came after I had worked for some time on the blossom, which to the ordinary teacher of the time was the only thing worth considering. I continued to write down an account, crude enough, of some of the things that I was finding, illustrating my notes with clumsy drawings. When I began really to need names for the things I saw the old professor dealt them out to me. He was rather niggardly about it: he did not pay me with one until I had earned it. I soon began to be proud of what I was finding. One day the old professor, after a word of commendation, said to me, cryptically:

"Perhaps you will discover something that no one else ever saw or knew about before."

This gave me a curious kind of thrill. I did not know it then, but it was the lure that has dominated the entire life of many a consecrated scientist. The farther I advanced the more interested I became. It was I myself who was making all the discoveries: it was as though I were exploring a whole new world I had never seen before.

I shall never forget the first few days after I was advanced to the use of the compound microscope. One of the first things placed on the slide was a drop of water from one of the weedy ponds in Doctor Beal's botanic garden. Here before my eyes were living creatures moving about, infinitely minute, infinitely graceful and beautiful, and wholly unknown to me. It gave me such a thrill of wonder as I have had only a few times in my life.

Native American

This is not the place to go farther into the details of my experiences, but from that time onward I could not get to Doctor Beal's laboratory soon enough, or stay too long. One great day in particular I remember. I had been following around a number of curious low forms of unicellular life, wholly invisible to the naked eye, and had finally learned that they were desmids, one of the water algae. I saw them moving about gracefully, actually propagating themselves by division before my eyes. The sight fascinated me completely and I began to make drawings of what I saw, jotting down, furiously, little descriptive and narrative notes. I did not stop at the end of the laboratory period, but kept on as long as the professor would let me. For I had had a curious and exciting idea—I think the first impulse of the kind that ever came to me. While I was seeing these wonderful and beautiful things that few people had ever seen or heard about—it was even possible I was seeing things that no one had ever seen before!—I began to have a sudden but powerful inspiration to tell about my adventures and discoveries. Perhaps other people, if only they could know, would be as interested as I was. That evening I wrote out a little article, and began working hard over several drawings, to make them as representative as possible of what I had seen. I kept correcting these notes and sketches for several days, with further observations through the microscope. When my little drawings and the article were completed I got up my courage to show them to the professor, without telling him what I wanted to do with them. I did not dare to do that! I could see that he was greatly interested not only in my manuscript, but in me. All he said was this:

What I Learned in College

"Go and look at them again."

However, I sent my manuscript to the editor of the *St. Nicholas,* then the most famous of magazines for young people, and it came back promptly with the kind of printed slip of rejection I was to know well in future years. It was the first "article" I ever submitted to a magazine. If only I had known it at the time, as a finger-post pointing unmistakably to my future vocation, I should have been saved many disappointments.

As a result of these experiences I began to have an affection for Doctor Beal and a faith in him that I felt in no other teacher I had ever known—except my father. I began, dimly, to see what he was trying to do. Long afterward when I had myself learned his method I read from a published address before the New York State Teachers' Association his own description of it:

"The longer I teach the less I lecture my students, and the talks that are given are mostly regarding things which the students have previously examined. As a rule I have to keep cautioning our instructors not to lecture so much. I have had some who apparently delighted to show their wisdom and would spend more than half the laboratory hour in telling students what they should attempt to discover for themselves. Students are inclined to like this plan, as it is so much easier and quicker to get information this way than to work it out themselves. They do not reflect that they are pursuing the study to learn how to work rather than to acquire information."

One prime defect in the method I did not, however, realize until long afterward. The doctor had explained that in his laboratory he was "simply giving the thirsty a chance to drink." The trouble was that so few in any class that came to him had any recognizable thirst whatsoever—unless it was, occasionally, a thirst for hard cider. It is never easy to accept the fact that in any college there are only a few men, at any one time, who reach the point where Doctor Beal began, of being willing, let alone anxious, to take their education into their own hands. They do not see that no man is ever really educated who does not educate himself.

In spite of this limitation, however, I am astonished, looking back across the years, at the number of men, my college mates, who sat in the early years under Beal, or worked in Cook's laboratory, or Kedzie's, who have carried the torch into new fields of science and education. In these days when men delight to trace their ancestry back to Bunker Hill or the *Mayflower*, I like to think of those fellow-students and of myself, as the intellectual descendants—grandsons as it were—of Agassiz and Asa Gray, and true-born sons of Doctor Beal or Doctor Kedzie or Professor Cook—carrying on, with honest pride of lineage, the work they began. One of the men trained in that school was Liberty Hyde Bailey, famous botanist of Cornell University and the author of many books on horticulture and agriculture, another was W. A. Taylor who, with Lyster H. Dewey, botanist, and several other men from Michigan, helped in the early days to build up the vast scientific work of the Department of Agriculture at Washington. Taylor was for many years Chief of the Bureau of Plant Industry. And there was Lyman J. Briggs, who is director of what is one of the most important scientific institutions of the United States Government, the National Bureau of Standards, and Ulysses P. Hedrick, director of the New York State Experiment Station at Geneva, and Nelson S. Mayo, one of the leaders and teachers in America of veterinary science. I must also mention Herbert Collingwood, editor for many years of the *Rural New Yorker*.

The leaven also spread widely in the educational field. To mention only a few of the many leaders—there was Eugene Davenport who was called to set up the first agricultural college in Brazil and became Dean of Agriculture at Illinois University, and Kenyon L. Butterfield, a truly constructive pioneer, who was president of three different agricultural colleges, and E. A. Burnett, Chancellor of the University of Nebraska, J. W. Toumey, Dean of the Forestry School at Yale University, Hugh P. Baker, who organized the forestry department at Syracuse University, and became President of the Massachusetts State College, and Dean Frederick B. Mumford, of the University of Missouri.

These men, and many others I have not room to mention here, were the true representatives of the great and original educational impulse generated there in Michigan in the earlier years. I take pride in thinking of them, even though I myself was a sad apostate!

Doctor Beal became my lifelong friend; I married his daughter; I learned from him the one thing I needed most of all to know. This was to *look* at life before I talked about it: not to look at it second-hand, by way of books, but so far as possible to examine the thing itself, and form my own conclusions about it.

Impatience, restlessness, were among the chief faults of

my youth. So much to hear, see, feel, think—I rushed at everything! The days were not long enough, the nights too long—I could get only glimpses. I tasted here and sampled there, always longing to go deep, often lured away by some new wonder. It was in Doctor Beal's laboratory that I began to learn that impatience is the enemy of thought, and restlessness of beauty, and that everything is in anything. Long afterward I came across a remark of Rodin, the sculptor, which I have quoted many times:

"Slowness is beauty."

If I did not devote my life to science as I was strongly tempted to do, I soon discovered the truth of one of Doctor Beal's homely mottoes: "An eye trained to see is valuable in any kind of business." It is as truly the fundamental requirement of art and literature as of science. How can a man write anything fresh or new unless he has seen, or heard, or smelled, or tasted newly? How paint, how model? This lesson, I confess in all humility, was a difficult one for me to learn, as all lessons must be that deal with the discipline of one's own temperament.

One more vital experience of those years I must here describe, since it nearly persuaded me to become a scientist. I went with my brother Charlie, two years my junior, who was just entering college, to hear A. R. Wallace, the distinguished British scientist and co-discoverer with Darwin of the doctrine of evolution. He was a godlike human being, as I remember him, with a noble countenance, a great white beard and the serenity, dignity, and simplicity of beneficent authority. His subject was "The Wonderful Century," and he outlined the progress in science in the last two generations, including the development of the doctrine of evolution. I remember the ardent conviction aroused in my mind that science was not only the greatest and most interesting subject in the world, but that it was destined, in no long time, to solve all the mysteries of the universe. It was one of those strongly emotional experiences which etch a moment or a scene or the sound of a voice indelibly on a boy's mind. The lantern pictures that were thrown on the screen remain as clearly in my mind as though they were this day before my eyes—tigers in a reedy Indian jungle to illustrate protective coloration—and I can hear the calm voice of that great old prophet, and somehow feel the tense interest in the darkened room. To my brother Charlie, sitting there beside me, it was the deciding voice of destiny. He was soon to be studying in the laboratories of Beal and Cook with even greater fascination than I had felt; for he brought to it a keen boyish interest in natural history; and this hour or so with the noble old British scientist gave him the final impulse. It was literally a kind of conversion. Science from that time onward became with him a religion: he devoted his entire life to it with utter singleness of purpose, he died for it. He was hardly out of college before he began exploring and collecting in Nicaragua and Cuba, he became a curator of the notable Brazilian museum at Para on the Amazon River, he studied the botany and entomology of Japan and the Malay States, he was largely responsible for organizing the scientific department of the University of the Philippine Islands and long served as its Dean. He built up one of the most extensive collections of tropical insects in the world, now housed in the Smithsonian Institution at Washington.

Native American

During all his later years he led the life of a veritable an-
chorite, spent all the money he could get for equipment the
University could not afford, or gave it to struggling scientists in his own field, especially during the World War when
many a devoted student in Europe was reduced to starvation. Even when his long residence in the tropics had under-
mined his health he refused to leave his work, and finally
died, worn out, at the age of fifty-five, and lies buried in a
Buddhist cemetery in Japan. He was a very great teacher.
While the university he served commemorated his work, he
built his real memorial in the hearts and minds of the many
students whose lives he fired, and whose love he won.

Although associated with no church, accepting no dogma,
and sometimes erratic and irresponsible in his personal affairs, he was one of the most truly religious men I ever
knew. In January, 1926, he published in *The Philippine
Agriculturist,* which he established and of which he was
editor, the essence of his creed:

"The World of Science knows no lines of race, nationality,
wealth, creed, caste, or cut of garments. It is the purest democracy on earth, a brotherhood from which poverty bars
no one—neither color of skin nor religious belief. Intelligent
devotion to the pursuit of scientific truth, and competent
effort, or support of effort, toward this end, automatically
enrolls one in the great company of the 'Fifth Estate.' One
may find in this real 'league of nations' some of the most
inspiring of human associations. In no department of human
activity has there been more devoted service, more superb
self-sacrifice, or greater contributions to human advance-
ment. The 'vow of poverty' is one of the prices one is often
called upon to pay for the great privileges of being a worker

What I Learned in College

in this field. On the other hand, here may be encountered some of life's greatest opportunities for service to humanity and certainly some of its greatest compensations. Happy are its devotees!

Charles Fuller Baker
Dean, College of Agriculture."

It was a glorious age I grew up in: the golden youth of scientific exploration and invention in America. The order of it: the beauty of it: the faith it engendered, and the hope!

The other day I read these words written by one of the greatest of living scientists, Sir James H. Jeans, the British astronomer:

"We cannot ignore the tragic fact that science has given man control over nature before he has gained control over himself."

☆ 23 ☆

I Meet Montaigne

I HAVE NOW to speak of one of the wholly non-curricular activities of the college I attended that had a considerable effect upon me. Many an outward event of that time that I regarded as important left me what I was: this one changed me.

It was entirely natural that I should have begun early to explore the college library. It contained many books that my Presbyterian father, much as he loved to read, had never harbored. I found some that ministered to a lively curiosity, and some that were merely amusing, but I also found Montaigne, two volumes in an old brown cloth binding with faded gilt lettering. It was the Florio translation, although at that time I had never heard of Montaigne, much less of Florio. But I knew as well by the first taste what I liked in a book as in a dinner; the moment I opened it my eyes fell upon a paragraph that dealt with the life and habits of cannibals and the way they cooked and ate their victims. Could I have stopped? On another page, opening at random, I read of the marriage customs of different countries, and of the relationships between husbands and wives, all prodigiously interesting and told without the slightest consciousness that such subjects as these in our family were unmentionable. I remember having a sudden sharp sense that I was doing something that my father would disapprove and of closing the book with a half-guilty feeling—and quickly opening it again. In fact I kept finding the most astonishing challenges to truths which I supposed were settled for good and all—as much settled, say, as the Ten Commandments. One of these related to the saving of money: it was a law, a part of the Presbyterian religion, one even prayed about it, and it applied especially to boys. And here was this writer quite dispassionately, and with humor, relating how, having tried that method, he had found it a failure and had adopted what seemed to me a most immoral course.

"I live from hand to mouth, from day to day, and have I but to supply my present and ordinarie needs, I am satisfied. If I lay up anything, it is for the hope of some imployment at hand, and not to purchase lands, whereof I have no need, but pleasure and delight."

The last sentence, especially, struck straight at my father who did save all his money to purchase land, which in truth he did not need, and which, for years, nearly beggared him. It seemed somehow disloyal in me even to be reading such a book. More than once I put it guiltily back on the shelf, resolved not to open it again. Once I broke my resolution on the ground that I wanted to find a story which had amused me very much regarding a man who was about to be hanged. This man "wished the hangman not to touch his throat, lest hee should make him swowne with laughing, because he was so ticklish." Having found the passage I went on reading with delight for an hour or so.

A deeper reason I felt at the time, but could by no means have analyzed, made the book seem disloyal to all I had known. In the world of my pioneer boyhood there were few half-truths. This was so: that was not so. This was right: that was wrong. My father knew and said so: my powerful old aunts laid down the Law as of the Medes and Persians: and the Presbyterian minister apparently never had a doubt in all his life. Well, here was this man in his book so honestly, so smilingly, so wittily, taking things apart and looking at them, telling so many things about them that a boy never heard before and giving reasons for his conclusions that were scarcely considered necessary in a Presbyterian household. He was irresistible: I began to like him very much indeed, even though I suspected I was a sinner for doing it.

In these early readings of Montaigne I balked on many a Latin quotation, I skipped many a complex paragraph and dry dissertation: I could not have told at the time, I think, exactly what it was the man had to say, but the saying of it, and the living spirit of the sayer, lured me onward. His daring, I remember, constantly astonished and shocked, but fascinated me. In the atmosphere of suppression I had known, if a boy could not avoid thinking of a vast world of the forbidden, he was at least admonished not to speak of it; but this astonishing man in the old brown book dared to tell the entire truth about himself, honestly, even exult-antly. What I read, page after page, gave me a delicious sense of new freedom. Why not be honest? Why pretend and conceal and deceive when it was so interesting and beau-tiful—yes, and amusing—to tell the whole story!

So I dipped into Montaigne and came back again and again to the quiet alcove where he lived and sat with him there, looking out through his eyes upon the troubled world of his day, hearing his dry comments upon the follies of it. It was not that I swallowed him whole, but at certain times, in certain moods, he was good for me, even though I was by no means ready as yet to accept his wisdom by acting upon it. I wished still to appear other, and much better, than I was.

I have been going back to Montaigne from time to time ever since, renewing my boyhood acquaintance. He is a recurrent need, not a permanent. He helps to keep me well linked to the earth, but never helps me fly. Mostly I have dipped into the wealth of his wisdom by way of Florio, whom I still relish best, but sometimes through Cotton and other more recent translators; and lately I have been reading a new "autobiography" made up by a clever fellow who has pieced together bits from the essays and letters to make a relatively connected narrative of the man's life. I am offended here and there by the license of inclusion and exclusion but the old fellow I knew is still there. However presented, if in his own words, his reality cannot be dimmed. He still continues to live richly and earthily. I can hear his voice and see the sly irony of his smile. He remains for me among the most authentic of human beings in this world, one of the freest and most veracious.

Nevertheless if Montaigne helped in my earlier years to teach me the invaluable lesson that I was all I had, all I ever would have, and that to be myself, honestly, was all that was required of me, he was never all I wanted. He was not everything. He could indeed deflate self-deception—who better?—he could purge pride, he could exorcise hypocrisy —this man who said of himself that he was "utterly material" and took "as current coin nothing but realities"—but I never went to him for the prophetic, nor the poetic, nor the mystical (or what I call the mystical). I have used him, and considered it no offense, very much as my grandmother used the steeped bark of the oleander for purification. I do not look among his acrid pages for such things as the "old and antique song we heard last night"—"the spinsters and the knitters in the sun, and the free maids that weave their threads with bones" nor anything that "dallies with the innocence of love." He is far too wise for many a thing in this world I love well.

I found much in Montaigne that seemed to me robust and wholesome. He gave me something of the same strong satisfaction that I found, some years later, when I first read Walt Whitman, who likewise lived robustly in his world and was not ashamed of it. He would entirely have approved Montaigne's dictum that "a man should speak as frankly of himself as of any one else."

Whenever I come at Montaigne, as recently, with the appetite of long abstinence, I find such delicious morsels of wit and sanity that he fairly takes the heart out of me as a writer. As he himself said of Plutarch: "I am vexed to be so tempted: I hardly ever finger him without stealing a wing or a leg." At the same time I am maliciously comforted, as we all are by the limitations of our friends, by the fact that in the well-steered course of his sanity he seems always, at one point, to drop his rudder in the deep sea. For he begins to heave and roll about, not knowing what port he is really headed for. It is, of course, the rock of Religion that he strikes upon. He will not have the Bible translated, nor the people at large trusted to read it!

I Meet Montaigne

I remember well, also, the mistake I made, some years later, taking a small volume of selections from Montaigne in my pack-sack for a tramp in the country. I soon found that he was no companion of the open road: he sat awkwardly at campfires, and lay down painfully under the trees at night. Was he too civilized? To his sanity how insane to climb needless hills, tramp long roads when one might better ride, stop to talk aimlessly (as I delight to do) with countrymen one comes upon. He cannot, I think, distinguish one tree from another nor any bird from any other bird, unless it be a pheasant to be shot for dinner; he does not know cabbages from lettuce—he says so himself—and there seems no beauty to him in quiet meadows or friendly hills. Apparently he never mused over the what or the why or the when of nature, save human nature: was never curious regarding the limitless vast or the immeasurably small. It was not of his age, the scientific spirit, however modern his perception when applied to human beings.

It was thus on this long tramp, pack on my back, that I realized acutely these particular limitations of Montaigne. I had another book or so with me, and gradually the old Frenchman, despite his wit and wisdom, seemed an alien in our party. I like my authors real men or none, and so, after many years of acquaintance, Montaigne had come to me to be. He was there, a person, dragged out into the wild country where he did not belong. No man with an infinitude of cultivated or crotchety habits, the love of petty comforts, the worship of trifling routine, has ever a place in the wilderness. He had no learning in such adventure, one of the first requirements of which is corporeal self-forgetfulness—a felicity, indeed, which no Frenchman ever quite attains.

179

Native American

It may seem ridiculous, but I began to hear—literally *hear* —his dry comments. Oh, he was courteous enough: what other author was ever more sensitive to human idiosyncrasies or more patient with eccentricities in the relationships of man to man! But there was a glint in his eye, a dryness in his tone, that I straightway found irritating. And why adventure? And why inquire? How much saner to remain comfortably at home.

The further I tramped the more irritating the old chevalier became. One night where I was forced to camp down in the woods I had difficulty starting my little fire, since the twigs were damp from recent rain. It came to me with such a thrill of satisfaction that I laughed aloud—and took Montaigne out of my bag, tore him up, dry leaf after dry leaf, every line of his wit, every word of his wisdom, and poked him under the smoking twigs of my fire.

"There," said I, "goes a bundle of quotations from Vergil, and there his observations on the eating of fish, and there his musty learning regarding old coaches. There are more uses than one for the classics."

I found that Montaigne blazed up marvelously well, for he was ever gifted with the genius for meeting any emergency in life, and made me a cup of hot tea. From that moment I travelled blithely with never a discordant note.

And yet here I am re-reading Montaigne with all the old zest. I do not remember past offenses. I take gratefully as of old what he has to give me: which is much: and think I shall go back to him when I am a hundred years old.

✩ 24 ✩

I Take to the Road

IN THIS queer college where I learned so much more than the faculty taught, we had a ten-day vacation in May, and since I lived so far away that I could not easily go home, I was left more or less to my own devices. During one such vacation, in my senior year, I think, I well remember getting up one sunny morning, leaning out of the window of my dormitory room into a "living glory bath of air and light," with the disturbing odor of lilacs drifting up to me—and feeling an irresistible urge to get away into new country. After breakfast the cook made up three or four sandwiches which I put in my pocket, and I started south by the nearest road.

It was a road that had long invited me: it went up a beckoning little rise of land to cross a bridge over the Cedar River and beyond that it turned away into a mysterious country I did not know. I swung into it with a sudden vast sense of freedom and joy, the first of innumerable such unpremeditated excursions which have blessed my life.

In the earlier days of my tramping experience I sometimes tried taking a good friend with me—some man or boy I really liked to talk with—but I soon found it never worked. He would never keep still, nor I either, while we looked at the world. Every impression was confused and divided between us, nothing vividly seen, heard, smelt, touched, tasted, nothing ever clearly felt or thought about. When I learned later that I often needed a companion on the road I took with me several men I knew, each in a little book that fitted easily into my pocket. I could thus have them out when I wanted them, and if they grew contentious or boresome, I could slap the covers together and put them back where they could no longer trouble me. This you cannot do with a living companion.

I remember little about this particular trip, save the sense of keen enjoyment I had. I did not then know I was a writer, and did not take a little familiar book in my pocket, as in later years, to write in. I was out three or four days. I had a vague idea of going to Hillsdale to see a friend of mine who was in college there. It was sixty or seventy miles off and I never got anywhere near it, but as in so many ex-cursions of later years, if I rarely reached my objective, I had a fine time on the way. I recall sitting under a shed, on a worn, last-year's hay stack, eating one of my sandwiches and looking out across the rich fields with the complete absorption of intense interest—the cattle feeding there, the birds drifting across the open sky, the yellow mustard and buttercups in the wheat. Almost everything I saw delighted me: almost every one I met as I travelled—farmers, truck-ers, agents, schoolboys—interested me intensely. I have liked always to talk with salty human beings, and amuse myself afterward by thinking about what they said, or put-ting them into the little stories I told myself.

It may possibly have been on this trip or a later one, I cannot now remember, that I went into a farmer's barn one afternoon, climbed up a dusty ladder into the mow, and lay down to rest for an hour or so before I went on to the village where I expected to stop. When I awakened it was in the pitch darkness of the middle of the night. I was chilled to the bone and half eaten up by mosquitoes. I lay there for a moment vividly awake. Everything about me seemed somehow alive: little rustlings, whisperings, in the hay. I could, or thought I could, hear something, or some one, holding its breath and then letting it out cautiously. Even the wooden beams of the barn seemed to be creaking and snapping as though stretching themselves there in the secrecy of the darkness. Overhead I could hear the rustling of wings and certain faint squeakings and flutterings. I never have liked bats or barn swallows; both are somehow uncanny.

I slid down out of the mow and fumbled my way out of the barn into the open air. The cows in the yard stirred sleepily. I heard a restless dog barking, somewhere, afar off. All about me, close to the earth, was the cool, moist, dark night. I looked up into the vast cold circle of the heavens, crowded with glittering stars. Suddenly, with overpowering intensity, such a sense of wonder and awe and terror swept over me as I can neither describe nor forget. A sense of heedless, chill immensity: boundless power without sympathy: and I standing there unknown, helpless, surrounded by cold darkness, not knowing which way to go or what to do. I tried desperately to reason that there was no danger, that the night would injure me no more than the day, but it did not avail in the least to modify that crushing sense of wonder, and of awe, or the helpless terror I felt. I must have stood there almost still for an hour or more, until the dawn began to break, and the stars to fade, and the way to open for me to go.

I have often gone back to that night, as one of the symbolic experiences of my life: a kind of datum plane in my effort to survey the universe, and find my place in it.

Often when I "came to" on these wonderful tramps, it was late afternoon and it seemed to me I was in a strange country, an immense distance from home. But when I stopped to ask the next man I met, "How far is it to East Lansing?" or in all the later years, "How far to Amherst?" he was likely to say, "Oh, 'bout six-eight miles," rarely more than ten or twelve. This applies, of course, only to one-day tramps. A friend of mine, who is a ferocious pedestrian, thinks nothing of walking thirty miles in a day—in one night he walked from New York to Princeton, New Jersey—and I have seen the glint in his eye when I spoke of my little excursions. But it is strange how far a man can travel in ten miles! It is not the number of steps one takes that matters, but the number of things one sees, hears, smells, tastes, and the intensity of his realization of these things. In recent years, since I have been growing older, I often go halfway to the unknowable before I get to Mount Warner, which I can see from my window.

I found such joy in this earliest excursion that I soon repeated it, and I do not think I have missed more than two or three Mays, during the lilac-blooming, in all the years of my life since that time. When I travel in May I am certain that of all the months in the year May is the best, but when I go out in October I am resolved that nothing could be finer than October. To the true tramper who has the longing in him, any month is a good one.

I developed, presently, a kind of tramping technique. Since I was often out two or three days at a time, sometimes as long as a week or ten days, I found I needed more room than my pockets afforded. I always took a few sandwiches and other necessaries and sometimes a small pail to make tea in, and I had to have room for a few books, one, certainly, to write in. So I began using a light Swiss rucksack I could carry on my shoulder. It held not only the requirements I have mentioned but I could put in a sweater, a light raincoat, and a pair of dry socks. I never despised the one-day trips, so often on pilfered time, but I much preferred the longer ones.

In the earlier years I sometimes tried tramping with little or no money in my pockets. I liked the curious necessary adventures of one who must take the chances of the road and live by his wits. I found by the compulsions I had to face that I could turn up strata of human nature both pleasant and unpleasant I might never have been able to meet in any other way: I came to know the men and women I met on far more intimate terms. Afterward I pieced together incidents of several such trips—the kindliest of them —in a little book called *The Friendly Road*. But it is the fate of any such penniless traveller that he is likely to have misadventures as well as adventures. After all, a tramp is a tramp, and he has to live down the reputation of his kind. In some cases I could not get near enough to a prospective benefactor to use my wits, or a chance to prove what a well-intentioned and helpful fellow I was, and if I were writing it again, I could add a chapter to *The Friendly Road,* narrating the dismay of a well-meaning traveller set upon by one farmer's ferocious dog and ignominiously driven off into the woods where he spent a cold and hungry night. And then there are the eccentricities of the weather and the road; I have been rained on until I was wet to the skin and chilled to the bone, I have been many times footsore and weary— once I was strangled and nearly drowned when I foolishly tried to swim a river I did not know with my clothing tied on my head—and I have had not a few bitter moments thinking what an ass I was not to have remained comfortably at home. Nevertheless, on a spring day when the irresistible longing came upon me to take to the road, to look freely again at the world I loved, I was up and off, and I can say without hesitation or reserve that my experiences afoot have been among the most interesting and deeply enjoyable of my whole life.

I finally gave up the practice of trying to live by my wits. I found I had greater freedom in looking at, listening to, smelling and tasting, the inexhaustibly fruitful world, and even in meeting the people I wished most to meet, if I had a few comfortable dollars in my pocket. One of these days I want to write a paragraph or so about the positively mystical power inherent in a five-dollar bill tucked away in one's inner pocket. Whether a man uses it or not, there it lies radiating the electricity of confidence, full of little bright sparks of self-respect and daring and power, even of generosity. It has no superior as a therapeutic for numerous psychological ills, and cures many a neurosis which is beyond the skill of the psychiatrist. I prescribe a five-dollar bill!

In the later years I have found nowhere, in no other way,

such a complete restorative for the spirit as the open country and the generous road. Whenever in my life a certain
weariness, a miasmic sadness, has begun to settle down upon
me I have known the sure remedy, and in spite of every
obstacle, I have practiced it—whether in summer or winter,
abroad or at home—and nearly always I have been able to
recover myself promptly, and to restore my tranquillity.

During the long months I spent in Europe while the Great
War was raging, and afterward at the Peace Conference at
Paris, I think I could not have continued to live or keep my
sanity, if it had not been for such restoratives as these. So
often, living or trying to live, in the midst of that vast
tragedy, I felt myself utterly drained with weariness, my
emotions battered and bruised until I was all one dull
misery. Most of us have understanding enough, love enough,
sympathy enough, to meet the small urgencies of the sweet
Auburns of our ordinary life, but I found that the impact
of the daily terrors and horrors of that time, the universal
suffering and cruelty I could not combat, the sorrow I could
not ease, left me bleak and empty. One cannot resign from
a war; he must learn how to live with it—or die with it. I
made many tramps in those times in England, in France and
in Italy, always in the country, and always with such a sense
of renewal and hope as I can never hope to describe. Sooner
or later, if I worked hard for it, I always recovered the sense
of proportion I was losing, always a renewal of the blessed
perception of the ease, the serenity, the patience, of nature
and natural processes. Time, time, my little man! Even the
shortest of these excursions was precious to me.

I think there is no other country in the world, save perhaps my own New England, so matchless for the tramper as

the British Islands. I never was in heaven, but I have tramped in Devon in April! I have walked up the hill at Harrow, and sat by Byron's grave and tramped by way of Pinner northward. I have gone out of Dorking with a heavy soul and tramped up Ranmore Common, and lain hidden for hours among the bracken, and gone back to smoky London a new man, ready again to take up the battle.

I remember days at Chartres and the cathedral with Henry Adams' wonderful great book open in my hand, as far removed from present misery as the bright sun from this little earth. I have walked the flinty roads out of Chartres and I know something—ever so little!—of the dour and flinty people of the neighborhood. Henry Adams knew architecture, he knew literature, he had studied the philosophies, but I looked in vain in his book to discover that he knew anything of the men and women, the common men and women, in those flinty fields, out of whom sprang not only the cathedral of Chartres but the democracy of France. *They* did not educate Henry Adams.

I could go on for a book or so telling of my tramps, one long ago from Jena to Weimar and back, and the wonderful rich day I spent in Goethe's little park, and several to meet friendly beekeepers in the English country, and no end of them here in America, but this is not a book of travels, but a chapter to set forth one of the deepest interests of my life.

Since I am on this subject and trying really to explain what I am and what I think about, I may as well go farther and set down a few illustrative passages from my notebooks, all of them written during May pilgrimages.

"Sunday May 21. Under my beech tree in the lower

woods, back to the earth, loafing with contented spirit—

I cannot see that the minute is not just as important and interesting as the immense. As I lean here with my back to the beech, all about me are young fern shoots, some pure green, some of a russet color, uncurling at the tips the rolled beauty of their verdure. One might crush half a dozen under a single footstep and never know it. And yet what beauty, what utter grace of perfection—young beech leaves almost red in color hanging on soft stems around me—young leaves of spotted violet and fine sword blades of grass, and within the space of a foot from my hand a dozen kinds of leaves and a flower or two of plants I do not know. Let them have their great world. Give me a day like this of sunny warmth and light airs and the small perfect things of life."

"May 19. Pin-cherries along the old fences all in bloom, and swamp blueberries, wild strawberries, violets, and in the deep woods the shy hobble-bush and the swamp-pink: also bellwort, adder's tongue, anemones. 'Oblivion here thy wisdom is.'"

"A crow. He sits in the top of a shag-bark hickory-tree, the last of all the trees to come to life in the spring. He sees me afar off across the pleasant fields. He raises his voice and tells all the other crows I am come newly into their domain. I am welcomed by a full chorus."

"I begrudge Form lest it twist Truth."

"I spent half an hour this morning watching honey-bees (perhaps some of my own) visit apple-blossoms: to see how many thrusts of the tongue a bee gives to each blossom, sometimes one, often three or four: to tell how near a bee must come to a blossom before deciding whether to test it at all. Is it wholly the sense of smell? Or partly sight? How many blossoms must a bee visit to secure a load? I counted in one case: twenty blossoms: and then lost the bee."

"I have been lying under a pine-tree on the shoulder of Mt. Warner: flat on my back with my hat over my eyes. There is dark green moss, thick and soft, and pine-needles, where I lie. A partridge has recently bedded here and left a feather to pay for her lodging, as I will leave a thought. Away off to the south, as I turn my head, I can see the rugged hazy outline of Norwottuck. A film of faint green, old rose and pink clouds, rises above the tops of the trees in the little marsh near at hand. A light breeze is stirring the tree-tops and all the valley is full of sunshine. I can hear a crow calling, a squirrel chickering, and somewhere, far off and dim, the drumming of a cock pheasant. What blessedness this—between hard labor and hard labor. What a thing to *live!*"

"I read to-day, with what a thrill, and would read a thousand times, a passage from Gilbert Murray's translation of *Hippolytus:*

"'We cling to this strange thing that shines in the sunlight, and are sick with love for it because we have not seen beyond the veil.'

"What old wistful longing! How this ancient poet, two thousand or more years ago, was thinking and expressing my veritable thought! He too felt the mystery of life: he was 'sick with love' to see beyond the veil. He too felt the nostalgia that is concealed in every musing spirit."

"Wait, be still! There is no hurry. Let T—— produce his novel a year, and W—— his play. Let B—— have his prizes. Literature is not a race, nor a fortune. Take time then, for time is yours to do with it what you will. Write a well-lived book. Accept without concern the charge of idleness, your own the most of all, work in your own fields, walk in your own orchard, tramp your own roads, and await the growth of your book."

☆ 25 ☆

What I Learned Outside
of College

WHEN I LOOK back, as honestly as I can, to the four years from the age of fifteen to nineteen that I spent in college, I see that my education was largely outside of my classes, quite independent of curriculum, regardless of guidance or administration.

The college had been a convenient and cheap lodging place with pleasant associations, provided with laboratories and books, where a boy could educate himself, or fail to educate himself. Outside of Doctor Beal's laboratory, already described, which was indeed a powerful factor in my education, worth the entire college course, and a certain amount of help from Professor Cook, I cannot now recall that I was much influenced or changed—that is, educated—by any other teacher, or in any other class, in four years of college life. This seems to me even as I set it down a harsh conclusion when I remember the many able and amiable and hard-working men who made up the faculty of that institution. Some of them no doubt did for my classmates more than they did for me: I can speak honestly and with knowledge only for myself.

Nevertheless, those four years were richly educative. I

learned more, I think, I learned faster, than at any other period in my whole life. Growth and joy are in beginnings! I have already related, in another chapter, something of my experiences in finding myself turned loose in a new library, better than my father's, and the discovery, to me somewhat revolutionary, of the two volumes of Montaigne's essays. I shall later speak of other books I found that really educated me. I have also written about my early adventures as a tramper, begun when I was a senior in college, which in later years not only enlarged my life but helped to make it happy.

These, however, do not begin to tell the story. I could write a whole book and still not exhaust the subject, since every moment in a man's life, call it education, or work, or play, whatever you will, if it is hotly lived, easily makes a chapter in itself.

I have always thought that I owed much to the fact that I grew up on the frontier. Pioneer life has been charged with intellectual barrenness, and with some justice, but its simplicities left much to whet a boy's curiosity. We were not surfeited, in the St. Croix Valley, with concerts or movies, or exhibitions of paintings and statuary—or automobiles or radios or flying-machines. There were voids which even the visit of an Indian chief with feathers in his hair, selling Kickapoo Indian remedies, could not fill.

It is probably rare enough in these glutted later days for any man to remember the first band he ever heard play: I can. Or the first dramatic performance he ever saw: I can.

My first band, although it came long before my college years, will illustrate what I mean. I must have been about ten years old when I heard, one morning, the strangest sounds rolling up from our village street. I ran down the hill as fast as my bare legs could carry me and there, in front of Jim Thompson's store, was a crowd of men, women and boys—a rare thing in itself—and in the midst of it one of the oddest spectacles I had ever laid eyes upon. Five or six men in gorgeous uniforms—or so I thought them at the moment —playing upon various instruments, the like of which I had never seen. There they were standing in the shade of Thompson's porch, one man with a great shiny horn that curled up over his shoulder, another with an astonishing instrument that he worked back and forth with a vigorous right arm—I had never before made the acquaintance of a trombone—and a little round fat man with a huge drum that he balanced on his belly and smote full-arm with mighty strokes. There were, besides these, a trumpeter rolling his eyes and making the oddest motions with his lips and cheeks, and a small boy in a cocked hat, scarcely larger than I was, who came in from time to time with brass cymbals which he beat together with energy and gusto.

What a thrill ran down my back and up into my hair: the delicious thin clear notes of the trumpet, the clashing brasses, the drum coming in with a bang just when it ought to, and the wonderful pump, pump, pump, of the big bass horn! I had never even dreamed of such wonderful harmonies: I was transported. While I stood there gazing, no doubt with my mouth wide open, a farmer's team, alarmed by such unexpected noises, ran away, tipping the driver out on the ground—I saw him lying there in his red mackinaw jacket—and disappeared, galloping up the street. I gave this incident, which at ordinary times would have been the saga of a day, hardly more than a glance, and turned back to the band—and the wonderful fat little drummer, and the thrilling clash of the cymbals.

It was one of the little German bands that occasionally appeared in the frontier towns of my boyhood. I suppose the uniforms were soiled and ragged; I suppose the musicians themselves were grimy and unshaven; I suppose the music was atrocious—but what a moment of heaven they gave me! I could not get over it for days; and it has lain in my mind ever since as one of the pillars of my beginnings.

My first dramatic performance came later and linked more directly into my college education. It was an amateur performance staged in Taylor's Falls, our neighbor town in Minnesota. I suppose I should not have been allowed to go —for the "theatre" was still under suspicion by good Presbyterians—if Joe Hawthorne, my Sunday-school teacher and a pillar of the church, had not taken a part. It must have been unspeakably primitive, but not for me. I lived every word of it, believed all I saw—marvelling at the tense moment when the hero, in his anguish, pulls the red and white cloth from the kitchen table, kerosene lamp and all, and the chimney smashes on the floor. I could not sleep afterward for thinking about it, and carrying on in my own mind the stories of the various characters. I was rarely satisfied, in those days, with the lesser people in the books I read —that is, if they had any life at all—and could only satisfy myself by rounding out their adventures to suit myself. I lived with this performance for weeks. I even tried, after that, to read the few plays that were in my father's library.

What I Learned Outside of College

Up to that time I had known Shakespeare only by sight; he was a kind of household god, for my father had a large old bookcase surmounted with a handsomely carved bust of Shakespeare, black and shiny (ebony, I think). I knew nothing about him save the name, but I felt the importance attendant upon such an idolatrous position in our family living room.

I asked my father what was "the greatest play in the world," and he answered with prompt decision, "Hamlet." I started immediately to read it, but the archaic words and the involved versification soon floored me. If only there had been some one to help me over the hard places when my eagerness and enthusiasm were ripe—until I began to feel the characters and action—I might have learned to enjoy Shakespeare years before I did. Incidentally I also found in our library a volume containing "She Stoops to Conquer" "with the stage business, cast of characters, costumes, relative positions, etc." and "London Assurance" and "Camille" and others (I have it here before me as I write), and because I felt instinctively that my old aunts might consider these plays improper for a boy to read, I tried hard to get through Goldsmith's classic, but without success.

I resolved early that if ever I got into a city one of the first things I did would be to see a real play. The opportunity finally came on one of my trips to college. I had to go through Chicago, and although a stop was not scheduled, I decided to spend the night there and go on to Michigan the next day. I picked more or less at random, since I knew nothing whatever about either plays or players. Fortunately I hit upon "Peaceful Valley" in which the leading part was

195

taken by Sol Smith Russell. It was the first time that I had ever been inside of a real theatre, but I was stuffed with books, and had read many incidents of theatrical life. I could spout Bulwer-Lytton:

"At Paris it was in the opera there
She looked like a queen in a book that night."

I remember before the play began of trying to decide what part of the theatre was called the "pit," of which I had read in English books. I do not exaggerate when I say that it was one of the great experiences of my life. Here again I entered absolutely into the story presented on the stage. I was in the top gallery, the cheapest seat I could buy, and there in the delicious darkness with the faint rustlings and the breathing of humanity all around me, I sat with my elbows on my knees and my chin in my hands, and laughed and cried with the best of them. What a play! What a play! Afterward I walked out into the raw streets of Chicago with my heart pounding and my brain on fire.

In later years I went to see Sol Smith Russell several times (I was momentarily the extremely poor dramatic critic of a Chicago newspaper), and while the first glory was tarnished, I came away always newly convinced that Russell was an unusually gifted actor. Only two or three times in later years have I been so completely carried away, out of myself, by actors—it is one of the supreme arts!—and twice by orators, as I hope sometime to relate. My greatest moment in the theatre, as I look back, was Edwin Booth as Cardinal Wolsey:

"Farewell, a long farewell, to all my greatness."

What I Learned Outside of College

One thing in that first night in the theatre made a lasting impression upon me. The hero as represented by Sol Smith Russell is seen as the curtain rises to be standing, galluses down, before a looking glass, *shaving*. A tin basin stands by to wash in, and a red-fringed towel to wipe on. It seemed all perfectly simple and real—I was as familiar with such scenes as with the palm of my hand—and yet the audience and I rocked with laughter. I cannot convey the astonishment I felt to see such a common incident presented on the stage—after reading, or trying to read, "Hamlet" and "She Stoops to Conquer" and other old plays, and being convinced that the theatre must, of course, deal with high and serious, or at least unfamiliar scenes. Here was the hero of the play shaving on the stage! I thought a good deal about it afterward, and I am convinced it stimulated my interest in the common things of everyday life, of which in after years I took so much delight in writing. In fact, all my life I have had more pleasure out of watching the commonest and simplest doings of life, birds flying, the wind in meadow grass, wild flowers on hillsides—oh, a thousand things seen, heard, smelt—than in almost anything else.

A walk to town: a moment in a country road: a good dinner: the odor of lilacs: a chance conversation with a teamster—it is possible to start a story anywhere! For stories somehow are not made, but lived. I get no end of amusement out of looking at horses, cows, hens. A cow can be one of the funniest things in the world; an old hen, of a morning, proudly and instructively leading her family out to breakfast, can be even funnier. When such a proportion of human existence is made up of common things—as common as shaving—I think it surely a kind of riches to any one if he can find them interesting or amusing.

In all the years I was in college I enjoyed, and richly profited by, a literary and debating society and a fraternity I belonged to. The long discussions we had, on all kinds of subjects, were of remembered value and amusement to me: and particularly those with certain boys whom I began to know at that time. Many friendships, especially those with my cousins Arthur D. Baker and Luther H. Baker, have lasted down through the years.

I also learned much as the editor of the college publication (then the only one) called *The Speculum*. This was not purely enjoyable, it had its difficult problems and controversies, and no end of hard work, but it was the kind of *directed co-operation* that a young individualist recently from the frontier needed much to learn. Even though I did not know at the time that I was a writer, the experience was of value to me in future years. I not only edited *The Speculum* and wrote everything in it that I could not get some one else to write—which seemed to be the secret of early college journalism—but I had really valuable training in Launt Thompson's print-shop in the practical problems of make-up, type, paper, printing. In those days we had no faculty supervision or prohibitions: we had the great advantage of having the entire responsibility—and labor—in our own hands. We could beg for as many advertisements as the bold business manager dared venture, and quarrel as hotly as we liked about what we should insert and how much we should discount the set rates.

What I Learned Outside of College

This activity, while not, under my definition, of the highest educational value, was excellent as discipline and training. I got a great deal out of it, and in later years, whenever I have had the opportunity, I have advised college students, especially those interested in writing, to take an active part in college journalism, even though the entire system seems to me now far too much regimented and directed from above.

More important and educative than any of these things to me and to many students of that college was the problem of scraping together enough money to pay even the ridiculously low charges of that more or less experimental state institution. I suppose three-quarters of the students in those days, perhaps a larger proportion, were sturdily "making their own way." This was in no way considered a hardship; I do not remember ever to have heard a complaint regarding this particular difficulty, for it was the accepted condition of students who were so eager for an education that they were glad to grub for it. A few of them every year were genuine backwoods characters. One man in particular was so poor that he went barefoot most of the time to save his shoes. When he entered, although far older than most of us, he had never shaved. He never wore a collar and played a fiddle with one string. Most of the men of this sort did not last long, not because they could not earn their way, but because education was not at all what they expected. It seemed foolishly impractical to them. Why waste years going to classes when they could easily "make a living without readin' books?" as one of them said to me.

I was in a somewhat different situation from many of the

other students. My father—as I knew better later than I knew then—could during the earlier years have paid all my expenses without too much sacrifice, but he had a stern philosophy regarding the upbringing of his boys, and I, being the oldest, was the first to face the practical application of it. "Cast the bantling on the rock!" He had made his own way, with never a penny of help, in getting such schooling as he could at Oberlin and the University of Wisconsin, and if he could do it, why shouldn't we?

"I believe," he used to say, "that one of the greatest things any boy can learn is the value of a dollar. And how can he learn it unless he sweats for it?"

At another time he said to me: "If you earn that education of yours, you'll really prize it."

Nevertheless, as I know now, he watched me and my brothers closely, and tried with real affection, but not always with success, to make sure that we did not reach the point of blank discouragement. He sent checks—and blessed checks they were—a little after they became absolutely necessary. I think now that he was too severe. I should have profited more if I had put somewhat less time into splitting wood at twenty cents a cord and more into my books and the laboratories. The cost of learning the value of a dollar may come too high. At fifteen or sixteen or seventeen a boy is still growing and if he must do hard physical labor a considerable part of every day, how is he to get in the requisite amount of studying? I remember often going to my room after supper so groggy with weariness, when I should have been getting up my algebra or history, that I tumbled into bed and slept ten or twelve hours until the breakfast bell rang. When my own boys went off to college I remembered these things.

In later years, especially during the great depression that began in the early '90's, my father could not help his sons and daughters—there were presently ten in all—as much, I am sure, as he would have liked, but every one of them went to college and every one he helped.

In those days the dogmatists of the laboratory method thought it could be as literally applied to agriculture and horticulture as to any other science, and they demanded a required labor period every day, usually three hours on the farm or in the fields. While we were paid the munificent wage of eight cents an hour, which somewhat took off the curse, the experiment was doomed to failure. A growing crop of corn to be hoed, an orchard to be sprayed, a field of cabbages or strawberries, go on their way far more responsive to summer sun and the rain than to a crowd of ignorant, blundering, more or less unmanageable students. Corn grows seven days a week, and every Sunday and on all holidays; strawberry picking does not wait upon classes in rhetoric or trigonometry. Two or three boys working every day all summer with a trained instructor might learn much, but three hundred boys sent out from one to four every afternoon come near being useless. When I entered college the work system had degenerated largely into the most routine of practice, hoeing corn, raking the college drives, lawn-mowing and the like, all with little or no educative value. In later years the whole system was abolished.

Well, I earned eight cents an hour from this work. I split wood for twenty cents a cord, I did chores, I worked in Doctor Beal's laboratory counting seeds for an experiment he was making, and finally, to my delight, the college librarian, who appreciated my interest in books, gave me regular work at ten cents an hour helping to make the first card-catalogue of the library. She had almost as little knowledge of the new system as I had, but we both "read up" and did the best we could. This experience was of great help to me at a later time, as I shall relate.

One of the most profitable things I did, financially, was to become the steward of a boarding club. It involved a great deal of attentive work that in the beginning was beyond my experience, and I made many embarrassing and one or two expensive mistakes which I kept wholly to myself. Think of a boy of seventeen hiring cooks and waitresses, buying food, keeping the accounts of forty or fifty fellow students, collecting the money (sometimes with difficulty), and holding down the board bill per student to $2.25 or less per week! For this service I received my own board free of charge, that is, $2.25 a week, but even this was a load lifted off my shoulders, for I could eat all I liked at every meal without feeling any compunctions.

Of all my money-earning activities, however, quite the most educative, and by all odds the most difficult, was my work during two winters as a school teacher; but this I must leave to another chapter.

☆ *26* ☆

I Teach a Country School

I COULD easily write an entire book about my experiences as a country-school teacher in southern Michigan. In some ways it taught me more about the actualities of life, especially of American farm life, by the process of hard knocks, than anything I got during my years in an agricultural college. Many incidents in the essays of David Grayson written years later had their origin in my adventures during those two difficult but profitable winters.

At the beginning of the long winter vacation of my sophomore year—I was then sixteen years old—I had to devise some way of making more money, if I was to go on with the spring term in college. When I began to look for a job I made the disconcerting discovery that there was an extremely limited demand for sixteen-year-old boys, especially in winter when farm work was slack. All the good places around the college had been filled by older classmen who were more mature than I was and much stronger physically. I knew that many of my fellow students taught country schools during the winter, but when I began to make inquiries I was discouraged on every hand. I was too young and looked it, I had never had any experience, the field was already overcrowded by better "men" than I was. More serious even than these limitations was the question always promptly asked me:

"Can you pass the county examinations and get a teaching certificate?"

I had about given up the idea when one of the older classmen said to me one day:

"I have just turned down an offer from a country school near Mason. It has a reputation for being unruly and, besides, they don't pay enough money."

I snapped at it like a hungry trout; I didn't care what kind of school it was, or how little it paid.

"Let me try it," I said.

He laughed at me good-naturedly, and, I could see, with complete skepticism.

I got up the next morning at five o'clock and walked the three miles to Lansing. It was in the first days of November, a dark morning, and the road was slippery with mud. I took the early train to Mason, the county-seat, and after buying a bag of soda crackers and a wedge of cheese at a country store, which I munched on my way, for I had had no breakfast, I tramped out three miles to the Hawley school. It was a little white one-room building in a farm neighborhood.

If it had not been for the fact that the season was late and that the trustees had been disappointed in finding a man teacher who could be had for $30.00 a month, I am sure I should never have been considered at all. I may say that they were insisting upon a "man" teacher because a woman teacher in a preceding winter had been turned out of the schoolhouse bodily. She was even said to have been set down in a snowdrift.

I Teach a Country School

"Have you got a teacher's certificate?" I was asked.

"No," I said.

"Kin ye get one?"

"Yes, sir," I said with a confidence I did not really feel. "I am sure I can."

The old farmer looked at me questioningly, my "beardless, cherubic face," as one of my students expressed it long afterward.

"Well, if you kin get a certificate we'll take you."

I tramped back into Mason and went at once to see the Board of School Examiners. The secretary looked me over with the kind of smiling skepticism to which I was becoming accustomed.

"Do you want an examination now," he said.

"Yes, sir," I said. I didn't care how skeptical he was: I wanted that school.

Whereupon he gave me a set of questions on various elementary subjects. As fast as I turned in my answers he checked them over, and finally, adding up my score, divided it by the eight subjects I had taken, and found that my average was eighty. It was just enough to let me by. I was considerably astonished myself to hear that I had passed; I did not know at the time how incredibly low the standards were in country schools.

"Well," he said, "I can't give you a regular third-grade certificate, but if they really want you at the Hawley school, I will give you a special certificate so that you can begin teaching there this winter."

He clearly thought I would not last.

I took the evening train back to Lansing, walked another

three miles to the college—making twelve miles that day—a tired but happy boy. I had got a school!

I have before me as I write the contract I signed with the Directors' Board on November 6 which stated that I was to receive "for the said services as teacher, to be faithfully and truly rendered and performed, the sum of $120.00" for the winter term.

I cannot exaggerate the pride and joy I felt at having become a school teacher, and that I was to receive the unheard-of sum of $30.00 a month for my services. I should not have felt so happy if I had known the difficulties soon to confront and all but overwhelm me.

I was nearly everything a teacher should not be. I was too young, I was ignorant, I did not know how to discipline a more or less unruly crowd of full-blooded farm boys and girls, some of whom were bigger than I was, whose tradition it had been for generations to make it just as uncomfortable as possible for each new teacher until he could by the sheer prowess of his good right arm, or by his wit, prove that he was their master. I was to find out later that one or two of the boys could be really classified as "bad" but several of them, however mischievous, had real ability. One of the brightest and prankiest, Vernon J. Brown, grew up to be the owner of one of the principal newspapers of the county, a member of the legislature, and finally Auditor General of the State of Michigan.

Even though I concealed my age, and by studying the text-books hard and long every evening, appeared to be much better prepared than I really was, I was near complete failure more than once during the first few weeks.

I Teach a Country School

Every one in the neighborhood, including the three school directors, told me that what was needed in the Hawley school was "discipline."

"Keep them boys down," said the chief director.

I began by trying to be entirely too stern and dictatorial: and soon had what an impartial spectator might easily have called a "mix-up" with two of the older of them. I was by no means sure I did not come off second best and injured my authority more than I helped it.

One of the numerous sources of trouble was my insistence upon teaching grammar. The school board, with the county superintendent behind them, had demanded it, but I soon found that grammar, not only in my school but in many others in that country, was taboo. The pupils hated the subject, and parents objected to buying text-books for the teaching of "any such nonsense." Soon after I began, an irate father came to the schoolhouse door and asserted loudly that he didn't want his boys taught "no such fool learnin'."

"Give 'em readin' and writin' and learn 'em to figger," he said. "I never had no grammar and I can talk good enough."

I remember one gloomy evening walking from the schoolhouse homeward to the farm where I boarded, as tired and hopeless and lonesome as any youngster ever was. I remember the snow in the fields, the bare trees, and the crows flying over Crittenden's cornfield, cawing disconsolately—and I wished I was anywhere in the world except in the township of Vevay. I felt that I was a complete failure.

What was I to do? I had been working as hard as I could, studying every evening, getting up early to go down the mile or more to the schoolhouse to clean it up, bring in the wood, and build the fire—for I was janitor as well as teacher—and then, all day, facing a crowd of wild young Indians often confined by the weather to the schoolhouse and getting their chief enjoyment out of rough and noisy practical jokes, coming as near to defying the teacher's rules as they dared. I also felt constrained, at first, at the farm where I boarded. They were most excellent people but they all lived in the kitchen and dining-room and while the farm meals were good and hearty, and the bed I slept in was comfortable enough, although the room, never warmed, was as cold as Greenland, I could not get away from the family, or chance visitors who might drop in, to do my studying and reading or the writing of letters. I paid $1.50 a week for my board and worked Saturday afternoons for the farmer—hard work, too—hauling up straw or cornstalks, or doing chores around the farm, to pay for my washing.

In short, I was completely discouraged. Walking there in that country road I began to think of my own home on the distant St. Croix, the joy and comfort of it, and especially of my father, and his inexhaustible resources for interesting and instructing his sons. I had a remorseful feeling that I had never appreciated him enough, that I had never tried in any way to express my gratitude.

With this the "man teacher," stubbing along homeward, felt, with humiliation, the tears streaming down his face. He was homesick for the first time in all his years.

So many times in my life my inspirations and my decisions have come like lightning flashes. It was so at this moment. My tearful thoughts of my father brought a vision of his way with his own boys, of his wonderful stories, of the books he read us with such delight, and above all, the dramatic surprises, some of which I have already described, which often attended his educational projects. He never forced a boy to learn: he made him *love* it!

I stopped suddenly there in the dark road, as though I had been struck. What was I doing? I was trying to get the best of the boys in my school, not by my wits or my enthusiasm, but by trying to prove that I could knock them down before they could knock me.

The apostle Paul on the road to Damascus was not stricken by a more blinding flash of understanding than I was at that moment. I knew exactly what my trouble was and how I was going to meet it—tomorrow morning at nine o'clock.

I don't know how long I stood there in the darkening road —I remember I was late to supper—but when I started onward again it was with a kind of exaltation, new courage, new resolution.

The mood continued still strong upon me in the morning, and I recall hailing one of the boys I met on his way with his dinner pail, and of taking him, to his surprise, by the arm. I could see it all now: I had been too fearful and too aloof: I had not shown them the stuff I had in me.

The critical moment came during a reading-class rather late in the forenoon. The school had begun to be tired and restless, with plain evidences that some sort of deviltry was afoot. On the previous day I should have feared it, and prepared to resist it by orders and force, if necessary. This morning I stopped in the midst of the dull routine of hopelessly bored and sleepy farm boys and girls reading passages from classic writers which they could only dimly understand, and often mispronouncing a good part of the words. I thumped on my desk: I don't know exactly what I said or whether I said anything at all, but in a moment I was in full swing with one of my father's more amusing and interesting stories of his boyhood. It was a complete surprise. In a minute or two I had every eye in the room fixed upon me—not only the members of the class before me, but every child there, little or big. One could have heard the dropping of the metaphorical pin! I remember the flood of exultant joy and relief that I had within when I recognized that those youngsters were doing exactly what we did when Father told his stories—subsiding into fascinated silence.

For a time it worked: it put me in a new relationship in that school. When some of the boys during the noon recess asked me questions about some incidents in the story I had told, I put them off laughingly, mystified them, just as my father used to do, made them itch for a continuation of the story. I firmly believe that most of them had never before heard any one tell a really good story.

I thought I had found the solution of my difficulties. I told other stories I remembered, and I began picking out short and amusing incidents from *St. Nicholas* and *The Youth's Companion,* which I either read myself—not too often—or got the pupils to read aloud. Instead of demanding that classes learn to spell so many words every day on pain of being kept after school I got up competitive spelling classes with an honor card for the victor: and I put up "mental arithmetic" examples on the blackboard, just as

I Teach a Country School

one of the teachers of my own boyhood had done, and tried to keep the class wide awake following them. I often used actual farm problems that they understood even better than I did, bushels of wheat and corn at so much a bushel, quarts of milk, pounds of seed to the acre—and welcomed the occasional disputes as to whether the price of oats should be so-and-so, or so-and-so.

Hard as I worked at these devices, however, there were boys in the school who, after the first surprised interest, seemed absolutely impervious. I could see that they had no home background, no basis whatever for understanding or co-operation. I visited one or two homes that were squalid and poverty-stricken. How could anything good come out of such surroundings?

One day I heard a rap at the schoolhouse door and upon opening it I found one of my school directors accompanied by the sheriff of the county. He was there to arrest one of my pupils! The boy had been in trouble not only in my school but in the neighborhood. He was taken away into Mason, the county-seat, and while the case was finally dismissed, he and his brother did not return to school—which was a great boon to me. I inquired long afterward about this boy; he continued to be a constant source of trouble in the neighborhood, was often arrested for drunkenness and disorderly conduct, and was finally killed in an accident at a railroad crossing.

The arrest and the dismissal greatly cleared the atmosphere for me. I was also becoming acquainted with the people in the neighborhood and found some of them as fine as any I ever knew. Out of this grew the organization of a

"Literary"—which held meetings at the schoolhouse to debate various questions. One I remember was this:

"Resolved that our country should prohibit the manufacture and sale of intoxicating liquors."

We also had lectures, and finally, the spelling bees in my school having been much talked about in the neighborhood, we planned to have a grand community spelling contest and invite all the adults as well as all the pupils of the school. Shortly before the appointed day a big red-bearded farmer came in to see me. He was a Scotchman named Angus Templeton. He wanted to know what book I was going to use in giving out the words. I thought afterward that I had made a mistake, but I showed him the school spelling-book with its long columns of words, some of which on the back pages were extremely difficult.

"And ye won't," he said, "be using any words that ain't in this book?"

I said that I thought that there was no one in Vevay township who could spell all those words. He went off with a grim look on his face.

When the great evening came the schoolhouse was crowded. We chose two leaders, one to stand near the front on one side of the room and the other on the other side. They took turns in choosing from the audience until every one present was standing up on one side or the other. The Scotchman, Templeton, who was not chosen until toward the last, loomed up in a row of boys and girls like a bushy crag. I put the words first to one side and then to the other and if any speller missed he sat down. The contest waxed fast and furious, and to the amazement of every one the two finally left on the floor were an unusually able woman who had the reputation of being "the most educated lady in the Hawley district," and the other was the Scotchman, Angus Templeton. I kept turning over the pages in the spelling book, getting to harder and harder words, and finally "the most educated lady" missed and sat down. I kept going for Templeton but could not floor him. Finally I remembered a word that had proved highly disastrous to me in a spelling contest when I was in school, and I put it to him.

"Aitchbone."

I could see that it was unfamiliar, and I hoped that it would finish off my Scotchman. But he looked at me keenly and said:

"May I ask ye, Mr. School Master, if that word is in yer little book?"

I had to admit that it was not. Every one shouted with laughter at my discomfiture and I had to declare him the victor. After it was over I learned that he had borrowed one of our spelling-books and learned every word in it. He was altogether an unusual character, self-educated, but richly endowed with Scotch wit. He loved to recite the poetry of Robert Burns, and was a tough customer in a cracker-barrel debate. His son later became mayor of the city of Lansing.

As I gained confidence I tried several other devices or surprises of the kind that my father might have originated. One of them proved a grand success. There had been talk of an elementary course in physiology and since I had recently taken that subject in Professor Cook's laboratory I was much interested. I found the proposed text-book, however, hopelessly dull as compared with the helpful accessories, such as skeletons, and models of the human organs we had used at college. I remembered in particular a small unarticulated skeleton, said to have been that of a Negro girl, which had been especially helpful. I took my courage in my hands and wrote to Professor Cook asking if he would loan it to me for a few weeks. College was not in session and I knew it would not be needed. I counted upon the fact that Professor Cook was a warm-hearted enthusiast, much interested in his students, and I was not mistaken. Some days later a substantial wooden box full of bones came for me. I worked them over in Mr. Crittenden's barn-loft to make sure I knew them all myself. I found that one femur was missing. I kept them back for several days, as my father used to do with his mysteries, giving intimations to my class of a surprise I had in store for them. This I repeated each day with all the ornate decorations I could think of until I had aroused them to the necessary heights of expectation. One morning the wooden box was on my desk, the subject of many questions. When the class was called I remarked that the time had come to present to them a strange visitor. I am afraid I played outrageously on the theme of the Negro girl. At any rate when I lifted out the skull I was rewarded with quite as much astonishment as I had hoped for.

After that, whenever "Physiology" was called I had the entire school in my class. We learned to lay out the bones on the table, putting each where it belonged, with a roll of newspaper substituted for the missing femur. It was not long before every pupil in the school, I think, except the very youngest, could name every bone in the body, as I held them up. I laugh still when I recall how they used to roar out:

I Teach a Country School

"Ulna, radius, occipital, metatarsus," and so on.

The introduction of even this faint semblance of the laboratory method in our school enlivened and sharpened the interest to a remarkable degree. Long afterward one of the students, then grown up, said to me:

"Do you know what I remember best from that winter's schooling?"

"What was it?" I asked.

"That skeleton of the Negro girl."

One Sunday when I was out on one of my usual long tramps—the one thing in a week of hard work that I really delighted in—I found on a windy hillside, blown bare of snow, the skeleton of a small horse. It was somewhat scattered about and bleached white with age. I examined it with great interest. I found that one of the long flat nasal bones in the skull had been loosened, and this I pulled out and put in my pocket with one or two lesser bones. When "Physiology" met I showed the pupils those bones, passing them around, to see if they could guess what they were. We had a grand time with them, comparing them with the corresponding bones in the human skeleton. In this way they got a first faint knowledge of comparative anatomy.

I went back to the college in March with about $70.00 in my pocket, after paying for my board and all other expenses. It was by far the largest sum of my own I had ever had. While I was glad to have earned the money, the winter had been a hard experience in which I think I learned far more than I taught. One of the chief rewards was an invitation from the directors to return, as teacher, in the following winter—which I did not accept.

Two years later in my senior year in college I taught another school, at Tompkins Center, near Jackson, Michigan. I was then eighteen years old and although the school was larger and in many ways more difficult—we had fifty-six pupils on the roll, in one room, ungraded, the oldest twenty-three, the youngest five—I benefitted by my former experience and on the whole made fewer mistakes. Even though I needed the money I earned—they paid me $40.00 a month instead of $30.00—I came to the conclusion, once for all, that I did not want to become a teacher.

☆ 27 ☆

I Become a (Poor) Business Man

So MANY wise observers, keen psychologists, all-knowing sociologists, have proclaimed that the adolescent period, ending say at seventeen, is the most difficult and dangerous in a boy's life. It was not so with me. I did not begin to have serious trouble until I graduated from college. The years from 1889 to 1892—from the age of nineteen to twenty-two —were for me full of doubt, frustration, unsettlement. I had not yet learned what I was good for, and I was torn between what I wanted to do and what I thought it was my duty to do. I was disturbed in my religious beliefs; I was halfway in love with three or four girls; I could see no prospect at least for years of earning enough money to set up a home of my own.

And yet, looking back, few periods in my life seem to me inwardly more exciting, more adventurous, more dangerous, more hopeless, more educative, than those years. I was putting out feelers in all directions, making all kinds of experiments—and mistakes—venturing where angels feared to tread. Although my outward life was usually dull enough, I was boiling hot inside, full at one moment of the most ardent hopes, the most glowing ambitions, and at the next overwhelmed with black discouragement. Once or twice I was near making blunders that would, I think, have unfortu-

nately determined, perhaps ruined, my life. At times I resolved to be a scientist, a lawyer, a grand new kind of
preacher-reformer, a poet, a novelist—but never a small-
town clerk or apprentice in business, which I really was.

When I left college I had only two vague purposes in
mind. One was to go home and help my father whose deafness, now almost total, made it impossible for him to handle
the perplexing details of his business. He needed some one
near him whom he could trust.

The other purpose was to go on, in some way, with my
scientific interests. With great care and difficulty I packed
up all the bottles of reagents, test-tubes, a Bunsen burner,
and other paraphernalia I had used in my last class in or-
ganic chemistry. These I carried home, a back-breaking
load, in my hand, not daring to trust them by express. I had
formed a nebulous plan of carrying on certain experiments
I had not completed. When I was on the train my package
began to emit a curious odor and when I finally opened it
I found that, in spite of all my care, the glass stopper of a
bottle of nitric acid had worked loose and had performed
numerous black, gray, and blue experiments of its own, incidentally eating holes in two pairs of my trousers. I soon
found I could get no gas for my burner, and no time whatsoever to devote to any experiments, in which, indeed, I soon
lost interest.

My feeling for my father had deepened with the years.
I was his oldest son, and we had corresponded during my
years at college with affection and in the fullest confidence.
He made one visit of two days while I was a student—two
days that will glow forever in my memory. I found recently

the notes I made in my diary relating to that occasion: naïve
but sincere:

"I spent a *splendid* afternoon and evening with Father.
His hair is very gray but he is as healthy and robust and
jolly as ever. He is now very deaf but he takes it as though
he did not mind it. . . . I don't know when I have enjoyed
myself as I have for the past two days."

My father was not, in his deeper emotions, an expressive
man, but I knew well by many little things he did or said—
the expression on his face, for example, when he bade me
good-bye at St. Paul when I went away to college—the
warmth of his affection. Few fathers, I think, ever confided
in a son more completely than he did in me, often writing
to me as though I were a brother or a trusted friend rather
than an immature boy.

I knew well that he hoped I would come into his business
when I graduated, taking over some of the burdens he must
before long begin to lay down. When I was sixteen years old
he wrote me a letter from Grantsburg, the county-seat of
Burnett County, where he went several times a year on
business:

"I wonder how many more years in the future I shall ride
during the bright May days over the winding weary road
along the river and then, the long stretch of jack-pines across
the 'barrens.' I wonder, too, who will take this annual ride
and attend to this business after I have taken it for the last
time. It may be you, my boy, who knows! . . .

"Heavy burdens are ready for your shoulders whenever
the shoulders are strong enough to carry them. This will be
equally true whether you return to me and my business or

whether you take an independent pathway in life. When the time comes I shall give you advice, but I shall never attempt to force or urge you into any position or calling which is at all distasteful to you."

I remember to this day the tears burning hot in my eyes when I read this letter, and the resolution I made never to fail him. He was destined to be disappointed: I did not know until long afterward how much disappointed he was. Neither he nor I knew it at the time, but I was not adapted to a business life and my able brother Harry, who ultimately took over the management, was born to it.

Well, I went to work in my father's office at $35.00 a month, living at home. I kept the books and took care of the bank accounts; I was the go-between in most of my father's transactions, and a buffer, well pounded from both sides, in a controversy ending in a lawsuit with a former partner. I made long and enjoyable trips with my father into the north country where I was often his ears, but never his eyes. In many respects it was a highly educative experience, since it gave me a familiarity with the fundamentals of business relationships that was to be of value in later years.

But I did not *live* in it, as one must do if he is to be happy and truly successful in any employment. In fact, I was from the first unhappy, unsettled, misplaced. For four years I had been in a highly stimulating atmosphere, doing interesting things. I had grown, but the town had not. I found no one to talk with on subjects which most deeply interested me. I remember trying to find some point of contact with a new minister who had come to town, and with a school teacher who seemed to have read a good deal. I recall the embarrassed pauses—"Well, I had that subject in college, but I haven't kept up." I had sometimes a sense as of having ventured upon an improper subject, like sex. The minister seemed vacant except in his religious fervor: he did not want to talk with me, he wanted to convert me to certain beliefs wherein he suspected my orthodoxy — rightfully enough. I had a feeling that he was afraid of any real discussion of religion, lest it shake his own faith. Some of the teachers, not all, had succeeded in getting just enough education to secure a teaching position—a "job," as they called it—and then no more study, or thought, or even reading. One of my distant relatives by marriage, George Ely, a much older man, liked to "argufy" as he called it, but he could talk only of Herbert Spencer and Henry George. One winter some of the women in town, vaguely discontented, organized a pathetic Chautauqua reading circle, and toiled over books they did not enjoy. Nevertheless, I think it really helped some of them: at least there was something outside the humdrum to talk about.

One man in town, generally as little respected as any one I knew, I occasionally enjoyed. He was a drunken printer, the scapegrace son of a clergyman. He contrived to keep sober long enough each week to get out the paper: the remainder of the time he was either in the process of getting drunk or of sobering up. One evening he and I were trying to warm up a hall for a meeting of the Sons of Veterans of which we were both members. It was a bitter cold night and while throwing a heavy chunk of wood into the huge stove, he nearly fell in with it. If I had not been close at hand I believe he would have been severely burned. It seemed somewhat to sober him up and he began talking to me with a brilliance and wit that astonished me. Although in his sober moods he was a dull super-patriot, when he was drunk he was as radical as any populist. This was the first of many hot arguments I had with him. In spite of the fact that I disagreed with nearly everything he said, he had seen so much more of life than I had, so much that had bruised and broken him, so much that he despised or hated, that he gave me many things to think about.

At first the deprivation of having no one to talk with upon subjects that most deeply interested me seemed all but unbearable, but as I became better acquainted I made the surprising discovery—I made it again and again in later life —that if I talked with the men and women I met casually about things that interested *them,* if I drew them out, I often discovered unexpected riches of character or experience, sometimes the most delightful or amusing oddities or absurdities. Every human being has a story in him—how he has come to be what he is, how he manages, after all, to live, just to live. And there is no place I have ever discovered that equals the frontier for salty human personalities. After a time I began to enjoy the people of the town—and some of them, in one guise or another in later years, I put into stories or books.

Nevertheless, I was lonesome and felt misplaced, I was not doing what I wanted to do, without knowing clearly what that really was. It seemed as though I was being pressed back into something I had escaped from: I felt suffocated. It was so in the town, it was so in the church, where I seemed irresistibly forced to conform to a round of activi-

I Become a (Poor) Business Man

ties that had changed in no whit since I was a little boy, I was *expected* into the Sunday school, and *assumed* into the creed, which I had begun to question.

Even in my old home, which I deeply loved, I felt as though I were being crowded back into a kind of cocoon from which I had long ago worked free, and flown. It was a curious experience. I slept in the very room that had been mine as a child, under the long sloping roof, with the deep dormer window opening out upon a fine grove of oaks and ash-trees. I began to have the feeling that I was stepping back, not forward. For some time after I returned home, I kept recalling, night after night, one of the earliest conscious experiences of my childhood, which the place, the room, the bed, brought back to me. I could not at that time have been more than five years old. Before I went to sleep, or sometimes when I woke up in the night, I had a strange sense of *going back* to something, to some place where I was happier than I was here, which I knew far better. It seemed familiar and homelike. It is not clear to me now, in detail—it was probably not clear to me then as anything but a bright emotion, or a dream—but it was incomparably comforting. It was a repeated experience, night after night. It warmed and comforted me when my mother put me away in the dark room—but left a triangle of light on the ceiling from the lamp that she left in the hall at the top of the stairs. My mind went back to this pleasant place, a place I seemed to know well. I don't remember what I did there: but I *lived*. It was warm and pleasant and comfortable. I liked it, longed for it. These nightly experiences must have lasted for a long time—months; years?—I cannot tell. But one night they stopped suddenly. I had awakened in the dark: broad awake and a little frightened. Everything was intensely still. I lay there for a moment and then, as usual, tried to go back for comfort and safety. *I could not go.* It was gone—the place, the feeling, the ease, the brightness. I remember struggling for a time wildly and in terror—I cried out in the dark —but the magical door was shut. I did not even know where it was. I could not get in: I could not go back. It was somehow vague and strange, but as vivid as any experience of my later life. I suffered acutely: I struggled: and yet I seemed to understand that it was inevitable, that it could not be changed: that I could never again go back.

As I say, I kept recalling this childish experience, and feeling somehow a repetition of it: the momentary longing to go back to the rich and beautiful years of my childhood, when my father was young and my mother living, and the boys all so full of youth and high spirits—and then the sudden revulsion, and the fear of somehow being suffocated. I could neither go back, nor could I see as yet how to go forward. I was most unhappy.

The old home itself was not what it had been: I could not recapture the glow and glory that I remembered. As far as my father was concerned I am sure it was much happier— and that in itself was a great thing to me. He had remarried fortunately, one of the most unselfish women I have ever known, who was completely devoted to him as long as he lived and who died, certainly of a broken heart, soon after he did. There were two children, two beautiful little girls— there were presently to be two more, boys—and the old home was full of life and activity. But it was not *my* old home.

I Become a (Poor) Business Man

Although nothing whatever was lacking in the regard and the kindness of every one in the house, I felt vaguely, but certainly, crowded out of it.

One deep tie remained, my delight in my father. He was now totally deaf, and instead of using a speaking-tube, he carried a pocketful of small white pads and a battery of short pencils. When any one wanted to talk with him he would thrust out a pad and the message would be written down—unless his caller happened to be a stranger, when petrification often set in. As he read the pads Father would strip off the pages one by one and lay them down or drop them wherever he happened to be. The result was that one came upon scraps of conversations from cellar to garret, out through the garden, in the barn, in the office—like picking up a series of cold telephone conversations. We could tell who had been talking with Father for days afterward. He never complained about his handicap, nor did it appear to affect his spirits. He even used to argue that there was entirely too much talk in the world, and that the best way to determine whether a man had anything important to say was to put a little pad in his hand and ask him to write it out.

My stepmother, through all the later years, was adept at writing to him and seemed to enjoy it. I have seen her sitting next to him in church reporting the points of the sermon.

"It's easy to get most sermons," said my father, "on a mighty small piece of paper."

Within a few months after my return home I began to be quite desperate as to what I should do. One day my uncle, Henry C. Baker, who lived at Hudson, a town some forty miles down the river, came to visit us. He was an older brother of my father, distinguished-looking, with the measured voice of authority, and occasional sallies of a discursive humor which I loved. He was an old-fashioned lawyer. His firm, Baker and Spooner, was the most notable in all that upper country. His partner, Colonel John C. Spooner, was an important political figure, had been a member of the Wisconsin legislature and later was to be United States senator, and to wage unceasing warfare against that "upstart," La Follette, and all that he represented.

My uncle was a great reader. While attorney for the "Soo" railroad, which was then building across the wild country from Minneapolis to the Sault Ste. Marie, he was absorbed in the novels of George Eliot and having to name some of the stations in our county he christened one of them Deronda. He, like my father, loved mottoes—but they were as different as the personalities of the two men. "When in doubt, charge," said my father, breathing fire and brimstone. *"Suaviter in modo, fortiter in re,"* placidly declared my uncle. He was always telling my father:

"Stan, you *can't* do that! It's illegal, it's suicidal."

And my father was always replying:

"Henry, I've done it already."

On this particular occasion my uncle got started on one of his favorite subjects, "the symmetry of the law." I delighted in his half-philosophical, half-argumentative representation of the Law—clearing his throat from time to time —as the most illustrious and learned of all the professions, its roots deepest in the past, its fruitage, the spirit of democracy and justice now expanding throughout the world. It was not only beautiful to hear: it was as convincing as

I Become a (Poor) Business Man

only absolute conviction, backed by the authority of success, can be.

I had had a vague idea of studying law—indeed, my uncle had himself suggested it on other occasions—and I now began to consider it seriously. I felt a shyness, which I cannot now understand, about asking my uncle's advice, since I must have known that he would help me with the greatest pleasure, but for some reason I turned to the president of the college from which I had so recently graduated. He had been a lawyer, a member of Congress, and had just been appointed Assistant Secretary of the newly created Department of Agriculture at Washington. His name was Edwin Willets. I had admired him as a student, although somewhat at a distance. I had had one class under him—in ancient history, of which I can now remember only one amusingly human incident. He was telling of the deep rootage and persistence of customs and habits:

"You see," said he, "the buttons on my sleeves, the purpose of which in early days was to keep back the sleeve and free the sword arm. And there are two buttons, now wholly useless, at the back of a man's coat which were placed there to hold back the long front flaps when the gentleman mounted his horse."

With that the president, who was a large, slow-moving man, turned his back to the class and fumbled for the two buttons. But one of them was missing! I remember the roar of laughter that went up, in which the president himself readily joined.

I finally ventured to write to Mr. Willets regarding my problems and my ambitions. I was delighted to receive, shortly, a typewritten letter (then a rarity) which I have preserved to this day.

Laws being the outgrowth of customs, he advised me to secure a thorough knowledge of historical backgrounds. The books he advised were Hallam's *Middle Ages* and *Constitutional History*, Robertson's *Charles the Fifth*, Sir Henry Maine's *Ancient Law*, Laveleye's *Primitive Property*, and O'Connor's *Manners and Customs of the Ancient Irish*. After all this I was to read Blackstone's *Commentaries*, Cooley's edition.

This thoroughgoing reading was to continue for two years, before I even looked into any books on modern legal procedure, such as Kent's *Commentaries*, Greenleaf on *Evidence*, Stephens on *Pleading*.

"When you begin study as study, do so for keeps," he advised.

It looked to me like a terrific program, but I went at it at once, ordering the books from a second-hand dealer in Chicago and beginning with Hallam's *Middle Ages*. I enjoyed *Charles the Fifth* the most, and the footnotes of Blackstone's *Commentaries*, but I soon found the going extremely difficult. My days were full of hard work, mostly desk work, and in the evening I was tired and sleepy and it was difficult to hold my attention to the task until I had the matter securely in mind. I tried getting up at five o'clock in the morning, but that often left me dulled for the work of the day. My eyes began to give me trouble, due largely I think to a miserable cheating oculist, and I hired an old aunt on my mother's side to read to me at ten cents an hour. She was perfectly delighted, although I think she did not understand

a single line of what she read, and mispronounced, fantasti-
cally, most of the hard words. I remember sitting there at
the window with her, inwardly boiling with irritation and
impatience, struggling to understand. It was plain, unadul-
terated hard work. I did not enjoy it—although much that
I got, studied "for keeps"— has been of use to me all my life.

When my eyes were too bad, or I could stand the strain
of my work no longer, I would rush out for the kind of country tramps I loved—down the river, over the rocky hills,
across the new farms, my spirits immediately rising. Everything I saw or heard or felt gave me a wonderful sense of
joy. Sometimes I rode one of my father's horses, which I
finally trained so that I could shoot partridges from his back.
Occasionally I went swimming or fishing, both of which I
liked. Most of these excursions I made alone because there
was no one of my age or of my interests whom I could take
with me and, quite frankly, I enjoyed myself much better
when alone.

If my time was too short for a tramp or a horseback ride
I would dash down the street for a call on old Strandberg,
the gunsmith, who was a real philosopher, gifted also in telling folk-stories of his native Sweden, or I stopped in the
doorway of John Comer's blacksmith shop to watch the
shoeing of a horse, or talked with Charlie Fisk or old John
Turnbull or Barney McCue. But these interests, which gradually led me to try my hand at writing, I must leave to another chapter.

I dislike, now, even to think of it, but I was sometimes
conscience-stricken at such a waste of time, and for the fact
that I found such delight in these runaway excursions and

friendships. I had in me, and couldn't help it, something of the old Presbyterian-Puritan suspicion of joy or ease or beauty—with sin all around me and in me, and death so near!

I did not know it at the time, but my bad eyes probably did me a service. If I had found a good oculist, as I did a year or so later at Ann Arbor, to fit me with glasses that made my vision perfect, so that I could read without tiring, I might have soaked in enough of the dry knowledge in my books to become a lawyer!

In the spring of 1891, just as I was coming of age, an odd character in the town with whom I had enjoyed talking and who had apparently taken a liking to me said one day:

"You ought to get into politics."

I laughed outright.

"I mean it," he said, "and you ought to begin early."

I thought he was joking but when the tickets for the town election were passed around—as they were in those good crude old days—I was surprised to find that I was down as a candidate for two offices, town clerk and, of all things, justice of the peace. I had a hot argument with my over-zealous friend, but finally surrendered and was duly elected. I knew little or nothing about town affairs and far less about the functions of a justice court, and I didn't at all like it when my friends began teasing me by calling me Judge Baker.

Only a few days after I was elected I had the shock of my young life. On Sunday morning a girl and boy called at our door and asked to see me. When I went out they looked at each other in smiling embarrassment and said:

I Become a (Poor) Business Man

"We want to get married."

I was about to send them to the Presbyterian minister when it came to me, the stunning realization, that they meant *me*. It had actually never before occurred to me that marrying runaway couples from Minnesota was one of the functions, in those days, of a Wisconsin justice of the peace. When I reached the surface, where I could get my breath, I invited them down to my father's office, thankful that it was Sunday morning and I could lock the door. I could have told something of marriage customs in ancient Ireland or in the Middle Ages: I did not know the first thing about what to do in St. Croix Falls in 1891. I asked the blushing young couple to excuse me for a moment and I went into a back room with the Statutes of the State of Wisconsin under my arm. I studied it feverishly, but could find no detailed instructions and little other information save that I was entitled to a fee of two dollars—which was comforting. "I've got to do it," I said to myself. When I returned I directed the couple, with great solemnity, to stand up before me, and on the spot invented a wedding ceremony in which afterward I took considerable secret pride. Having no Bible at hand, I had them place their hands on the Statutes of the State of Wisconsin—which seemed to do just as well. I forgot about the ring until the young man tremblingly began to finger for it, and they needed no prompting whatever to cement the bargain with a heartfelt kiss. The groom paid me, with gratitude, the two dollars, and I promised to send the certificate the next day. The fact was, I had never seen such a certificate, but I was able to get one, all covered with cupids and hearts, to fulfill my agreement. I have no doubt that the knot I tied was as enduring as most of those tied by constituted clergymen.

I had many other amusing experiences, including the custody of an itinerant circus with one elephant which irate creditors at the neighboring town of Oscela had attached in my court. I have always wanted to put the roustabout manager, as I came to know him, into a story. He was a round-barrelled, hairy, red-faced fellow with tobacco juice running down one corner of his mouth—and the most gorgeous gift of profanity that ever I heard in my life. He and I had a set-to before the lawyers agreed on a settlement—but he came roaring in afterward and gave me a handful of free tickets to his show. Sometime later a physician who was retiring from practice brought in sixty or seventy cases against former patients who had owed him money for years—and I had a deep look into what poverty and suffering in the back country might mean. The education I got out of these experiences, I am sure, was far more valuable than the money collected by the creditors of the circus, or by the retiring physician.

In the meantime I had been making hard progress with Blackstone et al. and had finally reached a decision as to the near future. My brother Harry, who was in college, had agreed to come home at Christmas time and take over the work in Father's office while I went down to Ann Arbor for the law course. I think, in all honesty, it was my passionate desire to get away from home, anywhere, on any excuse, rather than the decision to become a lawyer, that was the chief incentive in making the plan. In spite of many interesting activities at St. Croix, in spite of the fact that I had

I Become a (Poor) Business Man

begun to enjoy, intensely, certain secret attempts to write "poetry" and stories (of which I shall speak in a following chapter), I still felt myself unhappily misplaced.

I was, however, to have one more highly educative and in the afterlook, amusing, experience before I left home. In the summer of 1891 I was elected Secretary of the Polk County Fair Association. While this meant that I was to manage the fair held every autumn on the hill back of our village, I had really little to do except to make general plans and take care of the money—the latter, extremely important. For the county fair, like some of the institutions of the Middle Ages I had been reading about, was of ancient lineage. It had developed its own manners and customs, it had its experts in various activities—such as horse-racing, which I knew nothing about—so that it would almost have come to life and run itself without any youngster like me to interfere with it. I made at least one costly mistake, but I also did one new thing that people talked about all over the county. It was customary to have an orator as one of the attractions, usually some local celebrity, or some political aspirant with an ax to grind. I had higher aspirations! I had been reading Ignatius Donnelly's *Great Cryptogram,* in which the author tried to prove that Lord Bacon wrote the works of Shakespeare. I did not accept his arguments, but the book had made quite a stir and the man himself, as an orator and politician, was more than a local celebrity. I had also read his *Atlantis,* an account of the mythical island in the middle of the Atlantic Ocean referred to by ancient writers, including Plato, as the utopian home of a glorious lost civilization. Donnelly lived at Hastings, Minnesota, south

233

of St. Paul. I wrote to him and had a prompt response. He would come for seventy-five dollars and expenses, which seemed to me an enormous price. Upon further correspondence he came down to fifty dollars and wanted to talk on "The Mistakes of Ingersoll in Literature and Religion"—Robert G. Ingersoll being one of the great popular controversial orators of the day. I thought a subject dealing with agricultural conditions in the Northwest would please the farmers better, and Donnelly came. He was the first live author I had ever met—except certain scientific authors that I didn't count—and I was considerably awed. I studied hard on an introductory speech which I delivered, pretty badly, in the grandstand. Donnelly was a round, pudgy man then about sixty years old, with hair sleeked back, and a mellifluous voice. He had all the arts of the old oratory. I do not remember one word he said, but I have a vivid picture of the perspiration pouring down his face as he stood there in the hot September sunshine, and of his clenched fists rising and falling. He pleased the people and when, after the speech, I counted out his fifty dollars I recall the old courtesy of his bow and his exact words—as though he were concluding a letter:

"I am yours with gratitude and respect."

He was my first live author—but not my last.

☆ 28 ☆

I Begin to Write

IT WAS DURING the year 1891, when I was twenty-one years old—eating my heart out with loneliness in the little office at St. Croix—that I began trying really to write. As I have said before, I had begun keeping a diary when I was ten years old, and before I was twelve I had tried, hopelessly, to put down some of the stories my father told with such incomparable zest. While I was in college I had written a few essaylike articles which were printed in college journals, but the idea of writing for magazines or newspapers does not seem to have occurred to me until the year I have mentioned.

Looking back, I find myself surprised and embarrassed by the fumblings and flounderings of those early endeavors. It all seems so clear in the afterlook, that I should have written stories or essays or verses based upon my own true observations and experiences: what I myself saw, heard, felt, thought: what stirred and interested me most deeply, what fired my enthusiasm. Was not this the reasonable thing to do?

As a matter of fact, I did just the opposite. I could not somehow trust what I myself most enjoyed, nor disclose my deepest and truest thoughts, my loves, my doubts, my aspirations. In all the books and magazines I read I could find

235

nothing at all like my own life, my visions, or the stories I told myself, and judged that I must somehow be wrong, or at least odd. To say out loud, especially in such a neighborhood as ours, all that I thought and felt would have been at that time utterly impossible for me—an unknown clerk in a business office, a member of the Presbyterian Church, the Sons of Veterans, and the Good Templars, a Town Clerk, a voter in the Republican Party.

I kept secret all my early endeavors and whenever I sent out a story or verses which I considered the "real thing" I used pseudonyms, and sometimes took the most absurd precautions not to have the correspondence come in my own name—as though any one in the world was in the least interested! Even fifteen years later when I entrusted to the editor some of the little essays and stories that made up *Adventures in Contentment,* I hid behind what I hoped would prove an impenetrable nom-de-plume—David Grayson. This was not because what I had to say was shocking or revolutionary but because I was afraid to expose my deepest and truest thoughts and feelings, which I considered —I saw afterward how mistakenly—to be wholly different from what other people felt or thought. I was somewhat ashamed, also, because my interests were so common and trivial. I felt that I should talk about important, distant, thrilling things that people did not know about. I remembered the jeering remark of a neighbor of ours who had read a poor little poem, by some unknown author, about the beauty of our valley—and unusual beauty it was:

"Well, *I* ain't seen nothing like that around here."

So it was that when I considered writing a poem or a story

for the magazines I put into them only what I had seen in poems and stories I had read in magazines or books. I did not lay the scene of my first printed story in Wisconsin which I knew well, but in Iowa, which I did not know at all. Oh, I took care to use new names, new places, new combinations —but there they were, the familiar stories, nothing in them to offend, often designed to teach a "truth," or provoke a smile, or draw a tear, and coming out comfortably at the end. I was to wallow for some time, and deep, in this slough of futility.

I can best explain this paradox by remarking, in the first place, that I liked to write. I have always liked to write. When I really enjoyed an experience, when I saw or heard something which struck me as wonderful, when I met a man or a woman who interested me, whom I deeply admired or loved, I could not let these things go by with a glance. I clung to the brightness and beauty of them: I thought of them after I went to bed: I put them in little stories I told myself. Of all the ways ever I found for squeezing the last savor from an experience the best is to write about it, not for any one else, not even in a letter to a friend, but for one-self alone. An audience is fatal! I succeeded thus in living my experiences, enjoying my enthusiasms, not once but twice; and in all the years of my life, I have found no hours choicer in enjoyment than those I have spent on my note-books. Experience soon fades, thought degenerates into mus-ing, even love may presently wither, but the honestly writ-ten expression, hot from the penpoint, of the contents of one's mind, its observations, desires, doubts, faith, ambition and the like, becomes at length a kind of immortality.

Another matter seriously troubled me. All the stories I read came to an end, mostly happy, but if tragic, they came to an end. Mine never did or would. In my boyhood when my great old Aunt Hill told stories I can remember crying out, "what happened next?" When my father remarked some evening, after a grand session of story-telling: "That's the end of it. Off to bed with you," I *knew* it was not true. Wasn't Father there? Didn't he continue to live after he fought that battle, or won that war? If I couldn't get him to go on, why, I could and did, after I went to bed, tell myself what happened next. I knew, of course, that printed stories must stop, but how could I stop mine?

Still another element in the problem, somewhat related but vaguer, kept entering into my early plans to write stories. So many of the novels I read, almost all of them, were full of the most extraordinary crimes, catastrophes, coincidences, to say nothing of love affairs, and such wit and cleverness in conversation as I had never heard in all my life. While these things in a book often excited and held me, just as my aunt's early stories had done, they did not absorb me, fascinate me, as did my own deepest experiences. What I thought about oftenest, what seemed to me strange and wonderful, was the way that people, almost any man or any woman, kept on living, going along in spite of everything— eating, sleeping, working, loving, suffering, reading, praying, cheating. This I loved to watch. Even dying did not seem to end the business: the family went on, children grew up, got married, and had lawsuits. A strange thing I could never get out of my mind was that the man himself never seemed *entirely* dead. I had many stories with myself about

I Begin to Write

how this or that part of a certain man who had died went on living.

My notebooks of the time and for many years later are full of notes—sketches, an artist would probably call them—telling of things I liked most to see. Here are some of them:

"I like to see printers in small country shops, with green shades over their eyes, sleeves rolled up, smut on their noses, an old pipe lying on the edge of the case, and a cat sleeping under the stove. I can smell the printers' ink as I step in at the blessed door.

"Woodchoppers in winter: red-faced, and capable of eating for lunch six hard-boiled eggs, half a loaf of bread, two raw onions, a quart of coffee, a wedge of cheese, half a mince pie. And their fine sharp axes and the ringing strokes of them in the snowy forest! I have been with you too, O choppers. I love your husky occupation.

"I like the newsdealer in our neighborhood. No man in town knows as many people as he, not even the postmaster. The stone step of his shop is worn halfway down: there is a hole in the maple floor just where the town turns on its heel after buying a paper. I love his shelves all full of a miscellany of ink bottles, tablets, a vast variety of pencils, pens, erasers, all kinds of stationery, boxed and unboxed, toilet paper, school books. And in the cases there are cigars, gum, cheap candy. And the smell of that shop—no, you are wrong, it is not offensive—a bouquet of moist print paper, tobacco, molasses candy, licorice, and cheap perfumery. Some day I think I shall keep just such a shop myself—'Hello, Bill. How are you, George? How's the kid, Jimmy?'

"Why, I'd know all the babies in the town."

There were individuals in our village I was never tired of watching and enjoying. Each of them seemed to have a continued story somehow ravelling out behind him as he walked in the town road. I had endless talks, as I have already related, with Olaf Strandberg, the gunsmith, who had come to our country from Sweden, as poor as poor could be, unable to speak a word of English. He had known poverty and sorrow, but he had gone along, gone along. His first shop was built mostly out of dry-goods boxes the storekeepers had given him, to be taken home in his wheelbarrow. He soon had three little houses, all built with his own hands. Two he rented and he kept his shop in the third. When any one remarked upon his growing prosperity, he would say:

"It ist America."

"I get a little," he would say, "and get it for notting. It ist good to be von poor man among rich vons. In Sweden ve ver all poor."

As long ago as I can remember I loved to stand in his shop doorway while he worked the long sweep of his bellows and listen to the folk-stories he told, rich from his childhood in the "old country." He began them all, "Vonst der vast a man in Sveden," giving freely of his inexhaustible riches. One of them was a story he sometimes told when he heard people talk about "book-learning," which he did not much believe in:

"Vonst der vast a man in Sveden who should study to be a cook. So he vent to buy a big cook-book—I tink it cost about five dollars American money. And he studied and studied a long time on de book. And ven he tought he had

I Begin to Write

learned everyting der vast in de book he vent and bought a shunk of meat and put it on de kitchen table. Den vile he vast studying in de book haw to cook de meat, der vast a cat come in de kitchen and yump on de table and ran avay vid de meat. And den, det man who should study on a book haw to be a cook looked in det book to see vat he should do ven de cat run avay vid de meat. Ven it diden'ta stand on de book vat to do ven de cat run avay vid de meat and so he give up to be a cook."

It is impossible to convey the delight with which Old Strandberg told his stories, or indeed to reproduce the enchantment to my boyish ears of his Swedish dialect. Something of the latter I have been able to put down more accurately with the help of my brother Harry, who is gifted in telling Swedish stories.

"Vunst der vast two jung fallers in Sveden sum vast wery grate friends, ven after dey have grown up and marrit, dey vast away from each odder for many jears. By and by vun of dem fallers come on a wisit to de odder faller and stay vid him two-tree days. Ven he vast ready to leave, dey vast wisiting togedder in de evening and dat faller sum vast leaving he say to de odder faller, dat he haf a wery fine place and wery fine tings in it and a wery beautiful vife, and so on—but dat faller sum own de place he did-ent say anyting. After a vile ven de odder faller vast tru talking, he answer him:

" 'Do you see dat shoe?'—pointing to de shoe he haf on.

" 'Yes, I do,' de odder faller said.

" 'Isn't dat a gude looking shoe?'

" 'Yas, it is'—he answer.

" 'Val,' and he luk wery solemn, 'you can't feel how it pinch!' "

Strandberg was full of aphorisms which seemed to have come fresh out of his own hard experience. Some of them have remained in my memory, crystals of concentrated wisdom.

"Ven I feel like finding fault, I begin vit Old Strandberg and never get no furder."

"It's a good thing ven a man knows vat he pretends to know."

Not all of Strandberg's stories were remembered folklore. A good storyteller not only recalls, he also creates. Many of the old gunsmith's stories were founded on his own experience, and they were always the best because touched by the humor which made life livable to him.

"Ven I vast poor and carried dry-goods boxes from Jim Thompson's store, I used to vish I had a veelbarrow. Now I have four. Ven I had no house, I vished I had von. Now I have tree. I have tought I vould like a vife, but I have not dared to vish for von."

Old Strandberg was not much to look at. He wore the oldest possible clothes, often grimy with the smoke and oil of his trade, an old hat that came down over his forehead, and his hands and fingers were rough and cracked. But he had a lively blue eye and a smile of good humor, which I shall never forget. He was uncelebrated beyond our village; his name had never been heard "with plaudits in the capitol," but each time I met him I enjoyed him.

Among the people in our town I also liked well to watch was old Joel Nason, one of our most prominent citizens. He was from the state of Maine. He wore a long black coat, such as politicians and ministers of that time affected. It was threadbare around the collar. He had been a senator in the state legislature, and could sneeze louder than any other man in Polk County. Why did I like to watch him? I don't know.

Then there was John Comer, the blacksmith, a Swede. He was a magnificent figure of a man, great shoulders and arms, and a mat of curly crisp black hair to crown his head. To see him in his leathern apron, a red-hot horseshoe in his tongs, bending to lift the shaggy hoof of one of Bill Patterson's horses, gave me an unforgettable thrill. He has lain long in the cemetery on the hill, the place marked by an original and creative, yet appropriate, memorial: an anvil with a blacksmith's hammer lying across it. That is all there is except the name—as outright and simple as the man himself:

> JOHN COMER

I liked Emil Zorn, the stone-mason who built the walls my father delighted to plan; I liked to see Tom Peck, the carpenter, at work—he knew well what a good job really was; and Bill Patterson, the town teamster, standing in the middle of his great lumber wagon, legs spread apart, rattling down the road behind one of the finest teams of horses in the town.

I used to think I should like to spend one whole life going about just looking at human beings busily, unconsciously, and therefore happily, at work, listening to what they said to one another, the cheerful badinage, the amusing gossip; smelling all the good odors of work, the leather in the harness shop as the saddler took up his newest bridle to show me, the exquisite odor of shavings and new wood in the cabinet shop, the smoke of the out-of-doors fire at the wheelwright's. A great proportion of true workers will be found singing or whistling or humming under their breath, for of a truth they find a kind of poetry, harmony, music, in what they do. In unconscious, rapt employment resides much of the joy of life, and much of the sadness, weakness, evil, in this world are to be found in the idle intervals.

All my life I have loved to stop and talk with workers, if they would let me, and have liked such occupations as farmers, tinkers, blacksmiths, newsdealers, bootblacks, and the like because they have callings which permit of talk. And many a good and interesting story have I had from these: springing all fresh and rosy out of the fertile soil of life itself. Agassiz needed only a single bone to reconstruct his extinct fish: and one remark will sometimes disclose, with strange completeness and nakedness, a human soul.

Well, such were the things I was truly and deeply interested in: such was the material I had. But how could I put it into what I was trying to write for the magazines: and if I did, who would care in the least to read what I wrote?

I began, therefore, quite furiously, to write stories and verses that I thought the magazines might publish, and the people might read. I sent them away to *Century* or *Harpers* or *The Atlantic,* to all of which in later years I contributed, and back they came with the cruelly polite printed rejection slips. When the manuscripts were worn out and nothing happened I put them into the huge wood stove in our office —where they certainly belonged.

One evening after I had so consigned to fiery oblivion a story I had especially counted upon, and was feeling low in my mind, it came to me suddenly,

"By George, I had an idea in that story."

I went immediately at the business of rewriting it, finding that some entirely new things came to me as I went along.

The next day I started it and a little poem I had just completed on the rounds, beginning as usual at the top. Again they both came back, and came back—and I grew humbler and humbler. Finally I sent the verses to a magazine then published at St. Paul—I think it was called *The Northwest Magazine*—and to my astonishment and joy I had a letter accepting them. There was, however, a "but" in the letter: the magazine was scarcely yet upon a paying basis and could not compensate me for my admirable, etc., etc., but would gladly place my name on the subscription list for one year. I jumped even at this and looked eagerly in the next number for my verses. They were not there. A month or two later this ingratiating young magazine gave up the ghost and never appeared again. My verses were evidently too much for it.

Almost at the same time I was surprised to have the story I sent accepted by the editor of *Short Stories,* a magazine that then had a considerable following. He would gladly take it and pay upon publication. *Pay,* mind you!

I hung around the newsstands for the next number of *Short Stories,* and bought it anxiously. My story was not there. I tried to reason out my disappointment. Printing took time: and perhaps they wanted to illustrate it! I must be reasonable. So I waited and pounced upon the next number. My name was not in it. I thought of writing to the editor, but I was afraid he might change his mind, repent his purpose of paying me, and send my precious story home again. Month after month I repeated this anxious experience—for two years and a half. And then, when hope was almost extinguished, the story was published, May, 1895. If that editor had printed it two months after I sent it to him, I should have been his slave for life. I should even have thought it a pretty good story: but when it finally came, I had been working for two or three years on a newspaper and had become something of a cynical critic. I was ashamed of it! There it was, the old familiar plot-triangle, the dialect that never was on sea or land, the trick at the end—nothing in it that was deeply and truly my own.

But there it was—published! That fact was not so bad after all. I was on the cover—with Anthony Hope and R. L. Stevenson. I was in the table of contents: I was also on page 50: "The Red Scarf, by Ray Stannard Baker, Copyrighted."

Remains one sad chapter! It was to be paid for upon publication: but the check failed to come. I had seen that check in my imagination scores of times: and had spent it hundreds. I needed it in those days. It did not come.

I knew nothing of the methods of publishers and I was anxious not to offend my particular editor by reminding him of such an unpleasant subject as checks. He might want another masterpiece of mine. But I finally wrote to him and after another delay received a reply with not a word of apology in it. That didn't matter; it contained a *check*. I could not look at that check for some time. It was well that I put off the fatal moment as long as I could. The check was for Five Dollars!

When I had recovered consciousness I began to do a little calculating. I had bought *Short Stories* every month for at least two years and a half (I felt loyal to my editor: I had a sense that it was somehow *my* magazine) and paid twenty-five cents each month: total seven dollars and a half. Credit five dollars for my story. Net loss, two dollars and a half.

☆ 29 ☆

I Embrace, and Desert, the Law

IN JANUARY, 1892, I went to Ann Arbor and matriculated in the law department of the University of Michigan. I had tried hard to satisfy myself that it was the legal profession I was seeking, that after reading the solid volumes Mr. Willets had recommended, including most of Blackstone's *Commentaries,* I was convinced of the "symmetry of the law," and prepared to devote my life to the worship of it. It was so that I attempted, by main strength, to settle the unrest, the indecision, the sense of futility, I had felt during the two years and more in my father's office there in the north woods; but when I was at last settled in a little back room in State Street I found myself gloriously expanding in the kind of atmosphere I loved. I was finding men who shared something of my own interests to talk with, great music to hear, really good dramatic performances to see, new books to read. I was like one long starving who finds a splendid feast suddenly set before him.

I had saved enough money to pay my way for the academic year—tuition, board, room, everything—without the slavery of a "college job." Never before in my whole life had I felt so deliciously free. I went to hear Paderewski play the piano in the vast university hall; I drew in deep breaths of the scented air, I heard not only the glorious

I Embrace, and Desert, the Law

performance of the master, but all the little rustlings, whis-perings, echoings, in that great audience. I had to pinch my-self to realize that I was there, *I!* I heard Modjeska play Rosalind in "As You Like It"—oh, beautifully, perfectly, lovingly—and rushed out afterward, my head burning, to calm myself in the wintry streets. I have already spoken of an earlier experience, the first real dramatic performance I ever attended: well, this was nearly its equal. I shall never forget it.

I heard Grover Cleveland, who had been President of the United States and was to be President again, speak in the auditorium of the law department (Feb. 22, 1892), a great slow-moving hulk of a man, ponderous in what he said, but with something about him, some authority, some inherent power, that impressed me more profoundly than any other speaker I had ever heard up to that time. A few of us crowded timidly forward to shake his hand. I remember the thick, soft, warm feel of his fingers, like a handful of new-baked breakfast rolls. His subject was "Sentiment in our National Life." I tried afterward to set down in my notes some of the things he said. Of course he was a Democrat and anathema to my father and uncle—but I was now a free man and could admire where and what I liked. I heard John J. Ingalls, then one of the most popular of silver-tongued orators, much admired by my fellow law-students who looked for careers as criminal lawyers or politicians. He could, as one of my friends remarked, "make circles all around old Grover as an orator," but he made no such im-pression upon me of weight, power, greatness, as Cleveland had done.

249

Native American

I could not possibly have imagined at that time that in later years I should know personally two of this exalted company, Mr. Cleveland in his old age—I recall one peculiarly interesting conversation with him—and I knew Paderewski at the Paris Peace Conference in 1919.

My introduction to the law school itself, however, was a painful disillusionment. The emphasis in those days was still strongly upon the lecture system. I remember the distinguished, if bored, lawyer or jurist talking dully from the rostrum to classes of two or three hundred men, eager to finish as soon as possible and get back to Detroit. I remember the equally bored students, supposed to take notes, but usually contenting themselves with mimeographed digests that were sold on the street outside. In one case, at least, these lectures did not even have to be reported, since they were the same year after year. A book would have done as well, or better. The professors seemed to know scarcely any individual members of their classes; sometimes at quizzes, one student by agreement would recite for any one of half a dozen friends if they happened to be called upon, a deception rarely if ever discovered. Several times during lectures I saw groups of students playing poker in the back of the room—probably getting as much real education out of it as they would have gotten out of the lecture. It seemed to me an utter farce.

The great figure of the law school of that day was Thomas M. Cooley who had been a distinguished Chief Justice of the Supreme Court of the state of Michigan and was one of the most noted American legal writers. He was the outstanding authority upon "Constitutional Limitations." We all wanted to "sit under" him so that we could speak off-handedly about it afterward, but he was then an old man, so weak of sight that I doubt if he could distinguish us at all as individuals, and so thin of voice that we could scarcely hear what he said.

I had expected to find at Ann Arbor something of the enthusiasm of my uncle for the "beauty of the law." Before coming to the university, as I have already narrated, I had read Blackstone's *Commentaries,* Sir Henry Maine, and Hallam, and Kent—as much as I could stand—and I had seen something of the crude rough-and-tumble of the office of a country justice of the peace, and I now expected a stirring initiation into the mysteries of modern pleading and practice. I suppose my feeling of disappointment and boredom was due in part to the inner hostility, the sense of unfitness for the legal profession, however unacknowledged, which I really felt. But part of it, I still believe, was due to the old, dry lecture system. Certainly the law school of the university had an excellent reputation: and it turned out many good lawyers. But it was not for me.

I stood it for several weeks, growing all the time more restless, more dissatisfied. I had recourse to my usual restorative in such straits, long tramps in the country, sometimes with a sandwich or so in my pockets. It was the dead of winter, but the roads were not blocked and there was much to be seen and lived. Occasionally I struck out across the snowy fields beyond the Huron River, walking hard until I was all of a glow, and my mind had quieted down. Presently I would find that I was reviewing my experiences, not so much as personal difficulties, but because they were amusing or interesting in themselves. I recalled incidents in the classroom or in the studies of my friends, or in conferences with professors, as pictures or scenes. I began to put some of them into stories.

Indeed, the stimulation of my new surroundings had aroused every faculty. I began thinking of writing again. I revised some of the stories that had come back to me from unwilling editors and started them again on their rounds, and I contributed several little verses and articles, more or less secretly, to the university papers.

After a time I began to feel that I could stand the law courses no longer and debated whether I should leave the university entirely. I felt I was wasting my hard-earned money and getting little or nothing in return. Fortunately, a post-graduate literary student told me of the seminars conducted by Professor F. N. Scott, in which the lecture system had been dispensed with and the course was based upon discussion and conference. The subjects especially, as far as I could hear of them, interested me greatly: they dealt not only with literary subjects but with literature as applied to modern social problems. I went with fear and trembling to call on Professor Scott. I told him something of my problems and asked to join his seminar at the beginning of the semester in February. He had a glint in his eye that made me feel, at first, that he was laughing at me—I know how deadly serious I must have appeared!—but he asked such pointed and sympathetic questions that I was somewhat reassured. It was plain he doubted my preparation, felt that he ought not to take me away from the law department, and finally said that he already had applications from ten students (I

think he said ten) and did not care for any more. The more
he doubted, the more certain I became that I wanted to take
his course. He appealed to me as just the kind of man I
should like to know, and talk with—if I dared. When he
finally accepted me I took a long step further into the literary department by getting permission to take a course in
English Literature under Professor Demmon. It was conducted on the conventional uninspired information-from-
books method, with markings based upon what the student
could give back to the professor in response to quizzes. I
soon found it dull and uninteresting.

But Scott's seminars—I was soon taking two of them—introduced me into a new world. His method was everything
that the law course was not; a group of ten or a dozen, sitting
down together to discuss certain clearly defined subjects and
problems, led by a teacher who knew how to stimulate the
minds of his students. We were given subjects out of newspapers and magazines, sometimes reading lists at the library,
and came back loaded with ammunition. I remember the
meetings that followed as among the most interesting, even
exciting, I had ever known. Each day I went back to the
library, eager to follow up the new clues suggested—Scott
was gifted in sprinkling his anise-seed—going from book to
book, often far beyond the list suggested. There were days
when I could not even stop for lunch. The defect in my eyes
had now been completely corrected by an expert in the
medical college, and it was a joy to me to be able to read
almost indefinitely. One incidental reward from Scott's
courses was that I learned to read with more skill, to tell
quickly whether I wanted this or that book, and to add each

discovery I made, the essence of it at any rate, to what I knew before, or the author to my familiar company of friends.

Scott was unfailingly interesting. Although he slyly kept our discussions pointed, he was willing to follow them to their scientific, or philosophical, or social consequences. On one occasion he brought into the class an armful of a recent number of *Harper's Weekly* containing a new story by Rudyard Kipling—then the worshipful pattern of every youngster interested in either story reading or story writing. It was called "The Children of the Zodiac," a kind of unclear parable, extremely Kiplingesque. Without expressing any opinion regarding it, he gave each of us a copy and a series of pointed questions in regard to it, both matter and method, which we were to discuss at the next session. Nothing could have been more stimulating to me. I was a devout admirer of Kipling, and I had been trying my own hand at story writing—with no one to criticize me, or indeed, to direct my thought as to what a short story really was, and what it should, or should not, attempt to do.

Another thing that Scott did in one of his seminars was to ask each student to subscribe to a daily newspaper and to select some subject in which he or she was interested and be ready, once a week, to report on it *in writing* during the seminar—the notebooks being turned in to the professor, without opportunity of revision, at the close of the session. Few devices I ever knew were better calculated to test the students at all points than this. His product must rest in the first place upon his ability to read with understanding, upon his grasp, as well as his interest, in public questions, upon the backgrounds of his education, and finally, upon his capacity, within the limit of an hour, to express in clear English what he knew or had learned. Even if a student was not as deeply interested as all of our group seemed to be, no cribbing, or cramming, or bluffing, could cheat such a process.

I chose as my subject the relationships of labor and capital, which at that time, just at the beginning of the great depression of 1893, were much in the public eye. Workmen were everywhere organizing and strikes were frequent. *The Chicago News Record*, which I began to take, was full of both news reports and editorials regarding these widespread difficulties. I had been brought up on the individualistic frontier where such a thing as a strike had never been heard of, and I held strong opinions regarding the subject. The reports, therefore, interested me deeply and I came to the seminar loaded not only with the facts but with my own views regarding them—that is, my own editorials. I wrote with the greatest fervor, and awaited with impatience what Scott had to say at the next meeting. For the first time in my life I was getting honest and direct criticism—and it was like a draught of clear water to a thirsty spirit. Even though sometimes sharp, it was always helpful. It was exactly what I needed and wanted.

I think Scott began presently to be interested in me, and once or twice broke what I learned afterward was a rather stern precedent, by inviting me to his house. I must have poured out my soul to him—for he was the first person in the world I had met who seemed able to understand what was troubling me and what I wanted to do. He maintained, however, a kind of playfulness, a protective armor of irony,

255

which I somehow resented, but which, God knows, I needed.
He had once worked on a newspaper—*The Toledo Blade,* as
I remember—and he had tried his hand both at stories and
at verse. He was the author of one of the most popular of
college songs, "Romeo and Juliet."

> "Come now and listen to my tale of woe,
>   Of Romeo and Juliet
> Cribbed out of Shakespeare and dripping with woe,
> Never was story so mournful as that one,
> If you have tears now prepare to get at one,
> Romeo's the thin one, and Juliet's the fat one,
>   Oh, Romeo and Juliet."

I drank in all he told me, and must have demanded more
and more. I must have worn him out!

Taking it all in all, Fred Newton Scott was one of the
greatest teachers I ever knew, next to Doctor Beal, at the
college at Lansing, who taught me to look at life before I
talked about it.

For a time I kept on with the boresome law lectures,
thinking that I must, after all, get my degree, but presently
I dropped them entirely and never again went near the law
department. The months that followed linger in my mind as
one of the rich experiences of my life.

I did not make this break-away without many hesitations
and compunctions. I knew how disappointed my father
would be—and perhaps my uncle—not so much because I
was taking these literary courses but because I was not doing
what I had set out to do. *I was not going through.* I knew
he would consider it a kind of moral failure. To go down to
the university and spend all my money to complete a course

and get a degree, and then not do it! But I had begun to have a strong instinct that nothing now mattered, whether a university degree, or the approval of family and friends, or even the assurance of making a living, nothing but the business of trying to find out what I was good for, and then doing it. The more I thought of the matter the clearer it became that what had interested me in reading Hallam and Sir Henry Maine and Blackstone was not the development of the law, which my uncle found fascinating, but the strange ways of human beings. I was fascinated in the cases themselves, not in what they proved or what traditions and laws grew out of them; I was interested in the footnotes in Blackstone far more than in the text.

On one of my Sunday tramps I remember stopping suddenly by a little marsh on the Huron River and having all of my problems resolved, as by a blinding flash of light—as has happened several times in my life. I can see to this day the hooded skunk-cabbages, thrusting their green-brown heads up through the moist soil, and the red maples blooming, and I can recall a delightful sharp spring odor I could not identify.

My decision was made. I turned and walked rapidly back to the university, wrote a letter to the city editor of *The Chicago News Record* asking for a job, and posted it that evening.

The letter in response was not too encouraging, but intimated that if I came down in June there *might* be a chance for me. For the Chicago World's Fair was then in the building, business was booming and all the newspapers were expanding and prospering. No one knew at that time that the catastrophe of a great national depression was just around the corner. I did not know it either!

My doubts and hesitations were thus momentarily settled, but my real troubles were about to begin. I entered upon a life that proved to be as perplexing as it was absorbing, with unlimited hours, hard work, and, for many years, low pay; full of disappointments and mistakes, but perfectly suited to my deepest interests and capacities.

☆ 30 ☆

Chicago

IT IS NEVER without a touch of nostalgia—glimpses of the heaven of bygone adventures—that I think of my arrival in Chicago on that June morning in 1892. All the sights of that June morning, the very odors of it, the bouquet from the Chicago River and the stockyards, bitingly distinctive, not too unpleasant, are as clear to me today, I think, as they were on that morning so many years ago.

I had come down from Michigan on the night train, napping in a day-coach, for I could not afford a berth in the sleeper, and getting off at Polk Street soon after dawn. I had a brand new hat on my head, a brand new coat and shoes, and I carried in my hand a brand new bag. Several times before I had travelled through Chicago on my way to college, and once, as I have related, I stopped over for the night to see Sol Smith Russell in "Peaceful Valley," but I really knew nothing of the city, nothing, indeed, of any city.

The keen sense of my coming adventure had kept me awake most of the night. I think I must have felt much as did little David going forth with his sling to slay the mighty Goliath—fully as ignorant of giants, and quite as confident of my ability to slay them. I remember the cavernous and hollow-sounding sheds of the depot, the grimy buildings just outside and the slimy look of the early morning streets. A boy darted at me offering to carry my bag, but I clung to it with suspicious determination, and started to walk straight northward without much idea where to go or what, at the moment, to do. The only thing I wanted was to see Chicago.

I had thought of the various wonders one by one: the skyscrapers, the gray Chicago River, the ships and barges at anchor, the clanging trolley cars, the hurrying people in the crowded streets, and I now found them poured out upon me all at once with a lavish, overwhelming hand: confusing marvels, strange contradictions. I could get sharply detached impressions only here and there—the little tufts of white steam set like dancing cockades on the chimney tops of the marching city, a ragged man darting into the gutter to pick up a cigar butt, two flashily clad girls talking and laughing in the echoing streets. I saw with a thrill a boy crying the morning papers; he would soon, no doubt, another morning or two, be selling gems from my pen!

I walked and I walked and I walked. I was entranced. Sometimes I caught myself gripping the handles of my bag until my hands hurt. I stopped for a bit of breakfast, and bought a copy of *The News Record,* since I was soon to be a member of its staff—or thought I was. Afterward I started walking again toward the northward, having a vague idea of getting a room near the lake-shore.

My bag began to grow unaccountably heavy, and the spring sun hot on my shoulders. I began to be tired. In North State Street, in a barren row of cheap houses I saw a sign "Room to Rent." I climbed the wooden steps to the front door and rang. A heavy, dull, slatternly woman came to the door. She had a suspicious look in her eye. My second question contained the nub of the problem so far as I was concerned:

"How much is it?"

She looked at me appraisingly.

"I have one for three dollars a week"—adding after a pause—"in advance."

Well, I rented it; a hall bedroom, up one long flight of stairs, with a single narrow window opening on a dingy court. It was a close-pinched room hardly larger than one of the closets of my boyhood home, with a single gas-light set high above the bed, so high and so dim that when I read by it I had to stand up on my only chair. Even on that warm June morning, the atmosphere of the room seemed damp, and there was a sour, gassy odor. But it was only three dollars a week.

I cannot remember that I was in the least daunted, or even much concerned. I think I actually liked it. For this was The City: the dirty, clamorous, uncomfortable, wicked, fascinating city I had heard so much about. This was the real thing! What did it matter? I could sleep anywhere. Hadn't I slept in lumber-camps, and often and often on the hard ground of the north woods with only a blanket under me? It would not be for long: I should soon be earning plenty of money and I could look for a better place.

Mr. Yount, the city editor of *The News Record,* had suggested in his letter than I call after one o'clock. I did not even know at that time that a morning newspaper slept till noon. So I called after one o'clock. I waited for a long time in the warm, noisy, bustling city room with its strong odor of printers' ink. The reporters were getting their assignments and starting out for the day's work. I felt abashed and small.

Mr. Yount was a large, florid man with a bristling moustache, and a not unpleasant look in his eye. I forgot to say that I had carefully brought with me a paper-covered roll which I thought of afterward with embarrassment and chagrin. It was the last thing I should have done. But murder will out! I unrolled my college diploma and showed it to Harry Yount. I cringe yet when I recall the look in his eye and the slight disdainful wave of his hand. I was to understand later how infinitely inconsequential in those days was a college diploma in a newspaper office.

"What experience have you had?" he asked.

I could confess only to the editorship of a college paper, which did not seem in the least impressive to Mr. Yount, or even to myself when I thought of it in those overpowering surroundings. He cheered up a little when he heard that I had had some experience on a country newspaper and could "stick type." Even that gleam of encouragement would have been dimmed if he had known how little of that country newspaper I had had.

"Why do you want to be a newspaper man?" he asked me, I thought somewhat impatiently—and then added, "There are at this moment fifty pretty good reporters in Chicago out of a job—all ready to go to work."

I could see that things, decidedly, were not going well.

"I thought that with the preparations for the World's Fair, there would be plenty of newspaper work to be done."

"All the others," said Mr. Yount smilingly, "thought so too."

Chicago

Something in me suddenly began to get angry—and determined. I got up from the edge of the chair where I had been sitting, and rolled up my poor diploma with trembling fingers.

"I'm sorry," I said. "You wrote me I could come."

With that I started out of the room, hot, angry, and desperately disappointed. I must have made a ridiculous spectacle of myself.

"Hold on," said Mr. Yount. "Hold on there."

He had a delightfully ironical look in his eyes. He was positively enjoying my misery! It seemed to irritate him to think that any youngster—especially one who carried around a college diploma—held the profession so lightly that he thought he could practice, and even earn a living at it, without any training.

"One of the editors downstairs," he said, "sometimes asks the men who apply to him for editorial jobs, 'Why don't you practice medicine?' 'Why,' they always answer in astonishment, 'I never went to medical school.' 'Well,' he responds, 'you know as much about medicine as you do about the newspaper profession.' "

This hurt!—and it had never occurred to me at all. One wrote reports or editorials for a newspaper and that was all there was to it.

"Then how can a man ever learn?" I asked somewhat desperately.

At that time there were no such institutions as schools or colleges of journalism; and I soon found that many of the men still came up by way of the country newspaper, or the composing-room—the hard, slow way of the itinerant apprentice—the Mark Twain way, the Bret Harte way, the Walt Whitman way.

"Well," said Mr. Yount finally, "we may want to do something more with the Fair. Suppose you sit around the city room for a while and we'll see what you can do."

I jumped at the chance: I was soon to learn the utter weariness and discouragement of "sitting around the city room." I got only the crumbs that happened to fall from the banquet of the day. Mr. Yount or one of his assistants would look in at the door and ask: "Where's Ade?" (This was George Ade, afterward famous as a humorist and play-wright.) "Has McDowell gone out?" (Malcolm McDowell, one of the best reporters that ever I knew.) "Where's Field?" (Hollis W. Field, who had rare literary gifts, which he was too modest to put to the test. He became my life-long friend.) Their eyes would presently fall on me—and glance aside. I wouldn't do. So I continued to sit!

Fortunately it was the hey-day of June weddings, and the lively little society editor had her hands overflowing with work. I did not know at that time that assignments to report weddings were the lowest possible degradation a man could suffer; I was grateful for anything whatsoever to do.

I had never in my life attended a society wedding. Having been brought up on the frontier, I was ignorant of every nicety of such ceremonies, and more or less contemptuous of them. Your pioneer instinctively hates ceremonies; they make him feel uncomfortable. I did not even know the words with which to describe the bride's dress, the flower arrangements, the significance of the various attendants, as of bridesmaids, groomsmen, flower-girls and the like. Fortunately, much of the material was furnished in one form or another, and especially the lists of names, the description of the bride's trousseau and the like—and I worked hard at it. I found the shows themselves rather interesting, especially the church weddings, besides being, from my high and mighty point of view, not a little amusing if not ridiculous. I tried at first to put in a few original descriptive flourishes, but the next morning I found that everything that I had thought pretty good, especially everything I thought even a little entertaining or exceptional, had been ruthlessly cut out. I learned that a wedding, of all things in the world, was the most conventionally solemn. A funeral is nothing to it! I also watched how the other papers handled the weddings I went to: and finally learned the hard-and-fast formulæ.

It was well at the beginning of my experience that I had several hard-boiled desk-men to stand between me and such of the public as may have read what I wrote. I should have been promptly exposed for the hopeless amateur that I was. My ignorance was something to stand back and admire, for the very amplitude of it. I had come out of the frontier, where many of the accepted practices of the city were quite unknown. When I wanted to cross a street I crossed it: when I wanted to stop a man to ask a question, I stopped him. I was suspicious of "no-admittance" signs and tempted to find out whether they meant what they said. I had had little practice in the art of living in a crowded world.

I continued to sit in the city room. At the end of the week I supposed I would be paid *something* for the work I had done: and I was beginning to need the money. Nothing happened. Another week passed. Nothing happened. I got up my courage and asked one of the men in the office with whom I had become somewhat acquainted.

"If you are on space," said he, "you should take your string down to the cashier. She'll pay you."

Having learned what "space" was and that a "string" consisted of one's daily literary gems pasted together so as to make one long column, I took my poor little wedding paragraphs, and a few others I had written, down to the sympathetic Miss Dewey, who in later years became my good friend. I think she understood the situation instantly. She did not even smile. She measured out my "string" with a foot-rule as though I were a seasoned contributor and paid me, as I remember, $4.40 for two weeks' work. It was something even to be paid by the foot for my first real literary labors!

I continued to sit in the city room: but the boom of June weddings began to wear off. The crumbs grew more infrequent. One week I got down to less than three dollars. I tried various independent contributions, news items, editorial paragraphs and the like. They did not appear, and when I inquired I was blithely informed that they "probably went on the floor."

I began to be more and more pressed for money. I had been so sure of a job with pay when I left Ann Arbor that I put most of the money I had left into new clothes and the like, leaving only enough to get well started in Chicago. I was also horribly discouraged by a paragraph I saw in Eugene Field's column, "Sharps and Flats," which was then one of the notable features of the paper. Here it is in part:

Chicago

"Some time ago we took occasion to warn newspaper writers against the folly of coming to Chicago in the hope of finding employment here. We regret that the warning has been neglected by very many. This city has been overrun for several months by reporters (both men and women) vainly seeking work. The Chicago newspapers have for two years been getting ready for the World's Fair season, and their several departments are filled with competent men. Therefore others who come to Chicago now in the expectation of securing employment are bound to be disappointed; there are no places to be had; in every newspaper office at the present time applicants are standing about twelve deep in the outer chamber, with never so much as the prospect of a possibility to encourage them. Many of these people are suffering from want of money; they left employment elsewhere to rush to this city of the World's Fair, where they fancied their services would be snapped at. Most of these unfortunates will have to walk out of town or take to driving street cars for a means of subsistence."

This warning depressed me. I could see with my own eyes that it was true. Was I one of the unfortunates that would have to "walk out of town" or drive a street car? I must have let fall something of my disappointment in a letter to my father. I knew well that he did not approve of my venture in Chicago—what had it to do with my law-studies?—and I knew that if I asked him for help he would suggest that I come home at once. But he did believe that it was good for the "bantling" to be "cast on the rock." "Admit nothing to be a hardship!" His prompt response was characteristic:

". . . You have got what I knew you would get—a *hard job!* When the boys get onto the colts and they commence 'bucking' and I can see daylight between the boy's seat and

the colt's back, I yell 'Hang on!' 'Hang on!!' 'Stick to him!!'
. . . Make your own application——"

Here spoke the old soldier I knew and loved: it was
exactly what he himself would do if he were put to it.

Hang on! Stick to it!

So I continued to sit in the city room. It was not all gloom
by any means, even if I wasn't earning enough to pay my
room-rent. Everything I saw and heard was fascinating. I
was beginning to get a little acquainted: no one knew the
worshipful interest with which I watched what the various
heroes of the office were doing. I asked all the questions I
dared, and several times I went out to fires and on other
assignments with the older men, eager to help them, still
more eager to watch what they did and how they did it: and
the next morning I read their reports critically and compared them with the reports in other Chicago newspapers.

We had then a remarkably able group of newspaper writers in Chicago, both reportorial and editorial. I have already
mentioned three among the many on our own paper: Ade
and McDowell and Field. Peter Dunne, who became famous
as the author of "Mr. Dooley," was beginning to be a real
figure; and there were Brand Whitlock, afterward a successful novelist, mayor of Toledo, and Minister to Belgium during the World War; Frank A. Vanderlip who became a
great figure in Wall Street; John McCutcheon, the cartoon-
ist, Henry M. Hyde, Will Payne, "Dick" Little, Forrest Cris-
sey, Hugh Fullerton and many others who gave a good account of themselves in later years.

The most famous of them all, at that time, was, of course,
Eugene Field. He was the man, above any other, I most

Chicago

wanted to see, and if fate was kind, to meet and know. I had read his column avidly, and could quote some of his humorous verse. He had a little box of an office down the hall, but it was a week or more after my arrival before I caught sight of him. I heard him first: the slap, slap, slap of his heel-less slippers as he came down the corridor. When he appeared around the corner I was positively startled, he was so little what I expected. A rather tall, ungainly, solemn-looking man, almost bald, with a long neck, wearing a striped woolen coat such as a lumberman may have had. A few days later I saw him again, this time in his little cubby of an office, sitting on the small of his back with his feet hitched high up on the wall and a writing-board on his knees. It was thus that he liked to sit while he wrote in his beautiful clear script, sometimes with illuminated initials, the verses and paragraphs for his "Sharps and Flats." I remember seeing the hole he had worn in the plaster of the ancient building where his feet had rested. Some time later Mr. Lawson, the publisher, began making extensive repairs, among which were high wainscotings around all of the editorial rooms. These were of yellow pine, varnished and slippery. Field's feet would no longer stick when he put them up and began his day's work. Accordingly he brought down a pair of old slippers with dependable heels and nailed them just at the right height to the beautiful new wall. He could slip his feet into them and work again in comfort. I must confess that I myself never saw the famous slippers on the wall, but it was a story currently told, and since it would have been entirely characteristic of the man, I quite believe it. Field was a character, a person, a book lover, a hard-boiled practical joker, a comic actor, a soft-hearted lover of children. Much as I should have liked it, I never came to know him more than casually. He was the bright particular star in our editorial firmament, when I was the dimmest of asteroids. Moreover, he was then passing the zenith of his powers and his health was wretched. Two or three years later I attended his funeral, and felt proud of being entrusted with the writing of the memorial article for *The Record*.

There were other activities that somewhat relieved the tedium of sitting in the city room. When I was sure that there would be nothing for me to do in the evening I sometimes went to the theatre which I intensely enjoyed. I sat always in the top gallery where the seats were the cheapest: and I am ready now to take up the cudgels with any man to defend my conviction that the gallery is really the best of all places to see most plays. Illusion is the secret of dramatic art, and where is the illusion more perfect than it is in the dim, misty reaches of the topmost gallery? I can make a case for it from experience!

When my money began to run dangerously low I had to give up even the galleries; but I soon discovered a scarcely less delightful diversion, known to many an old bookman, wholly new to me. This was the acquaintance I made with the second-hand book-shops of Chicago. It was interesting, and it had the further advantage of costing nothing—except once, as I shall relate. I had been brought up on books and I loved to stand at the shelves and look into this and that, some new, some old, and when I liked the flavor, to stay on for the banquet—if the keeper did not close his shop and turn me out. My adventures in this delightful field would make a

Chicago

chapter in itself—but I must confine myself to the one great day of my memory, my supreme experience in a Chicago book-shop.

Book-shops thrive on wintry weather—with the rain and the wind and slush in the streets—for then the devotee may creep in where it is warm and dry, and find himself soon a traveller in Arcadia or lost on Parnassus.

But this, my particular visit, was in July, warm summer weather, when even bookworms love a touch of the sun. I remember the shop was all but deserted when I, standing there all unknowing by the populous shelves, reached up and took down Walt Whitman's *Leaves of Grass*. I had heard of it before. An upper-classman in college had brought it to my room, with a smirk of unholy joy on his face, a book he said he wanted to show me—I was for throwing it out of the window——

I opened *Leaves of Grass* as I stood there by the quiet dusty shelves on that summer day in Chicago, and I came upon the poem entitled: "Whoever you are, holding me now by the hand." I shall not forget the moment of that reading in the stuffy shop with the sun coming in at the dirty window, nor the very smell of the old cased books, nor the drone of two Jews talking somewhere in the back of the shop.

"O despairer, here is my neck;
By God! you shall not go down! Hang your whole weight upon me."

I had a strange impression, such as one may have once or twice in his life, if he is fortunate, but only with the greatest books, I had the impression of the writer actually speaking in person: a great, calm, brave, wise presence. I could *feel* him; and I had suddenly a sense that I had done him an injustice, that it was I who had misunderstood——

I turned a page or so and read, "Are you the new person drawn toward me?" with such a sense of directness of contact as I have rarely had with any writer whatsoever. So I stood reading and reading, forgetful of time and space, and want of money and want of work, thinking only of the great joy of having found a new and potent friend in my small world.

Some of the pages of that edition of the book were uncut and, in my absorption and impatience, I drew out my knife and began to cut them—a wholly unpardonable sin in any book-shop. A touch on my shoulder recalled me to reality: the owner of the shop was protesting.

"Oh, I'll take the book," I said and so stood, still reading, until he closed the shop. I paid for it half a week's wages— which I owed to my landlady. It was one of the best investments ever I made.

I also followed one of my other enthusiasms, that for taking long tramps, especially in spring weather, explorations in every part of that great city, all so new and wonderful to me. It was thus that I made my first acquaintance with mean streets, unemployed labor, and the tragedy of "accepted poverty," as I heard Jane Addams once call it—but of all that I shall speak later. It made a deep impression upon me, and in some measure influenced my entire attitude toward life.

One night after I reached my lodgings in North State Street I counted up my money, all I had left. It amounted to sixty-five cents. What should I do? Already I was behind on my rent, and the slatternly landlady was beginning to look threatening. I could save carfare by walking to the office, as I had, indeed, been doing, but where was my food to come from?

On my way out to breakfast the next morning I came across Alexson sitting on the steps. He was a careless, gay, offhand young fellow who lived on a small allowance sent him monthly by an uncle. He pretended to be studying art.

"Baker," he said, "come now, loan me a quarter. I haven't a cent left to get breakfast. You'll get it back. My remittance comes next week."

I explained my own predicament; I already knew that his allowances were spent before he got them.

"I know a place," said he, "where we can get a real fill-up for fifteen cents."

It was a little Swedish restaurant in Division Street; we really got the "fill-up," and I paid for it.

"Alexson," I said, "how does it feel not to know where your breakfast is coming from in the morning?"

"Baker," he said, "you don't know what life is until you have had that experience, and have had it every day for a week or so."

I began to think I was myself about to learn what life was! I knew that something radical must be done. It was well enough to "hang on" and "stick to it," but one had to have at least one good meal a day, and manage to avoid being turned out by an irate landlady. I thought of Eugene Field's warning: was it time for me to get a job as a street-car driver?

☆ 31 ☆

Pawn Shops and Potato Salad

WHILE my discovery that I had actually reached the point of not knowing where my next meal was coming from considerably startled me, I do not remember of being in the least frightened, or even anxious. My feeling, I think, was one of astonished incredulity. *Me*—hungry! *Me*—turned out of my miserable hall bedroom! *Me*—having to "walk out of town," as Eugene Field had prophesied. It was something that simply did not happen outside of story-books, not in America. And here I was facing it.

I knew, of course, that if worse came to worse, I could go home; but when I thought of my father and what he would say—at least what he would think—I knew I could and would stand a considerable degree of starvation before I surrendered. The same applied to my many friends in Michigan who had watched me, so short a time ago, starting off with flying colors, for Chicago. How could I confess defeat?

Curiously enough, it did not seem at all a hardship. Something about it even lifted one's spirits. It was an adventure in hard realities; it aroused everything a man had in him. It was, in short, something to be enjoyed—almost! I even began thinking of writing a story about it, when it was all over.

Pawn Shops and Potato Salad

Having got down to total assets of thirty-five cents, and with little prospect of having much of anything coming to me on payday at the newspaper office, I knew I must do something at once. But what did a man do in such an emergency? Borrow, beg, stand in the soup-line? In recent weeks, since I had been in Chicago, I had seen poor fellows practicing each of these humiliating methods. I dismissed them instantly, and my mind turned at once, and as usual, to what poverty in the old novels, Dickens, say, commonly did. The pawn shop!

I was just then in Clark Street where I had seen such a shop. I paused in front of it, looked both ways, and slipped in through the shaded doors. It was a gloomy place, full of strange commodities, violins, clocks, jewelry, firearms, overcoats (in summer!), books—everything that misery thought it could temporarily dispense with.

I pushed my precious silver watch through the little opening in the grill-work. It was a good one that I had purchased out of my earliest earnings.

"What do you want on it?" asked the surly man behind the grill.

"Ten dollars," I said boldly.

"Huh," he exclaimed contemptuously, pushed it back at me, and turned away without a word.

I was both angry and crushed; I walked a block or two farther down the street and slipped into another pawn shop.

"Vell?" asked an oily-looking old man.

I had learned my lesson. "How much will you let me have on this watch?"

275

He looked it over with a kind of cynical distaste, and seemed on the point of handing it back.

"Two dollars," said he.

I took it at once and walked out with the money and the little yellow ticket he gave me. It was something! It would keep me along for a day or so. That noon I made my first visit to Burcky & Milan's restaurant, then one of the most famous of Chicago's "hash-houses." Here they served a heaping plate of potato salad, a roll, and a cup of coffee, all for ten cents. It was momentarily filling—and that is about all that could be said for it. I even tried eating it twice a day until the odor, to say nothing of the taste, of the purported "olive" oil in the salad became nauseatingly unbearable. For years afterward I could not look at a potato salad with any comfort.

In the midst of this predicament, I found something I could laugh at most heartily. I received a letter from my father, who was suspicious of the city and all its works, earnestly advising me to be sure to hang on to my savings: to avoid wasting them on "unsubstantial amusements." I wished he could have seen my savings, and my principal daily amusement—the potato salad at Burcky & Milan's!

A man out of work, with no money, looked for a paying job, didn't he? That afternoon, when I had made sure that my sitting in the city room would be unproductive, I looked into the want-ads in the early afternoon papers, and after marking several that looked hopeful—just as I had more than once seen the seedy-looking men on the lake-front busily doing—I started out.

If one cares to examine the unvarnished, cold, cruel, hopeless, back-door life of a city, especially at the beginning of a great Fair and a greater Depression, let him try to get a job by answering want-ads. He will get a large and possibly useful dose of reality. If I had not been so densely ignorant of cities and city life I should never have tried it; as it turned out, I was glad I had the experience. There was usually a line, often a long line of men, ahead of me—reaching out into noisome alleys or up dark stairways, ordered about by rough special policemen, cowed by raucous-voiced managers, the men ahead gradually turning away with hopeless resignation. I shall never forget the look of blank defeat on some of the faces I saw on those unhappy mornings. Whenever I got near enough to the "company-hirer" to speak to him at all, I was usually turned off contemptuously with a single glance. I soon found I had almost nothing to sell, in terms of experience or training, that any one wanted to buy. In a few days I learned more about the so-called labor problem in America than I did during all the sessions of Scott's seminars at Ann Arbor, where I had made labor conditions in Chicago, as reported in the newspapers, my especial subject.

I can give only glimpses of this experience: I could write a whole chapter about the technique of the want-ad, and the psychology of its devotees. When my own search proved utterly discouraging, I began to look elsewhere. One morning I read in the newspapers that Doctor Poole, he of *Poole's Index,* who was directing the Newberry Library, then a grand new institution, was about to begin cataloguing several large collections of books that had been recently acquired. I put on my best clothes and went to call on Doctor

Poole. He readily invited me in. He was then an old man, but vigorous-looking, with white hair and widely flowing side-whiskers: a benevolent and distinguished presence.

I presented as good a case for myself as possible, though with fear and trembling, for I had in mind so many recent rebuffs. I explained that I had helped catalogue the books in my college library, and had assisted one spring in lettering the diplomas for the graduating class, this to show him that I knew something of the art of the pen. The old doctor still seemed skeptical.

"What have you read?" he asked me quite unexpectedly. He was a wise old man! There were good reasons why he had become one of the most distinguished of American librarians; he knew that relatively few in his own field were real readers of books: that to a large proportion of them the library was merely a business, or an occupation, not a true profession.

While I knew well that I did not wish to become a librarian, I could tell him truthfully enough of my interest in books, of my father's library, and of my experience in two college libraries. And I wound up with the naïve, but honest, declaration:

"I am a lover of books."

I think this remark helped more than anything else: I saw the amused, interested, tolerant look that came in his eyes. I was very young!

"Well," said he, "talk with Mr. Nelson, and make me a few sample cardings. We'll see what you can do."

I worked hard at it—and went away, after handing in the samples, somewhat encouraged, even though Mr. Nelson told me that it might be some time before he could let me know. Of one thing I felt certain: not many men among the thousands of unemployed in Chicago could catalogue books.

But I couldn't wait! While I was still getting little driblets of money from my work on the paper, they were not enough to keep me alive from day to day. I therefore continued looking for a job where I could begin work at once. I finally went to see a distant relative by marriage of my mother, W. F. VanBergen, then the ticket-auditor of the Northwestern Railroad Company. I did it only after overcoming my fear that the news of my joblessness would get around by way of the family grapevine telegraph to the folks at home. Mr. VanBergen and his wife and several other members of the family, the Ballards, who lived in Oak Park, were most kind to me. How I did appreciate the bountiful Sunday dinners they presently invited me to. They made me homesick!

Mr. VanBergen had a large staff in his employ, but there was, or seemed to be, no chance for me.

"Sometimes they die," he said, "but no one ever resigns."

So I continued to sit in the city room. I continued to look for a job, I ate ten-cent luncheons with utter repugnance, I read my Walt Whitman standing on the chair under my one gas-light, and I managed to keep from being thrown out of my hall bedroom by giving the now angry landlady an occasional dollar. I was near complete hopelessness.

Quite suddenly, one day, the unexpected happened. I had a note from Mr. VanBergen, saying that he had a vacancy in his office and I could have the job if I could report at once. Could I? It almost made me cry. I ran, literally ran, to the Northwestern offices, and went to work the next morning.

I was to have the munificent wage of $40 a month, eight hours a day, with a free luncheon in the railroad-building at noon. The luncheon was a main argument! At the moment I wanted that luncheon more than anything else in the world. And it proved to be good, if almost spartan in its simplicity. Plenty of milk, bread, cold meat, and everything clean: I could really satisfy my hunger.

It was a large room I worked in with thirty or forty clerks at long tables, sitting side by side. In the morning I had a pile of railroad-station returns placed before me—schedules about two feet long and two feet broad with a list of stations along the top and down the side, and entries in ink giving the number of tickets sold and the amounts collected by the station agents. These were to be footed, first down, then across, and made to balance in the lower right-hand corner. It was one of the most wearying, monotonous tasks that ever I had in my life—adding long columns of figures eight hours a day! And being in a great open room, where every one, including the chief clerk and the auditor himself, could see everything that was going on, we soon became fearful of leaving our seats too frequently, let alone stopping to rest or to talk.

I had determined, no matter what kind of temporary job I got, to report every evening, and on Sundays, at the newspaper office on the chance of getting a few assignments. I must not, I felt, lose touch with the editors, however slight it might be. But I soon found that nature was too much for me. Even though I was a youngster of robust health, the long days of confining and wearisome work left me so utterly

Pawn Shops and Potato Salad

worn out that I had to give up for the time being the ritual of "sitting in the city room." I hoped soon to get enough money ahead to enable me to "resign" from the railroad office, even though my friend, the auditor, said no one ever did. He spoke with some authority, for how could the poor, hapless clerks get far enough ahead on $10 to $15 a week to make a change—especially if they happened to have families, as most of them did.

I was soon to have a deep look into some of the individual aspects of that employment. Just across the wide table from me sat a middle-aged man, gray-haired, dull-eyed, who was lame in one leg so that he had to rest heavily upon a cane and walk with a swinging gait. He looked hopelessly weary.

After a few days I saw him watching me furtively. I had tackled my new job, as men did on the frontier, with all my might. It was of the law and the prophets, in my boyhood, that a man was to be judged by the amount of work he could "turn out." He was to "rise," he was to "get ahead"—without making it clear as to what he was to rise to, or of whom he was to get ahead.

One day when we were going to lunch the man with the cane and the swinging gait took me by the arm. He and I had previously exchanged only a few words.

"Young man," he said, "do you want a hint from a clerk who has been a long time in the auditor's office?"

"Why, yes," I said, "I'd appreciate it."

"Well, you're doing too many of them schedules a day."

"What do you mean?" I asked in astonishment. How could a man do too many?

"You're a young fellow, and you've just come into the

281

office. Some of us old ones have been here a long time. We don't do more'n thirty (say thirty, I cannot remember the exact number), and you're already doing (say) thirty-five, and one day you did (say) forty. You're doing more'n you ought to."

"Do you mean," I asked, "that a man should do less than he can?"

"Don't you see," he said, sharply, "if you and a few of the younger fellows begin to raise the tally, it'll just put some of us old fellows out of a job. They'll fire us: that's what they'll do: they'll fire us."

I turned to look at him: there was a blaze in his dull eyes, and he spoke with a stress of passion I could not then understand.

"You don't know what that means, do you? You haven't got a wife and children. I have, and I'm trying to support 'em. What could I do if they turned me out: what could my family do?"

I was completely bowled over. I had never before heard this argument put forth. I was to hear it enough times later! But my own experiences since coming to Chicago, trying to get a job, gave it a meaning I could a little understand.

I made a hasty and foolish response: "Why don't you organize?" This was what thousands of workers everywhere, especially in Chicago, were just then doing. It was in the air.

"Organize!" This time there was positive anger in his voice. "Organize! Do you want to get us all fired? With 50,000 unemployed men in Chicago, ready to jump into our places!"

There was something both beseeching and menacing in his voice when we parted:

"Take my advice, young fellow. Don't do too many of them schedules."

This problem stirred me deeply. I was faced with a personal situation that had never even occurred to me before. If it had been merely my work in the railroad office that had been called in question, it would have been a minor matter, since I was determined to get out of it at the earliest opportunity; but the attitude of my fellow-workers, and the meanings I saw dimly behind it, struck with force at some of the deepest principles I had learned there on the frontier, chiefly from my father. He would have called them the "essential moral plan" that lay beneath individual success in life. Taken in connection with my own bitter recent experiences in trying to get a job that would keep me alive, I was completely mystified. What was I to do? What did it all mean?

A day or so later, again on the way to luncheon, I got the opportunity of putting up the problem, in part, to another clerk with whom, fortunately, I had become acquainted. This was Stoughton Cooley. I had been warmly attracted to him from the first. He was then a cripple, walking with crutches, but there was something so smilingly sincere in his face, and he had such gentle courtesy of manner, that we soon became friends—and continued friends for forty years, until his death. I have known few men more unselfishly devoted to the cause of the good life, or who worked harder to bring it about, than he.

I poured out my little story, I think over-impetuously, winding up with the question:

283

"How many schedules should a man do in this office?"

He looked at me smilingly. "If I could answer that question, with all its implications," he said, "I'd be solving the whole social problem."

He paused a moment.

"What do you say! Let's talk about it."

"I'd be more than glad to," I replied earnestly.

With that he invited me out to his little home in Maywood (he could live cheaply in Maywood because he worked for the railroad and could get a pass) and we spent the evening discussing the problems of creation, as exemplified in a small corner of a great railroad office. I met his wife and two delightful little girls. They had a garden and a hive or so of honey bees: and the way they lived, the simplicity and the beauty of it, making no complaints about low wages and hard conditions, made a strong impression upon me. Here, I knew, there was something precious.

Cooley, I soon found, was an ardent single-taxer. It was his religion: it explained all the difficulties of the present age: it gave hope for a perfect, or nearly perfect, future world—if one had faith. Cooley had that faith: it was what I had seen in his eyes when I first met him. He was already writing articles on his favorite subject for *The Chicago Daily News* and sometimes getting them published. He was later to become an associate of Louis F. Post and Mrs. Post, in editing *The Public,* which for years was the most interesting, if not the most important, single-tax journal in the country.

I had been slightly interested in Henry George and his ideas for some time, having read parts of *Progress and Poverty* when I was in college—a book that I knew was anathema to my father, who was himself a large landowner, and who represented the owners of many great tracts in northern Wisconsin. Cooley invited me to go with him to the Chicago Single Tax Club where I began to hear discussions of all the problems I had been dimly struggling with. Some of the addresses and debates were most able, for there were at that time no better prepared or more reasonable reformers in the country than the single-taxers. And yet, such was the turmoil of controversy in the country at that time—the ground swell of the coming depression and echoes of the populist and free-silver movements in the West—that there was often a "lunatic fringe" even in these meetings. One night, I remember, a wild-looking man began speaking in the back of the crowded room. We all turned to look. He was almost inarticulate in his vehemence.

"Who is he?" I asked Cooley.

"His name is Prendergast," he replied, "we can't keep him out."

The next year that man assassinated the mayor of Chicago, Carter H. Harrison. Some time later I saw him hanged.

While I was intensely interested in the work these men were doing, and I could admire and even envy the all but religious devotion of many of them to the teachings of Henry George, I did not join their society. I remember copying in my notebook a passage from Henry George that seemed to me to set forth a great truth: "To educate men who must be condemned to poverty, is but to make them restive; to base on a state of most glaring social inequality political institutions under which men are theoretically equal, is to stand a pyramid on its apex." This, I felt, was good diagnosis, but would the remedy Henry George offered really cure the disease?

I felt that I did not yet know enough to be sure. I wanted, almost passionately, to understand, but I had already found that the more I understood of the myriad problems I saw, the less I felt like accepting any one solution and trying to strait-jacket the world into an acceptance of it. I can see now, sometimes a little sadly, that this was to become the pattern of my life. I should have been glad to preach with the prophets and suffer with the martyrs: but I was destined all my life, when I saw a thing that seemed true, to look around another corner. I have found life boundlessly fascinating; I have never yet been able to "solve" it. I was never quite converted to anything: I never joined.

With all this, and the long tramps I took on Sundays or in the long summer evenings, I became more and more deeply interested in labor and social problems. I not only liked to walk, especially to explore every part of the exciting city of Chicago, but it gave me a chance to see the streets of the "permanent-poor" of the west and south sides of the city. It may seem strange—it seems strange to me in the after-look—that I should have found poverty so arresting. I think it was because I had never before in my life seen any real poverty.

We had plenty of people on the frontier who were poor, and who often looked poor, with their rough clothing and unshaven chins, but they would never have thought of themselves as problems or admitted being poverty-stricken. For they were full of hope: whatever privations the present held, the future glowed with promise. Land was to be had almost for the asking, logs were at hand for their houses, all the streams were full of fish, and all the hills full of game, with no game-laws yet in force. There was everywhere plenty of work, building roads and dams, cutting down the vast forests, plowing up the virgin soil. All they needed were willing hands: and willing hands they had. Almost the only idle or unemployed men I knew as a boy—and even they were not wholly unemployed—were a few more or less broken-down veterans of the Civil War who lived on pensions from the government.

In short, we of the frontier did not recognize poverty. Once, as a small boy, I heard an animated discussion among several good ladies (including one of my old aunts) as to how to get rid of several Christmas baskets that one of the newcomers in town—an uneducated newcomer!—had insisted upon providing for the "poor." What poor? And what would happen if one dared to distribute baskets?

Years afterward I tried to put into a story a Mrs. "Penny" Daniels (though this was not her real name) who performed a most important function in one small pioneer community I knew. Almost alone and unaided she was the poor whom we were supposed to have always with us! She was a rather jovial soul, but on occasions such as Thanksgiving and Christmas she could curb her natural outpourings, and look as deserving of charity as any person ever I knew. If it had not been for Mrs. Daniels' devoted faithfulness, our Ladies' Aid Society might have perished miserably of undistributed turkeys and pumpkin pie. We always pitied the little Daniels —poverty comes hard on the children—because, after every holiday they always wore a painfully stuffed and suffocated look, but we could appreciate warmly what a self-sacrificing public servant Mrs. "Penny" Daniels always was.

What I found in Chicago, or seemed to find, was a cheapening of human beings. The great teaching of my youth on the frontier had been the incomparable preciousness, the value, of a man: of a personality. *One soul.* It was the teaching of the religion of my youth ("the lost sheep"), it was inherent in everything I saw and heard. But in Chicago the man seemed lost: I myself felt lost. One became a part of the crowd; there was no anxious family looking on, no real neighbors. This, at least, was my powerful early impression, somewhat corrected later, against which I fought in vain. The miserable living conditions, the long hours, the low wages, the universal insecurity, tended to tear down the personality, cheapen the man.

But life on the frontier was never cheap—though the romanticists have sometimes tried to make it seem so. It was too precious; it was to be preserved. Life was good, not doubtful: no one was "tired of life." While it was rough, and often dangerous: while men suffered and struggled, they also hoped.

I soon discovered Hull House where that saint of the slums, Jane Addams, was beginning to widen her remarkable sphere of influence. There was something about Miss Addams herself, whom I came presently to know, and about her work, which seemed to me infinitely helpful. She was not preaching a doctrine: she was living a life. By making new understandings there among the people who were the poorest and most crowded of any in the great city, she seemed to be pioneering toward a new method of living together in a crowded world. I often stopped in at Hull House meetings and later, when I began to find my own place, I wrote many little paragraphs and articles about Miss Addams and her work.

In the meantime, while I was finding life daily more interesting, I seemed to be getting nowhere in my chosen work. I was earning scarcely enough to support me; my ambition seemed blocked at every turn. Probably Eugene Field was right—and there really was no place for me in Chicago.

One evening, coming home tired from the wretched struggle with the railroad schedules, I found on the hall desk in the rooming house a letter with the address of the Newberry Library in the corner of the envelope. I seized it eagerly: the world changed for me before I could even open it. Doctor Poole asked me to "drop in some day soon."

I dropped in at the earliest moment on the next day. They could use me if we could "make it a test on both sides." While I could see that they were uncertain as to my usefulness as a cataloguer, this tentative arrangement suited me exactly. I asked if they would let me work, at least for a time, only in the forenoons—thus allowing me to try again for assignments at *The News Record*. To this they readily agreed, and I immediately resigned from the railroad job— though I never resigned from Stoughton Cooley.

After my experience in footing schedules during endless days, it was a delightful change into quite another world— leisurely, easy-going, and interesting. I met fine and charming people—and no one of them wanted me to do less than I could! I had always liked to look into strange books, and this was an unlimited field. At first I had a shelf full of miscellaneous volumes, and then, one day, I was given a great pile of volumes dealing with the life and times of Horace Walpole. I had read little or nothing of Walpole and this gave me a wonderful opportunity for making his acquaintance.

It is true I did not make much money—not as much as I did at the railroad office—but I worked only half a day, and I hoped I could add enough from my newspaper work to keep going.

☆ 32 ☆

I Get My Chance

IT WAS so that I began again to "sit in the city room"; but it was with a somewhat different point of view and a far more confident interest. I was better acquainted with the men in the office, and I had become much more familiar with the city itself, in part due to the long tramps I was taking. I read the newspapers devotedly, noting what was going on, and becoming familiar with the names, at least, of the prominent men of Chicago, whether politicians like Carter Harrison, or great merchants like Marshall Field, or natural-born boss saloon-keepers like "Bath-House John," or "Hinky Dink." On Sundays I went to hear eloquent preachers like the Reverend Frank W. Gunsaulus, whose oratory one morning on the subject "If I Had a Million Dollars" so interested Philip D. Armour, the great beef-baron, that he went up afterward and said:

"Doctor Gunsaulus, if you will give five years of your life, I will give that million."

Gunsaulus immediately agreed, and built the Armour Institute, which became a famous industrial and technical school. Chicago, in those days, was like that. It had its magic!

I had also begun to turn in "pick-up" stories, glimpses, street scenes, common little incidents of the daily life of a great city, which could be treated more or less lightly or humorously. To my surprise, I found that these unpretentious sketches were in considerable demand in the office and sometimes made the first page. I was much set up one day when Mr. Yount saw me in the city room and said:

"Baker, take a turn around and see if you can't find a few pick-ups to lighten up the paper. It looks like a dull Sunday."

It was exactly what I liked best to do—looking at human beings and discovering the many surprising things they were doing and thinking. I found that one of the good hunting-grounds was the railroad stations of the city, where there was always movement and color—men and women going somewhere. Of all the cities in America, there was never, I think, a more interesting crossroads for travelling humanity than Chicago.

One morning, scouting in the Grand Central station, I happened to see in the waiting room a quiet, dark-eyed woman in no way remarkable except for the large bundle on the seat beside her. This was covered with heavy paper and firmly tied with string. She had evidently come a long distance, and the paper was torn so that a furry tail, or what looked like a tail, stuck out of it. This was enough for me. I sat down beside her, and we were presently talking most amiably. This was easy and natural for me to do: it was the friendly way of the frontier. I soon discovered that she was from Humboldt County in northern California and that the paper-covered package contained three beautiful wild-cat skins, which she presently opened to show me.

What surprised me most was that she herself had shot the animals. She gave me the most delightful account of her life in the West: and I had only to ask a new question to get a new story. I went back to the office full of it, and wrote with keen delight. The "story" made three-quarters of a column in the paper the next morning. Here was the headline:

SHOT MANY WILDCATS

HOW A BRAVE LADY USED A GUN

Mrs. L. W. Hower, on Her Way from the Woolly West, Talks of Her Adventures in California—Riding a Broncho— Killing Beasts

---

"Full of the fearless western spirit of independence, Mrs. Hower travels unaccompanied except for the bundle of wild-cat skins and the motherly canvas bag. It is the first time she has been east since as a bride she followed her husband over the prairies of the west and settled with him in a lonely little cabin among the redwoods of northern California. . . .

"Her stories of her adventures sound like passages from some exciting romance. They all begin with the little cabin which her husband built as soon as his wife arrived. In those days, the forests were full of wolves and wildcats, to say nothing of deer and antelope. Sometimes in the winter a huge grizzly bear or wildcat, driven out of the mountain by hunger, would prowl around their cabin trying to steal a stray sheep. Mr. Hower was away a great part of the time and his wife soon became an expert with the rifle.

"There would be a commotion in the flock of sheep browsing near the house. Mrs. Hower knew in a moment that a wildcat had been skulking down. Dropping her sewing, she would seize her rifle, vault upon the broncho standing always saddled near the door, and dash up the rocky road. The bleating of the sheep would guide her. Presently there would be a glimpse of a dark object bounding heavily from crag to crag under the weight of a live lamb. The broncho would be brought to a sudden standstill. A rifle deliberately leveled, a quick report, and the dark marauder would fall back with a snarl of pain."

I will not reprint more of it. It is a sufficient sample of the kind of "pick-up" that helped me to find a place in the newspaper office. However tinged with the newspaper jargon of the time, the editors liked it.

Although I was still a "sitter," not a member of the staff, with a microscopic income, I was beginning really to enjoy myself, and to feel that sooner or later my chance would come.

It did come at last, one dull afternoon which promised at first nothing important. It seemed, afterward, like sheer chance.

As usual all the "regular" men had gone out promptly after one o'clock on their assignments. As it happened, and it did not happen often, I was the only man left in the city room.

I saw the city editor look in at the door.

"Where's McDermott?" he asked.

McDermott was the reporter who "did" labor. He had already gone out.

The city editor finally motioned to me. It was as plain as though he had told me aloud that I was a regrettable last resort.

"Baker," he said, "some of the waiters at the Blank restaurant (I have forgotten the name) in Monroe Street have struck. It probably doesn't mean much, but go over and look at it. Come in early."

I went as fast as my legs could carry me. Sure enough, a considerable crowd was gathered around the Blank restaurant. Men were rushing up out of the basement entrance: there were shouts of "Come on out, waiters, come out." A cook in a white apron with a large spoon in his hands was standing on the top step; two policemen were hurrying down from State Street. Many people were still at the tables, with their luncheons only ordered or partly served. I found the proprietor rushing about in the wildest excitement, crying out in anguish:

"They've struck on me: they've struck on me."

I talked with the amazed and angry customers. I found the leader of the strikers, a lively, black-eyed little fellow, with curly hair, behaving like Napoleon Bonaparte. It was confusing, but interesting and exciting.

Presently the strikers began moving down the street, shouting, "Pull out Smith's: pull out Smith's."

I marched with them, as near to Napoleon Bonaparte as I could manage. At Smith's, more excitement, much shouting, all the waiters tumbling out, some still in their aprons, many lunchers angry and hungry. Policemen, crowds!

This continued most of the afternoon, winding up finally with a grand meeting and much oratory at the dingy union hall, up a long flight of stairs, in Lake Street.

Nothing could possibly have been more fortunate, or more interesting to me. Labor problems, labor unionism, labor leadership, as they existed in Chicago, had been the subject I had chosen, as I have already related, for Scott's seminar at Ann Arbor. I was well grounded, after weeks of reading the newspapers and hearing the discussions at the Single Tax Club and elsewhere, in the fundamentals of the Chicago situation. I knew many of the leaders by name and one or two I had met. Here was an actual demonstration, before my delighted eyes, of what really happened at a strike, what the men themselves did, how they looked, what they said, how the employers reacted, and not least important, the activities of the police—always a controversial matter. There was also the important attitude of public opinion, as expressed by the hungry customers, and the gaping or cheering or laughing crowds outside the restaurants.

I was so much fascinated that I kept delaying my return to the office. When I did get in I was greeted with gruff impatience:

"Why didn't you report earlier?"

The afternoon newspapers, then on the streets, had played up the strike: it appeared to be the news of the day. I was full of the story, but when I tried to describe what I had found, I was met with the chilling order to "turn it over to McDermott."

"He'll write the lead."

I was crushed. Here was my chance, and I was to be cheated out of it! I don't remember exactly what I said, but I was angry. I remarked that I had been sitting around the office for months; now for the first time I had a really good "story."

"It's early yet," I argued. "Let me write it. If you don't like what I turn in, there'll be time enough for McDermott to do it."

I Get My Chance

The city editor was plainly irritated, but he finally said grudgingly,

"Well, go ahead."

I was also wonderfully well treated by McDermott: he remarked, generously,

"Go ahead. You've got the story."

One of the greatest moments in the life of a newspaper man is when he sits down, late, at his desk in the noisy city room with the consciousness that he has the most important or interesting "story" of the day. At that time there were no such things as typewriters in editorial offices: we wrote on pads of soft paper with number two pencils, turning out the copy swiftly page by page and throwing it aside, to be picked up by watchful office boys, and hurried in to the night copy-readers. In few other occupations is there a greater stress of intense labor, or more joy of complete fulfillment.

One precious moment of that night, after I had been writing furiously for an hour or so, I shall never forget as long as I live. I saw Armstrong, the assistant night editor, coming in. He was a stocky, rather grim, slow-spoken man. His sleeves were rolled up and he had a green reading shade over his eyes. I don't think we had ever, since I had been around the office, exchanged a dozen words.

"Great stuff, Baker," he said, "great stuff."

I've had fine things said to me: never a finer than that. How I did need it, and what a thrill it gave me! I knew well, also, that it was not lightly said: few men I know are less given to flattery than newspaper men.

I found my "story" on the first page the next morning with wide headlines. When I reached the office I was one of the first to get my assignment.

"Better go on with those strikers," said the city editor.

I will not enlarge upon the days that followed. I wrote many columns regarding the strike and all its implications, I interviewed the leaders, I put in as many amusing sidelights as I could gather.

At the end of the week when I "pasted up" my "string," I had a roll so big that I could not get it into my pocket, and felt embarrassed to carry it in my hand.

".Well!" exclaimed Miss Dewey, the cashier, when I placed it somewhat hesitatingly on her desk.

This time she got down her yard-stick, instead of the foot-rule which she had always used before. That yard-stick was as good as a diploma or a medal. When I left her desk I had something over forty dollars in my pocket. All earned in one week!

Well, I paid off my landlady—to her joyous amazement—I redeemed my watch, I got my hair cut, and to make sure of the immediate future I bought a meal-ticket at King's restaurant—and had money in my pocket when I next went to the office. Never before or since in my life have I felt so genuinely rich.

I set down these monetary details without compunction or apology. They are not trivial or unimportant: they were of the essence of my life at that time. The redoubtable Micawber of *David Copperfield* long ago feelingly described the importance of being on the right side of the bread-line. I had now made the discovery on my own account. I had been on the wrong side. I was now, for a glorious moment, on the right side. I would not willingly, for anything I know, forget the understanding, the *feeling* of that experience, common enough then and still more common since to a large part of the human race. It was true, as my quondam friend of the rooming house had said:

"You don't know what life is until you wake up every morning for a week or so and find you haven't money enough to buy your breakfast."

It's a noble experiment—if it doesn't go too far!

A day or so afterward I found a note in my box at the office:

"Please come in and see me. C. H. Dennis."

Charles H. Dennis was the managing editor of *The News Record,* and one of the ablest men ever to sit in a Chicago newspaper office. He was the editor of Mr. Lawson's morning paper, *The Record,* afterward of *The Chicago Daily News,* for more than fifty years. I treasure many years of friendship with him.

At that time I had never met him or spoken to him. Who was I that I should? I had seen him in his little office, bent low over his desk, as was his custom—working harder than any man on his staff. His note somewhat alarmed me. What did he want? I knew I must have become something of a nuisance sitting in the city room so long and so persistently. What did he mean to do?

When I went in, he shook hands with me.

"Pretty good work you're doing," he said.

I must have stammered some response.

"You had quite a string last week."

"Yes," I said guiltily.

"Maybe you'd like to come permanently with us on the staff," he said.

Would I? Would I?

"Well," said he, "we'll put you on salary beginning this week."

I went out with my head in the clouds. I resigned immediately from the Newberry Library and Horace Walpole, and awaited, anxiously, the coming payday at the newspaper office. There had been no indication as to what I was to receive. I had no idea as to what a "beginner's salary" might be, but since I had earned over forty dollars the week before, it couldn't be less than twenty-five dollars—and I was already planning what I should do with such a prodigious income.

When Miss Dewey handed me my envelope on Saturday —no more yard-sticks for me!—she said:

"I'm glad you're coming with us permanently."

As soon as I got around the corner I opened the envelope with eager fingers. It contained twelve dollars.

That was newspaper work in Chicago in the roaring days of the World's Fair! But I was so greatly rejoiced in being recognized, and in finding at last a permanent place, that it bothered me not at all. I could live on twelve dollars a week.

Now that I was really on the staff I had no more "sitting" to do. It was a hard-working office, and if salaries were low, they had to be earned. I did anything and everything that came in sight, except politics. It being an election year, Cleveland versus Harrison, with Illinois a doubtful state, there was a great body of political news every day, but all of this work went to experienced men who knew the politicians and the candidates, and understood the inner workings of the machines and the bosses. In after years I became

deeply interested in the political scene, but in those early
months I did fires and murders and robberies and sermons
and lectures and banquets and obituaries. I wrote about
champion watermelons, and sad tales of the orphans' court,
and golden weddings; about an elephant that escaped from
a circus, and an elopement in high life, and a banquet for
the "four hundred" among the dogs of Chicago.

To some of the older men in the office such assignments
would, I know, have been boresome. Many newspaper men
tend to become cynical, to look upon life, or pretend to, with
an incurable sang-froid, and regard a show of excitement
or hot interest as the sure mark of the amateur. Some of the
best of them presently, when they begin to look at life slowly
and deeply, pass through this more or less sophomoric period
and begin to count as real writers. I remember a remark that
Mr. Dennis once made to me:

"It is not superficial or noisy action that really makes the
best news: it is the meaning that underlies the suffering or
the happiness of everyday life."

As for me in those early days, amateur or not, I was passionately interested. I had come out of the frontier: I had
known nothing of cities: all this was new to me. It was one
of the most absorbing periods of my whole life. Excited? Of
course I was excited, even if I did try to hold my tongue in
the city room.

I had a wonderful feeling of not being dependent for my
knowledge of what happened upon hearsay, or upon specu-
lation, but by actual contact. The sense of being taken into
the event is surely one of the greatest lures of journalism: the
satisfaction of the appetite for knowing life at first-hand.

Native American

Another thing I soon noted: my own strange detachment even under the most horrifying or shocking circumstances. I remember going out to the crowded Milwaukee Avenue district to report an unusually brutal murder. I had never before had an important murder story. I saw everything, heard everything, smelled everything, eagerly storing up my impressions for my report. I did not need to make notes: I could not have forgotten a single fact. I looked at the horror of the wounds: I saw the wrecked rooms and the blood spots on the floor: I talked with the weeping women: I noted the cold objectivity of the police. I did not feel shocked, but vividly interested. I did not think of it as a crime to be punished, a wrong to be righted, a tragedy to be wept over. It was an event to be intensely seen and immediately written about. I rushed afterward to the office and wrote my report —columns of it—without as I remember any emotion or repugnance. I remember beginning the narrative quietly, descriptively, as one might write fiction. I had had hot discussions in the office with seasoned reporters who asserted that an important story should begin with a sharp, brief statement of the main facts—names, places, dates. And this was, indeed, more or less the office practice. "But," I had argued, "that is the job of the headliners. They've already put the startling facts in big type. Why repeat them in small type?" Moreover it seemed to me that the imaginative perception of the event was enhanced by approaching it calmly, quietly, as men commonly approach the unexpected and unusual.

I took the chances, and wrote the story as I wanted to, knowing that the copy-readers might recast it. But they printed my "lead" just as I wrote it:

302

I Get My Chance

"No one could ask for a quieter place than North Paulina Street of an ordinary Sunday morning. The trim wooden homes of the workingmen stand in crowded rows, with a few shops and stores sprinkled between. An occasional spire with a gilded cross rises out of the monotony of well-to-do homes. The Bethlehem Evangelical Lutheran church is one of the larger structures on the plain thoroughfare. It stands near the McReynolds Avenue corner, in the thick of the German settlement.

"Across from the church is a homely little two-story place with the number 723 on the transom. The roof is low and peaked. There are cheap curtains in the windows. A short flight of steps leads from the street to the front door. This house is like many another in the humble block.

"Until yesterday the people who lived there were not known more than six doors away. They were hard-working Germans who persevered and saved and kept themselves out of the world. Herman Siegler was a wood-carver with a frugal wife, a stout youngster of a boy, and two little girls. The wife's parents, Henry Sietz and his wife, lived in the same house. Henry was a decrepit old German, and his wife was a withered matron with wrinkles and gray hair. The people who lived on either side of 723 heard and saw nothing to indicate that the household was not contented and happy.

"Yesterday morning the little two-story building became a slaughter pen."

And so on and so on for several columns! Afterward, at two or three o'clock in the morning, I went home and to bed. I could not have slept more than an hour or two when I found myself sitting up, trembling, hot and cold.

"I didn't get that story! I didn't get that story," I was saying aloud, over and over again.

Native American

It seemed to me, for the first time, that I realized this for what it was—a *murder*. All the gruesome bloody incidents flooded back into my mind. I began to see, and above all to *feel*, the crime in its true meaning. The horror of it! It began to spread out in all directions, backward into the youth of the murdered man (why hadn't I tried to look more deeply into that?). Was it due to a twisted youth or a bitter upbringing (why hadn't I looked into that?)? Was it an unhappy marriage (why not that?)? Was it money? Work? Or was it, possibly, the result of years of the attrition of hostility, jealousy, suspicion? I could see how it must affect a wide circle of other human beings, not only the wife and daughters, who now began to awaken my sympathy, but relatives and friends far remote, even to unborn children.

If one could really understand a murder, all of it, down to the roots and responsibilities! Could any reporter, working under high pressure for immediate publication, ever do it?

I can here report only haltingly and imperfectly the intensity of my revulsion of feeling or the rushing torrent of my thoughts. I could not explain it at the time, but it was there, a problem to consider.

Again and again in after months and years this experience repeated itself. I could see and hear and smell with extraordinary clarity at the time. I could remember. I could report. But I seemed at the moment to have no real pity or sympathy; I could not feel deeply, or suffer, or enjoy, until afterward.

One other element in my early experiences on the newspaper—although they were far from being the most important, as I shall show presently—gave me a great deal of pleasure. I had an all but passionate, even somewhat ridiculous, interest in seeing and hearing and, if possible, talking with more or less noted people, especially writers whose books I had read. It was probably due in part to the fact that my boyhood on the frontier had been starved in this respect. For some reason the city editor had discovered this liking, and I was sent out, that first winter, to attend many lectures and dinners, and to interview various "visiting celebrities." Such a variety there were of them; and although few were important from the news point of view, I was quite content to cut down my reports to a "stick or two" in order to see and hear them.

I have already related my boyhood interest in the Hindu doctrine of re-incarnation of souls, and here I was sent out to meet and to report on an address by Annie Besant, the most important leader of the modern theosophical movement. I enjoyed the experience, without being any more of a convert than I was before.

Two speakers on the problem of the Negro in America attracted me greatly. I had been brought up on the woes of slavery and the struggle to abolish it. My father, an officer in the Northern army, always spoke of the Civil War as a holy crusade to "abolish the greatest evil known to man." His family had been a link in the "underground railroad" in western New York, and two of my great-aunts had been among the earliest volunteers to teach in the freedmen's schools in the South. Frederick Douglass, the first great American Negro leader, had been often referred to or talked about in our family—and here I was, sent out one wintry night to hear him speak to a thousand colored people in Quinn chapel. I found him all I expected: a benign, notable-looking old man, with a great beard and a mass of white hair. He had a genuine gift of tongues:

"The Negro like the Jew cannot part with his race. Call us mulattoes, octoroons—what you will—we are Negroes still. The black man will be respected nowhere while he is not respected in the United States. Our work is to make ourselves respected."

A little later I went to hear Albion Winegar Tourgee, whose book, *The Fool's Errand,* was second only to *Uncle Tom's Cabin* among the books relating to American problems which I knew as a boy. He was also a strong defender of the Negro.

"His old bonds of slavery are not yet gone. He still suffers many of the old indignities. Furthermore, these cruelties have left their scars on the perpetrators. . . ."

These and other addresses and discussions I heard that winter (some at Hull House) sharpened my interest in the Negro problem, and years later, when I found the right opportunity, I travelled widely in America, not with any solution or panacea, but as a kind of maker of understandings, which I hoped might lay the foundations for better relationships. I spent nearly two years studying the problem, and I wrote a series of magazine articles afterward published as a book called *Following the Color Line.* I never believed in quick solutions of this or any other deeply seated social problem, nor in mere legal inventions and compulsions. Real changes are slow and deeply rooted.

I Get My Chance

I delighted that winter in hearing readings by three men whose books had charmed me: F. Hopkinson Smith, F. Marion Crawford and Thomas Nelson Page. The last named I came to know personally many years later when he was Ambassador at Rome. I always thought that his well deserved literary fame was dimmed by his appointment to this high place, where he was ill-equipped to shine, and where he had many troubles.

I went to interview Nordica, the famous opera singer, who had come to Chicago to sing in "Aïda," at her spacious apartment at the Auditorium Hotel—and lost a new pair of rubbers. It was a stormy night and a hard-worked reporter had no opportunity to dress for such a call—even if he had known how. When I found myself in the anteroom of so much magnificence I was acutely conscious that my rubbers were muddy. I slipped them off. When I came out they were gone, and I did not dare ask for them. I remember well the charm of the interviewed, and the awe of the interviewer:

"Are you," I asked, "an optimist or a pessimist on the outlook for music in Chicago?"

I am thankful to say that she heard me with a twinkle in her eye!

I heard the man who was probably the most famous popular orator of the day—Robert G. Ingersoll. The old aunts of my boyhood spoke of him always as though he wore horns and a spike on his tail. I hoped he would give his audience one of the "atheistic tirades"—as my family called them—say the "Mistakes of Moses." But his subject was Robert Burns, upon which he lavished the eloquence of a true lover, and wound up with a quotation from a poem of his own.

307

Native American

"Though Scotland boasts a thousand names
Of patriot, king and peer,
The noblest, grandest of them all,
Was loved and cradled here.
Here lived the gentle peasant prince,
The loving cottar king,
Compared with whom the greatest prince
Is but a titled thing."

I was affected, however, far more deeply by an orator of quite another sort: a hard-hitting, knock-down-and-drag-out speaker he was, full of high-keyed western jokes. This was a bold young fellow, then somewhat known for his books on western ranch-life. He was also United States Civil Service Commissioner at Washington and something of a local leader in New York State politics. His name was Theodore Roosevelt. He spoke at a dinner of the Hamilton Club to a noisy group of Republicans who insisted upon proposing a toast to James G. Blaine, the "plumed knight." He began his address with a pouncing assault upon the "mugwump" in politics, whom he heartily despised. He described him as "a man who has small hands, small feet, a receding chin and a culture much above his intellect."

It was the first time I had ever seen him, and I was greatly impressed by his vigor, his directness, and his fearlessness. He was the perfect pattern of a leader for the youth of a nation. Cowboy, hard rider, straight-shooter, bold speaker, champion of the people, gifted in telling the rich old fellows, many of whom were present on that evening, to say nothing of the cultured "mugwumps," where they got off! I was later to become his friend and loyal supporter. I was not the only

308

youngster who believed in the "strenuous life": there were
thousands of us who had recently come from the frontier,
and the farms, and the plains. Not a few of us felt that we
had something to do in saving an America that seemed to us
to be going astray.

Some years later I wrote for *McClure's Magazine* one of
the earliest biographical articles regarding Roosevelt, which
I know he greatly appreciated; I wrote many other articles
along through the years, which he considered helpful. Afterward, because I thought he did not live up to his own pro-
gressive program (champions of the people also get tired!)
and seemed to me to have become more interested in retaining his political power than in advancing the social program
he had espoused (perhaps I was wrong in this, for who can
judge any man's motives?), I went over to La Follette of
Wisconsin, and later to Woodrow Wilson.

While I found all of these experiences highly delightful
and profitable (from the educational, not the financial,
point of view) they did not strike down to some of the conditions in Chicago which began to be serious during the first
winter before the World's Fair, and grew worse during the
second winter. Some of these, of which I shall speak later,
seemed to me to be of paramount interest and importance.

☆ *33* ☆

"This Infernal Profession"

AROUND A CORNER OR TWO from the newspaper office I often
visited a little hole-in-the-wall restaurant kept by a man we
called John or Johnnie. He had thick curly hair, smiled
broadly, and was always saying: "You bet: d'reckly." I
never knew his surname, nor had occasion to. There was a
counter with a few stools along it, and dim tables against
the side wall near by. It was a hospitable place, open twenty-
four hours a day, and for these reasons, as well as the cheap-
ness of its excellent hot coffee and "short orders," and in
spite of certain evidences of economy with the scrub-brush,
it was much frequented by newspaper men, not from our
staff alone, but from all the offices in Chicago.

I suppose that there is or was just such a "joint" as this
in every newspaper row in America. The newspaper man is
notoriously a night-hawk and the most irregular of men in
his meals. He likes a place where he can drop in at two in
the morning as well as two in the afternoon and while drinking his coffee find a fellow sufferer or two with whom he can
discuss the general decadence of the press in America, and
the niggardliness of the pay allotted to those who are really
making the paper.

Just now, when I began writing of Johnnie's place, I
found my mouth strangely watering. For I recalled the huge

German coffee-rings he served. They were artfully twisted or braided, with the top baked brown and crusty with sugar and grated nuts. Sometimes there were a few raisins in them. To a hungry man, after long hours of hard labor, at two in the morning, they were the last word in gastronomical satisfaction. Once, long afterward, when I enlarged upon this experience, I was met with the exclamation:

"What! Did you eat the *whole* of one of those rings?"

"I did."

"A big cup of coffee and an indigestible coffee-ring at two in the morning! Could you sleep after that?"

"Like a log!"

I don't think I was fully believed: but it was a fact. In those days I could eat anything, anywhere, at any time— except potato salad!

One of the newspaper men who often drifted into Johnnie's place was an oldish, rather sallow, sad-looking man. He was not on our staff: I think he was a *Herald* man. I had been out with him on several small assignments, and we had had some talk from time to time, but I knew nothing whatever about him. He had seemed to me, in some sort, interesting.

Late one night I went into Johnnie's and took a place at one of the side tables. I was in the midst of my coffee-ring when I saw the man of whom I have spoken coming over with a cup of tea in his hand to sit with me.

He had a pleasant, deprecatory way with him, and something—manner, cultivation, distinction—not common among the rough-and-ready newspaper men I knew best. We had some little talk and then he surprised me greatly by remarking:

Native American

"I wish I could feel as much interest in anything in this world as you apparently do in everything."

I was somewhat taken aback, since I did not realize that he knew anything about me. We were soon in deep conversation of the kind I liked. I found that he had been a great reader all his life, and once he was aroused could talk with a delightful, half-ironic charm. Many of the men I commonly met were of the old-fashioned up-from-the-composing-room type, more numerous then in the Chicago offices than young college upstarts like me, and like George Ade and John McCutcheon who had come in only two or three years before from Purdue. Many of them were characters gifted in one way or another. I recall a broken-down lawyer who, when properly fortified, could make as witty an after-dinner speech as ever I heard; a doughty retired English army officer of uncertain antecedents, two or three former editors of country newspapers who had seen life whole, if never quite steadily. I must include the towering figure of Opie Read, who came from Kentucky and had edited *The Arkansas Traveller*. He could tell stories all night long, and good stories too, without once faltering. I heard him first at a 'possum dinner, cooked by an enormous colored woman he had known in Kentucky and who now kept a little basement eating place in lower Chicago; and nearly fifty years later —he lived to be eighty-seven years old—Irving Bacheller and I sat on the stage when he made his farewell appearance. He had no intellectual quality whatever, and little or no social interest, but sitting in the midst of a congenial company, his huge low-hung pipe in his hand, to be used for humorous emphasis, he was a "natural," a born genius. I heard him tell a story once—but if I start on Opie Read I shall never get back to the far more interesting friend I started to tell about.

I suspect that this entire race of newspaper men has now disappeared from the offices of America, and their places have been taken by able young college men, most of them specially educated in schools of journalism. I suspect that the product of these bright, knowledgeable, sophisticated young men is of a much higher quality, better informed, more judiciously set forth, but something of the old flavor of newspaper life—its originality, its casual genius, its extravagances, has probably disappeared.

To many of these older men "book-learning" was positively anathema, or any special knowledge, particularly anything literary; they were still more or less of the frontier. My new friend and I often talked about the various men we knew, and of how many of them had come from other professions or employments.

"You know," said he, "that the newspaper office is the haven of shipwrecked ambitions."

He said it a little sadly, ironically, and somewhat later I learned that he was generalizing on his own experience—as we all do. I found that he had once been a successful pulpit orator with a large following. What it was that caused his downfall and retreat to the "haven of shipwrecked ambitions" I never knew. It was not drink, which was the curse of some of the older men I came to know. It was something subtler and deeper. I thought I caught a significant clue in one of his favorite expressions, often used after we had had a warm discussion. He would hesitate, his eyes would take on a reflective look, and he would say:

"Maybe so, maybe not."

Was it the advisability of a strong position in the current presidential campaign, was it the demand for cutting down immigration from Europe, a subject then much discussed, was it the immortality of the soul?

"Maybe so, maybe not."

He was a lonely man, and I soon found, behind a defensively gruff exterior, a world of gentleness and natural affection. We met often at Johnnie's or at King's, and I could see that he took a warm interest in me.

"If you're going to be a writer," said he, "don't stay too long in newspaper work."

"Why not?" I asked hotly.

"It's a great school—nothing in the world better to let a man into the realities of life and possibly give him facility with his pen—I'm not so sure about that, either—but it's a poor profession. Many a good man I know has been ruined by it."

At another time he burst out with unwonted vehemence:

"Facts, facts, facts—superficial facts! Facts are one thing, truth is quite another. Reality is quite another."

In the inner pocket of his coat he kept a long black leather wallet, much worn at the corners and stuffed with clippings from newspapers, soiled bits of memoranda, a photograph or two so worn that one could not make out the faded faces. It never harbored a dollar bill—that I saw.

One evening he took out a piece of paper and handed it over to me.

"You see," said he, "what Schopenhauer says about journalism."

314

"This Infernal Profession"

I read it with deep interest:

"The object of journalism is to make events go as far as possible. Thus it is that all journalists are, in the very nature of their calling, alarmists. This is their way of giving interest to what they write. Herein they are like little dogs; if anything stirs, they immediately set up a shrill bark."

"You see," he said, "what you and I are. Little dogs, barking shrilly every time anything stirs. How make any literature out of that?"

On another occasion he delved in his shabby wallet for another quotation.

"You should see this—it is from John Stuart Mill's autobiography. Steady now, I'll find it."

The paper was almost worn out: he had evidently had it for a long time.

"This is particularly for you," he said.

I laughed and read it aloud:

"Writing for the press cannot be recommended as a permanent resource to anyone qualified to accomplish anything in the higher departments of literature or thought: not only on account of the uncertainty of this means of livelihood, especially if the writer has a conscience, and will not consent to serve any opinions except his own; but also because the writings by which one can live are not the writings which themselves live, and are never those in which a writer does his best."

I have kept a copy of that quotation down through the years.

When I was called away from Chicago to help my father, and was not certain as to when I could return, my friend bade me good-bye with tears in his eyes, and my hand in both of his.

"Remember!" he said, trying to smile, "don't wait too long: get out of this infernal profession."

That was the last I ever saw of him.

It was curious, but these discussions chimed in with some rather painful exchanges I was having with my father. He had been indulgent enough when I went to Chicago to seek what he considered to be temporary money-making employment for the summer vacation. While he knew of my interest in writing, he was so sure that the law was my real objective it seemed never to have occurred to him that I would fail to complete my course at Ann Arbor.

"Your business," he wrote me, "is very erratic and the tendency is to break up all regular habits." Irregularity, disorder, with him were moral delinquencies. "A year more of quiet study would be beneficial to you."

In later letters he became still more outspoken and specific:

"It strikes me that your present methods of work and the high pressure under which it is done, and the rather sensational and lurid style required of you, is hardly conducive to the formation of the *simple, neat* and *elegant* style so much commended by old Blair, whose rhetoric I used to study in college."

The underlining is his own.

In other ways I could see that he did not at all approve of what I was doing and thinking. He seemed anxious and somewhat alarmed. I wrote him often and at length, since he was not only my father, but the best friend I had, and in

"This Infernal Profession"

some letter I must have referred to my attendance at the Single Tax Club, with comments regarding labor conditions in Chicago as I was seeing them. Worse still, I must have expressed my belief that the result of the recent presidential campaign, which resulted in Cleveland's election, was the best possible thing for the country. I even think I told him that if I could have qualified as a voter in Illinois I should have cast my first presidential vote for Cleveland. Well as I knew him, I could not have realized how such views must have shaken the pillars of his temple. Henry George to him was an "economic heretic," a "disturber of settled institutions": and any one, like Cleveland, who was no better than a "carpet-bagger," who challenged the beneficent rule of the Republican Party, and the necessity of a high protective tariff, was a danger to the nation. It was as though some one had attacked his religious beliefs! Even more, perhaps, he must have felt that I, his oldest son, was not worthy of the care he had bestowed upon my education.

He wrote me more than one high-tempered letter, in which, as he said, he would not "mince matters"—and he did not!

"I was amused at your remarks on politics. After you have watched politics of this country carefully for thirty years I believe you will be less certain about the "voice of the people" as indicated by an election. In the first place a large majority of the voters of this country have no *intelligent* or *clearly defined* opinion upon the question of tariff or any other of the great national questions of the day; of course they are ready enough to *express* an opinion but a moment's talk with them will show that it is wholly superficial—based on neither facts nor arguments. . . . You never were more

317

mistaken in your life than when you think that the election of Cleveland means *free trade* for this country. The more intelligent Democrats have never had the *remotest intention* of repealing the McKinley bill—they will *tinker it some*. The Republicans would have done the same to about the same extent had they come into power or remained in power. This nation is now and will remain for some time one of *high protective tariff!*"

He went on to say:

"Don't be too sure about the *death* of the "Grand Old Party." If you watch it carefully for the next four years you will observe it to be a remarkably lively corpse. And as for the wonderful *new* party you talk of, don't take too much stock in it; it is not hatched yet and the chances are three to one that it will get badly addled before it has strength enough to break its shell."

He was also not unwilling to hit at me directly and vigorously:

"Many young fellows with beards of sparse and recent growth are very much inclined to be *sentimental* and *optimistic* in regard to matters political. That is all right and quite proper, in fact it is one of the *principal* and *peculiar attractions* of youth. Young chicken is much more desirable and admirable than aged rooster—excepting on occasions of a well-contested cock-fight; then give me the *old cock* every time."

These things irritated and troubled me deeply. My affection for my father, and his for me, were deep and abiding. I had always followed, or tried to follow, his advice; and I recognized that what he said contained much robust sense.

"This Infernal Profession"

He had the assured force and cogency which goes with settled conviction. He was sure—and I was not, as yet.

I travelled a weary round of argument with myself. Every time I tried to accept his settled point of view I began to see with painful clarity the conditions that existed all around me in Chicago—the unemployment, the poverty, the strikes, the radical meetings, the widespread hunger—*actual* hunger —and the suffering from cold, during the winters that preceded and followed the grandiose hullabaloo of the World's Fair. I was a night newspaper man, familiar with dark and windy streets, and I saw it for what it was in all its ugliness, long after the "honest citizen" had gone to his warm home, had eaten his generous dinner, and was resting in his comfortable bed. Chicago was being advertised as perhaps no other city in all history was advertised before. It was itself for the time being the greatest show on earth—greater by far than its enormous circus on the lake shore. It was rich, prosperous, powerful; every one was making money, or pretended to be. It would have been outright treason to suggest that everything was not for the best in the best of all possible worlds. Had not Chicago itself crystallized its philosophy— and that of its time—in the swaggering motto: "I will."

But I was lifting a flap of the gorgeous tent, where the music was, and the warmth and the feasting, and looking into the cold, wet streets and littered alleys outside. It was not because I was a more than ordinarily benevolent young man, but because I was profoundly *interested,* yes, and indignant. It seemed to me really the greatest news of the day, even though the newspapers were more or less playing it down. Any one could write of what was going on at the

319

World's Fair: few took the trouble to describe what was
going on behind the scenes.

I was sent out one day to report a complaint of the coal
dealers of Chicago, that their storage yards were not being
given sufficient police protection. I talked with several of
them, and they seemed to make out a pretty good case for
themselves. There were too many coal thieves in Chicago! I
could have stopped there and made a pretty good and, indeed, truthful report of it, but I wondered why it was that
coal stealing had become so widespread. I tramped down
into the black railroad neighborhoods, and called at the
little wooden houses. This was part of the report I wrote:

"They live in the poorest of the shanties, where the icy
wind gains easiest admittance. Their clothes are the thinnest.
Their families are the largest. Their cupboards are the
emptiest and their stoves the smallest. They have no way of
procuring coal unless they steal it. Large numbers of them
hold tickets from the county agent and the various benevolent societies. Yesterday they stood shivering in line for
hours, but their tickets drew no coal, for it was not to be
had in sufficient quantities, even by the county authorities."

This my newspaper published: it did not publish what I
myself was wondering and thinking. I did not as yet feel sure
enough to put it down on paper. What *was* the matter, I
asked myself, why was it that a great city like Chicago,
which, with its brave "I will," could build the most won-
drous fair the world had ever seen, should find itself unable
to supply thousands of shivering people with the coal they
desperately needed? If there was really no coal, why police
officers to prevent the stealing of it?

"This Infernal Profession"

Many of my "stories" of that time dealt with these bitter conditions. Here are some of the headings:

"HOMELESS AND HUNGRY. HOUSED AND FED BY CHURCHES."

"EVICTIONS OF WOMEN."

"Hundreds of women and children are suffering for the necessaries of life in the district west of the river and south of Van Buren Street, comprising much of the 7th and 19th wards. Here evictions of women with large families of little children are of almost daily occurrence, in spite of the fact that the poor in this part of the city receive more than one-half of all the fuel and food given out by Cook county. Among these evictions there are numerous cases where the father has grown discouraged and deserted his family, and the mother and children must receive aid from charity or die of hunger and cold."

"CHILDREN SET ADRIFT. ORPHAN HOME OVERCROWDED."

"PLATOONS OF HUNGRY. FED BY THE SALVATION ARMY."

I reported a ragged parade I saw which carried this placard:

> BLACK SLAVES OF 1863.
> WHITE SLAVES OF 1893.

I knew that my father had no realization of such conditions—and had never had. He and all our family, for two hundred and fifty years, had been pioneers. If any one was discontented in one neighborhood or found it hard to make a living, all he had to do was to load his belongings into an

321

ox-cart and go west, where there was plenty of free land, free water—a free sky!

I clipped out and sent some of my "stories" to my father: I wrote him a number of long letters giving him glimpses of what I was seeing—behind the gilded glories of the World's Fair. They seemed to make little or no impression upon him. I expect he thought some of hem lurid! "I have heard," he said casually, "that Chicago has become a lodestone for tramps and hoboes." At another time he asked me,

"Why don't they get out of Chicago? There's plenty of room in the West. All they've got to do is to use their brains —and little at that—with some elbow-grease."

I did not realize it at the time, but here spoke the pioneer, who did not know that the frontier in America had gone forever. My father's only heartfelt advice was what he had given me when I myself was meeting the problem of getting hold in Chicago:

"Hang on, stick to it, fight it out."

The trouble with me was that while I could see the conditions and could feel their seriousness, I did not in the least know what should be done to remedy them. I could report what I saw: I did not, and could not, get any light from soap-box orators, or find any hope in the many organizations that were being formed to deal with the problem. Even the Single-Taxers, and my friend Cooley, who, on the whole, were earnest and thoughtful men, seemed not to see the urgency of the problem, and to be talking, while men were starving, of complicated reforms which could not at best be instituted for years.

For a time I was strongly tempted to throw everything to

the winds and go home. There was much that seemed soundly practical in my father's advice. He did not suggest that I give over my ambition to write, but simply to recognize that I could not make a (respectable) living at it. "Go on with the law and do your writing as a side line." Many writers had done that with success and with honor. More persuasive still, he suggested that I come home and become a partner in his business. I could have, almost immediately, an assured place and a good income. I could marry the girl I was in love with, and build a little home in the country.

Another element in the situation also made a strong appeal to me. My father was getting on in years. He was greatly handicapped by his deafness, and recently he had been feeling the depression which had begun to creep across the country like a plague, without in the least understanding what it meant or how deadly it was to be. In short, there was every good reason why I should give up my work in Chicago and go home.

I am pretty sure—fate often hangs by a slender thread—that I should have done it, if it had not been for one of the strangest incidents or accidents of my entire life. This incident concerned an unimportant person—presumably unimportant—who stepped into my life one wintry night, and soon stepped out again, after having left an indelible impression upon me. This must be left for another chapter.

☆ 34 ☆

The Potato-Car Boy

I HAD BEEN trying hard, as I have said, to get some understanding of what the conditions in Chicago really were. This seemed to me to be the real news of the time; and besides, I was deeply interested. I spent two or three nights in cheap lodging houses, where "beds" could be had for ten cents, so that I could meet the down-and-outs; and talk with them, man to man. It had not been a pleasant or comfortable experience, and it was not really fruitful. So many of these miserable lodgers seemed to have been beaten into a kind of insensibility. Some were suspicious, some drunk. I could not seem to get at them.

I had indeed become accustomed to meeting such men on the dark and wintry streets of the city—shuffling men with their coat collars turned up, and their hands deep in their ragged pockets.

"Please, mister, I ain't got any place to sleep tonight. Can't you spare me a dime?"

A dime was almost the universal request. Sometimes it was a wheedling demand for "a few cents" to get a cup of coffee. At first I had given the dime, but I soon found that the need was bottomless: and I did not myself have too many dimes to spare. Moreover, I took pains in some in-

324

stances to see what the recipient of my dime did with it. In quite a proportion of the cases he headed straight for the nearest saloon. I felt positively relieved one night when a man who stopped me said gruffly:

"Mister, give me a dime: I must have a drink of whiskey."

I gave it to him.

The good people of Chicago were indignant and alarmed by this tremendous influx of what they called the "riff-raff of humanity." But they had flung an invitation to the world to come to their fair. They had experts who were geniuses at advertising and publicity, and the pictures they painted of the beauty, the variety, the miraculous cost of their wonders, and the richness and prosperity of the city in which they were displayed, lured not only the rich and comfortable, but the poor and discontented. They should not have been surprised at that, for these hapless ones argued reasonably enough that if all this money was being spent in Chicago, with such evidences of prosperity, surely there would be jobs for a few more men. They came by thousands!

All of these experiences and observations of mine seemed to culminate on one especially bitter night—an icy night with a raw wind that cut like a knife, blowing off Lake Michigan. I had some business at the City Hall—I forget what—and I pushed my way into that great old mausoleum of a stone building through one of the double-swing doorways.

As I stepped into the dimly lighted corridor I was all but overwhelmed by a rush of hot, heavy, fetid air.

I stopped just inside the doorway. Dante in his Inferno never bettered the sight I saw there. How could he? He lived in an age not so civilized as ours! Every inch of the stone floor of the corridor was covered with the bodies of men. They had nothing under them except, occasionally, a few newspapers, and they were using their hard wet shoes for pillows. A nobly generous city, however, had increased the heat in the corridors so that the men could sleep, though restlessly, with muttered oaths when they tried to turn over. There were some 300 of them in that stone corridor; they lay in every conceivable and painful attitude so that it was impossible to go down the hall without stepping over the ragged bodies. Miserable, shivering specimens of outcast humanity! Incidentally, the heat made the atmosphere of unwashed bodies almost unendurable to the outsider. It *stank*. This is not a pretty word, but no other seems strong enough to describe the reality.

I am almost ashamed to tell what my first powerful reaction was: I have never been able to forget it. It was one of anger; not pity, not horror: anger. And it was no abstract anger either: at a "society" or a "system" or an "institution" —it was anger at these men themselves personally and individually. Afterward, I was astonished to recognize it as being exactly what my father would have felt.

Here they are, he would have said, a lot of bums, tramps, hoboes—drunkards, probably criminals! Why are they lying here like beasts, on the stone floor? Why don't they get out and hustle?

This was also my first overwhelming reaction. I stood for some time looking at that nightmarish spectacle. Presently I found myself asking: What should be done, what should be done?

The Potato-Car Boy

I could not answer my own question, I could think of nothing whatever. It was as though I were in a bad dream, and knew it for a bad dream, but could not wake up.

Possibly it was this feeling that something must be done and done at once that led me to step up to a young chap sitting on the lower step of a stairway with his head on his arm, trying to sleep. He was sitting up because there was no room to lie down. I shook him by the shoulder.

"What are you doing here?" I asked—probably with some of the anger I still felt in my voice.

He stood up quickly; he was young and rather good-looking, with the rugged countenance and clear eye of a farm boy—I knew the kind well—but he was also dirty and looked cold and unutterably tired. He did not say much, only that he couldn't find any other place to sleep.

I don't know quite why I should have done it, but I took him roughly by the arm.

"Come on out of here," I said.

When he held back, I marched him along.

He came with me, somewhat hesitatingly and fearfully, but he came. I took him to a near-by night lunch counter I knew about, and ordered hot coffee and, afterward, hot soup and everything else he could eat. I had never before in my life seen a ravenously hungry man. There had been times when I myself, as I have related, did not get enough to eat, but it was not like this. This was wolfish.

The blood came up into his face: the pinched look disappeared. It was a kind of miracle which I watched with fascinated eyes. He began to appear more definitely what I had first thought him: a sturdy, hard-working farm boy. His powerful hands showed that he had husked corn, and dug potatoes, and milked cows.

His tongue soon loosened. He said he was from Iowa and had come to Chicago in a carload of potatoes.

"A carload of potatoes!"

"Why, yes, at this time of year, some one has to go along and keep up a fire in a little stove, or they'd all freeze."

In answer to my inquiries he told me much of his home, his father and mother, and brothers and sisters, how much schooling he had had and what wages he could earn. I understood him down to the ground. I had been brought up among just such farm boys.

"Are you expecting to go back to Iowa?"

"Well, no. You see, mister, I thought if I could only get to Chicago, I could better myself. I could get a good job. So I came with only a little money, and that's all gone."

I remembered, with strange emotions, my own too-recent escape from just such a situation.

"Have you looked for a job?"

"Have I? *Everywhere*. No one wants a man like me"—he said it with sudden profound discouragement in his voice.

That, too, I remembered, when I had tried answering "want ads"—as I have related.

Something in me—not quite myself, perhaps my father— spoke up:

"Well, I'll get you a job."

His face instantly lighted up.

"I'll give you money for a bed tonight and for breakfast in the morning. You come to this restaurant at noon tomorrow. I'll be here to meet you, and I'll have that job for you."

The Potato-Car Boy

I went home that night thinking of all I had seen and saying to myself over and over:

"I'll make this a test."

While I scarcely admitted it to myself, I knew that it was to be a test of my father and his point of view, as well as a test of the real conditions in Chicago. I did not plan it: it was there.

I thought much that night of the potato-car boy and wondered how many of these "bums, tramps, hoboes" were just like him. Two lines out of my new copy of *Leaves of Grass* kept coming to me:

"You there, impotent, loose in the knees!
Open your scraf'd chops till I blow grit within you."

The next morning I got up early and started out. This time I was not going for myself, and I was not dependent, and therefore fearful, if I did not succeed. I had the authority and the privileges of a great Chicago newspaper behind me. I could walk up to the employers themselves, explain the situation, and testify to the worth of the boy I was interested in. While I knew that this, after all, was not a fair test, it would have to do. If it failed it would be all the more impressive.

I tramped hard all that forenoon; I saw and talked with a number of key employers—and got exactly nowhere. While the men I went to were patient enough with me, because I was a reporter, they said with one accord that there was absolutely no opening.

"We've got a waiting list of fifty men"—or a hundred, or five hundred—"and some of them have been at our hiring

329

gate every morning for weeks." In one or two cases they asked:

"What can he do?" or "What experience has he had?"

I had to acknowledge that all he had was good health, strong muscles, and I believed an intelligent and willing spirit.

In some cases I got the names of other employers who might give at least one man a chance; these I put down in my notebook.

At noon I went to the little restaurant as I had promised —a chastened young man. I saw my potato-car boy afar off. He was standing at the curb with his overcoat buttoned to his chin—he did have an overcoat—stamping on the sidewalk to keep warm.

"I didn't get that job this morning," I said as cheerfully as I could, "but we'll do it yet."

We ate lunch together and I gave him the list of names.

"You start in and call on all these people, see what you can do yourself. Go to it hard all this afternoon and tomorrow morning. Meet me here again at noon."

That day and the next morning I also devoted all the time I could spare to visiting various charity and benevolent organizations of the city—both the old established ones and some of the many new ones that were trying to grapple with the emergency. I even called on Miss Addams at Hull House whose judgment I greatly respected. I got plenty of information and good advice, but no job.

"What shall I do then?" I asked in desperation.

"Send the boy back home."

When I met the boy that noon, I found, what I had entirely expected, that he had met only rebuffs and disappointments in his search for a job.

"I tell you honestly, mister, I did everything I could. There were always hundreds of men ahead of me."

"I believe you," I said.

He looked at me, his face a picture of forlorn and questioning helplessness.

"Why don't you go home to Iowa?"

"I haven't any money for railroad fare."

"I haven't either," I said, "but I'll get you transportation."

I did exactly that, through the combined efforts of a charity organization and a good friend of mine in the Northwestern Railroad office—and the potato-car boy stepped out of my life. I never even heard of him afterward.

Well, I had failed completely and miserably: the father who was in me had failed completely and miserably. Something that neither he nor I understood was terribly wrong!

I thought a great deal about that potato-car boy. A few days later, walking home from the office through the dark streets, it came to me with a flash:

"Some one ought to write a novel with a boy like that as a central character. One could explain this whole miserable mess in such a study. He could rip it all open: he could make it so hot that people would shrivel up when they read it—and resolve to change it."

I stopped suddenly in the middle of the pavement. A strange, solemn feeling came over me.

"I will write that novel myself," I said.

Before I got into my hall bedroom that night I had made an outline, in my mind, of what the novel was to be. It was to start, of course, in Iowa, with a wonderful picture of the old pioneer farm life—I felt I knew it well enough already—and then proceed to Chicago (in a potato car) and the remainder of the book was to deal with the desperate struggles, sufferings, and failures of my hero. Incidentally I could present all the problems I had begun to see, and the strange, tragic, comic, futile efforts of civic organizations, chambers of commerce, churches, and radical groups—flying about in desperation of futility—to deal with them. In the end I was to come off, grandly, of course, with the true solution!

I did not sleep all night. I was red-hot with the idea. By morning I had decided to start at once on "the great American novel."

I did start at once. I spent all my spare time on it. I made voluminous notes. I tried to get assignments from the newspaper that would enable me to investigate working-class conditions. The advancing crisis of 1893 and 1894 gave me overwhelming material. When Coxey's army of discontent marched from Massillon, Ohio, to Washington in the spring of 1894—a so-called "petition in boots" that wound up, beaten by the clubs of police officers, on the lawn of the Capitol at Washington—I was with them, as the representative of my newspaper. What a story out of a book of nightmares that was! When I got back to Chicago the greatest railroad strikes the country ever knew were under way, centering on the "model town" of Pullman—where I saw workmen and their families starving in the model houses. I saw Eugene Debs, Socialist leader of the strike, arrested; I visited him in prison; I testified in his behalf when his case came up in the courts of Chicago, not because I was a So-

The Potato-Car Boy

cialist—I was not—but because I liked and admired him as a man, and believed he was not getting justice.

The President, Mr. Cleveland, apparently fearful of outright revolution, ordered the Federal troops into the panic-stricken strike neighborhoods. I saw men shot down at Hammond, Indiana. I attended meetings that were positively revolutionary in their oratory. I began to write for the *Outlook* of New York, and other magazines and newspapers besides my own, brief articles dealing with the subjects I was so deeply interested in.

Incidentally, the problem of my own future, my father's criticisms, and the proposal that I return home and join him in his business, dropped instantly and wholly out of my mind—as though they had never existed. They no longer troubled me in the least. The idea that I could do my writing as a "side line," neat little stories, elegant little verses, polished little essays!—I dismissed indignantly. A man who had anything real to write needed all and more than all the life he could give it.

Other things, however, did trouble me. The more intently I looked at the chaotic American scene, the more I tried to follow my poor potato-car boy stumbling through all its mazes, the more difficult the task began to seem. It was like life itself, as vast as life, and as kaleidoscopic: I could not get hold, except of ravellings here and there, vivid moments, tragic or humorous incidents.

In the beginning I had thought earnestly of old Doctor Beal's method (Agassiz's method before that) of getting at truth. I recalled my own enthralling experience in Doctor Beal's laboratory at college. disappointing at first, then completely satisfying—which I have described elsewhere. By this method one *looked at life,* looked at it again, kept looking at it. One avoided being satisfied with names—names being merely the symbols other scientists made when they were weary of looking. Above all, the inquirer was to be wary of conclusions until he was sure.

If only one could apply this beautiful and simple method to social problems—looking at them as though he saw them for the first time, taking no one else's observations as final, accepting no conclusions founded upon them! After all the wild talk I was hearing, it seemed to me, momentarily, a complete and original method of examination. For science is not primarily valuable for its results—these may or may not be worthless—but for its method.

I believe today, after nearly fifty years of observation, and a certain amount of thought (the best I am capable of), that the principle underlying the Agassiz-Beal method is as sound in the realm of the social as of the natural sciences. If only people would stop and look, and think!—and not jump at conclusions, nor accept shibboleths and slogans, nor wind themselves up in organizations and parties for trying to do wholesale what can only be done a little at a time. For I have never been a reformer, nor desired to be. I have never accepted any cut-and-dried program for social reorganization. I have never been a Socialist, nor a Communist, nor a Single Taxer. I have never belonged to a political party, nor, since my boyhood, to any church. I am suspicious of those who would change institutions without changing the understandings upon which they rest. What I have wished most, if it can be expressed in a phrase, was to be an introducer of human beings to one another, to be a maker of understandings—those deep understandings which must underlie any social change that is effective and permanent. When men come really to understand one another—if that time ever comes—war will end, poverty will end, tyranny will end, and this under almost any sort of government, almost any economic system.

I soon discovered the deep-seated difficulties of the method I envisioned—which I may sometime, I hope, develop more fully. It was not only the complication of the problems themselves and the difficulties of human beings trying to act collectively, it was the complexity and perversity of *me,* the observer. I could sit calmly with a microscope under my eye and study with joy a plant of the blue lupin. In this field I could make satisfactory discoveries for myself, knowing well that my own life would be little disturbed, one way or another, by what I found. But when I studied the potato-car boy, and his roots and his leafage and his flowering, I found my own eyes colored by my background; my observations blurred by my education, and complicated by my loyalties; warped by my selfish interests; short-circuited by my emotions. I was myself, in some sort, the potato-car boy!

I will not go into all this more fully here. It is sufficient to remark that I did not write the "great American novel," nor yet the saga of the potato-car boy. But the days and months, yes, and the years, that I devoted to the subjects I should have had to master in order to write such a book, gave me a clearer foundation of understanding when, a few years later, I began to write the so-called "exposure" or "muck-raking" articles for *McClure's* and *The American*

Magazine. When such words as Progressivism, Insurgency, Socialism, and the Square Deal and the New Deal, began to dominate public discussion, I knew, far better than I might otherwise have done, where I stood regarding them, and what I believed—so far as I had gone. And I had a good reason when I began writing the adventures of David Grayson, under a nom de plume.

My father was presently reconciled. My brother Harry, who was far more gifted as a business man than I was, became his loyal assistant and afterward took over the business; and I know that in later years my father came to approve of my profession, though he never admitted it in so many words.

It is certain that a man is happiest when he has found his own place in the world, and is doing what he is best fitted to do.

J